In The Hand
Herrmann The Greats World
Magic
The History Of Magic #3

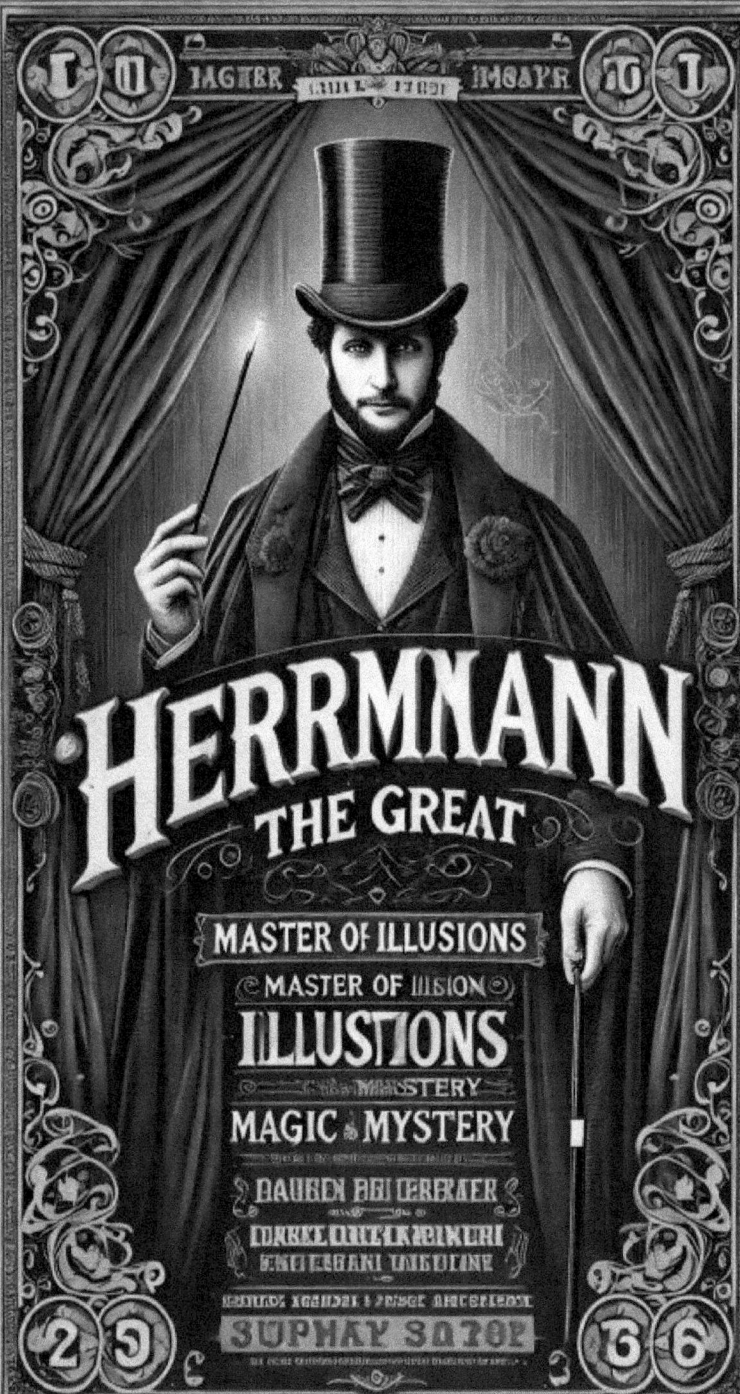

In The Hands Of A Master Herrmann The Great's World Of Magic

The History Of Magic, Volume 3

Robert Jakobsen

Published by Robert Jakobsen, 2024.

While every precaution has been taken in the preparation of this book, the publisher assumes no responsibility for errors or omissions, or for damages resulting from the use of the information contained herein.

IN THE HANDS OF A MASTER HERRMANN THE GREAT'S WORLD OF MAGIC

First edition. November 6, 2024.

Copyright © 2024 Robert Jakobsen.

ISBN: 979-8227688255

Written by Robert Jakobsen.

Table of Contents

The Magic of Alexander Herrmann 1
The Early Life of Alexander Herrmann 11
Humble Beginnings 23
Training Under His Brother 35
The Rise of Herrmann the Great 47
From Apprentice to Master 59
Touring Europe 71
Sleight of Hand: The Art of Deception 83
Mastering Sleight of Hand 95
The Influence of Magic Manuals 107
Magic on the World Stage 121
International Fame 135
Signature Illusions 147
Herrmann and His Rivals 161
The Competition 173
Magic Wars 183
The Golden Age of Magic 195
Magic's Popularity Boom 209
Innovating the Art 223
Behind the Curtain: Life Beyond the Stage 237
Personal Life 249
Building a Legacy 261
The Final Act 273
Herrmann's Legacy After His Death 285
Remembering Herrmann 297

The Magic of Alexander Herrmann

The Enchantment Begins

Alexander Herrmann's fascination with magic began at a young age, fueled by the captivating tales of wonder and mystery that surrounded him. From the time he was a child, Herrmann felt an inexplicable pull towards the art of illusion. The enchanting stories of mythical sorcerers and legendary magicians cast a spell on his impressionable mind, igniting a spark that would eventually grow into a passionate pursuit. His thirst for the unknown and the inexplicable shaped his early years, leading him to experiment with simple tricks and sleights of hand. His playful curiosity and boundless imagination turned ordinary objects into vessels of wonder, as he sought to unravel their secrets and harness their hidden potential. Herrmann's enchantment with magic allowed him to escape into a world of endless possibilities, where the laws of nature bent to the will of the conjurer, and extraordinary feats defied logic and reason. He immersed himself in the rich tapestry of magical lore, soaking up every story and legend like a sponge, infusing his young mind with the belief that anything was possible through the power of illusion. As he delved deeper into the realms of mystery and marvel, Herrmann voraciously consumed every book, every anecdote, and every whispered rumor about the art of magic, eager to unlock its elusive secrets. His journey into the enchanted realm of magic symbolized a profound revelation—a calling that beckoned him to unravel the enigma of the impossible and to share it with the world. It was this insatiable thirst for wonder and enlightenment that marked the beginning of Alexander Herrmann's lifelong love affair with the captivating world of magic.

A Childhood Wonder

Alexander Herrmann's childhood was filled with a sense of wonder and curiosity that would later shape his illustrious career as a magician. Growing up in a small village, young Alexander often found himself captivated by the ordinary yet magical elements of everyday life. Whether it was the way sunlight danced through the trees or the mesmerizing patterns in the night sky, he developed a deep appreciation for the enchanting mysteries of the world around him. It was during these formative years that Herrmann first began to recognize and appreciate the power of illusion. His keen eye for detail and his natural ability to see beyond the surface of things allowed him to perceive the extraordinary in the seemingly mundane. This unique perspective would eventually become the foundation of his magical artistry. As a child, Alexander would spend hours lost in thought, pondering the secrets of nature and marveling at the inexplicable beauty hidden within the simplest of phenomena. His early experiences with the enigmatic allure of the world ignited a passion within him, driving him to seek out ways to bring this sense of wonder to others. From an early age, it was clear that Herrmann possessed an innate gift for cultivating awe and fascination in those around him. Friends and family alike were drawn to his magnetic personality and the captivating stories he spun from the threads of his vivid imagination. His uncanny ability to weave tales of magic and mystery cast a spell over everyone fortunate enough to hear them, leaving a lasting impression on their hearts and minds. The seeds of his future vocation had been sown, and the restless spirit of a budding showman began to stir within him. Even in his youth, Alexander Herrmann exhibited the qualities that would one day make him known as "Herrmann the Great" – a masterful entertainer capable of conjuring joy and astonishment wherever he went.

Discovering the Art of Illusion

As Alexander Herrmann's childhood wonder continued to flourish, he found himself increasingly drawn to the enchanting world of magic. His insatiable curiosity led him to immerse himself in the art of illusion, eagerly devouring every piece of magical knowledge he could find. From his earliest encounters with sleight of hand to witnessing grand stage performances, Herrmann was captivated by the mesmerizing allure of magic. He spent countless hours practicing and perfecting his skills, honing his ability to weave a spellbinding narrative through each meticulously crafted illusion. With unwavering dedication, he delved into the rich history of magic, studying the timeless techniques passed down through generations. It was during this formative period that Herrmann discovered the transformative power of magic; its ability to transport audiences to realms where the impossible became possible. Every moment spent exploring the intricacies of illusion filled Herrmann with an unshakable sense of purpose and ignited a fervent passion within him. Discovering the art of illusion proved to be a defining chapter in Herrmann's life, shaping the trajectory of his extraordinary journey and laying the foundation for his future as a master magician.

The Influence of a Magical Family

Alexander Herrmann's upbringing was steeped in the world of magic, with his family playing an integral role in shaping his future as a renowned magician. From a young age, he was surrounded by relatives who were themselves accomplished magicians, and their passion for the craft ignited a deep-seated fascination within him. The familial influence provided him with invaluable exposure to various magical techniques and secrets, allowing him to witness firsthand the artistry and dedication required to captivate an audience through illusion. This environment of enchantment and mystique nurtured a profound sense of wonder in Alexander, fueling his desire to master the intricacies of magic and follow in the prestigious footsteps of his family members. Moreover, the familial support enabled him to delve into the rich history of magic, learning from generations of accumulated wisdom and honing his skills under the guidance of those who had already left an indelible mark on the world of illusion. It was within this nurturing and supportive environment that Alexander Herrmann's unwavering commitment to becoming a magician of unparalleled distinction took root. With his family's magical legacy serving as both a source of inspiration and a guiding light, Alexander embarked on a journey that would ultimately redefine the art of magic and establish him as one of its most eminent proponents. As he matured, he drew upon the collective knowledge and experiences of his magical lineage, transforming his boundless admiration into an unwavering dedication to preserving and enhancing the enchantment associated with the craft. The influence of his magical family permeated every facet of his performance and persona, infusing his mesmerizing acts with a timeless allure and a profound understanding of the transformative power of illusion. Indeed, it was the foundation laid by his family that propelled Alexander Herrmann towards achieving unprecedented feats in the realm of magic and shaping a legacy that continues to inspire and enthrall audiences to this day.

Captivating First Audiences

Alexander Herrmann's magnetic stage presence and mastery of illusion quickly garnered attention from audiences far and wide. As he embarked on his journey as a magician, he captivated first audiences with unparalleled charisma and an uncanny ability to transfix and astonish. Each performance was a symphony of artistry and enchantment, leaving spectators in a state of spellbound wonder. Whether it was a small gathering or a grand theater, Herrmann had an innate talent for connecting with people and transporting them to a world where the impossible became reality. His genuine passion for magic shone through every trick and flourish, creating an atmosphere of awe and excitement that lingered long after the final curtain fell. Witnessing Herrmann in action was not merely a form of entertainment; it was an experience that ignited the imagination and kindled a love for the mystical. Audiences were left breathless, eager to unravel the secrets behind his mesmerizing performances yet simultaneously content to be immersed in the mystery and allure of his craft. With deft sleight of hand and an unwavering dedication to perfection, Herrmann wove a tapestry of wonder that resonated deeply with all who had the privilege to witness it. His early shows marked the beginning of an illustrious career that would leave an indelible mark on the world of magic, drawing in crowds with the promise of bewilderment and delight. From intimate parlors to opulent theaters, Alexander Herrmann's capacity to captivate and mesmerize served as the cornerstone of his magical legacy, igniting a flame of fascination that continues to burn brightly to this day.

Crafting His Unique Style

Alexander Herrmann's journey to master magician was not solely marked by the mastery of tricks; it was his unique style that set him apart from his contemporaries. Crafting his own brand of magic, Herrmann enveloped his performances with a captivating blend of charm, sophistication, and mystery. His stage persona exuded an aura of enigma that left audiences spellbound, eagerly anticipating the next marvel he would unveil. What truly distinguished Herrmann's style was his relentless dedication to showmanship and presentation. Every movement, every gesture, and every word was meticulously choreographed to weave a mesmerizing narrative, drawing spectators into a world where the impossible became reality. He strived not just to perform illusions, but to create an immersive experience that would linger in the minds and hearts of those fortunate enough to witness his artistry. Moreover, his attire and stage presence were carefully curated to evoke an air of elegance and grandeur, befitting the wonder and spectacle of his performances. Each detail, from the adornments on his costume to the design of his props, reflected a discerning eye for aesthetics and theatrical impact, elevating his acts to something more profound than mere sleight-of-hand. Yet beyond the external trappings, it was Herrmann's innate ability to connect with his audience on a deeply personal level that truly defined his style. His charismatic rapport with spectators cultivated an atmosphere of intimacy, as if each individual in the audience had been personally invited on a journey of astonishment and delight. This genuine connection infused his performances with an emotional resonance that transcended the boundaries of mere entertainment, leaving a lasting imprint on the hearts of all who beheld his magic. Herrmann's unique style was not merely a product of skillful manipulation, but an alchemy that fused artistry, passion, and a profound understanding of the human longing for wonder and enchantment. It was through this extraordinary blend that he etched his name in the annals of magic history, forever remembered as a luminary whose indelible mark on the art of illusion continues to inspire and captivate generations.

Beyond Tricks: The Philosophy of Magic

Alexander Herrmann's journey in crafting his unique style delved deep into the heart of what magic truly means. Behind the wondrous spectacle of his performances lay a profound philosophy that shaped not only his artistry but also his worldview. Beyond the mere mastery of tricks and illusions, Herrmann sought to convey a deeper message through his magical performances. At the core of Herrmann's philosophy was the belief that magic had the power to ignite wonder and inspiration in the hearts of the audience. He viewed magic as a conduit for transcending the ordinary and inviting spectators into a realm of enchantment. Through his carefully curated acts, Herrmann aimed to awaken a sense of childlike awe and curiosity, reminding audiences of the limitless possibilities that exist beyond the boundaries of everyday life. Central to this philosophy was the intention to evoke genuine emotion and connection with his audience. Herrmann understood that the true magic lay not in the mere execution of tricks, but in the emotional impact they could deliver. Every sleight of hand and illusion was meticulously designed to touch the hearts of those who witnessed them, leaving a lasting imprint of wonder and joy. His performances were infused with a palpable sincerity, creating an intimate bond between performer and audience that transcended the stage. Furthermore, Herrmann believed in using his magical prowess as a force for positivity and inspiration. He saw himself not merely as an entertainer, but as a purveyor of hope and delight. Through his art, he sought to uplift spirits, spark imagination, and instill a sense of belief in the extraordinary. This commitment to spreading joy and wonder through magic was a defining element of Herrmann's philosophy, shaping the very essence of his performances. In embracing the philosophy of magic, Herrmann also recognized the responsibility that came with wielding such captivating power. He understood the need to uphold the integrity and ethics of magic, ensuring that the mystique and allure remained untarnished. His dedication to preserving the purity of magic's enchantment set a standard for generations of illusionists to come. Indeed, beyond the allure of entertainment, Alexander Herrmann's philosophy of magic resonates as a testament to the transformative potential of wonder and the enduring impact of heartfelt connection within the realm of enchantment.

The Heartfelt Connection with Fans

Performing magic is not just about the illusions, slight of hand, or captivating performances. For Alexander Herrmann, it went beyond the stage and deep into the hearts of his audience. He understood that the real magic lies in creating a bond, a connection with those who witness the marvels unfold before their eyes. Herrmann had an innate ability to make each person in the audience feel like a part of the show; he made them believe in the impossible and reignited that sense of childlike wonder. Whether performing for a small gathering or a grand auditorium, he approached each spectator as an individual, taking the time to connect with them on a personal level. It was this genuine and heartfelt connection that set him apart from his contemporaries. The ripple effect of his performances extended beyond the realms of magic; it left a lasting imprint on the hearts of those fortunate enough to experience his artistry. Herrmann's dedication to his fans and his genuine appreciation for their support and admiration became a hallmark of his illustrious career. His humility and gratitude towards his audience created an unbreakable bond, transforming mere spectators into devoted admirers. Letters poured in from all corners of the world, expressing profound gratitude and admiration for the moments of enchantment he had shared. These letters were cherished by Herrmann, each one serving as a testament to the incredible impact his magic had on countless lives. Even after the final curtain call, his legacy continues to thrive in the hearts of the individuals whose lives he touched. It is a testament to the extraordinary bond he formed, bridging the gap between performer and audience in a way that transcended mere entertainment and created lasting memories that would be etched in the hearts of generations to come.

Magic Redefined: Herrmann's Legacy

Alexander Herrmann's impact on the world of magic goes far beyond his captivating performances and revolutionary techniques. His legacy is one that has redefined the art of illusion, inspiring countless magicians to push the boundaries of what is possible and captivating audiences around the globe. Herrmann's dedication to his craft was unparalleled, and it was this unwavering commitment that set the stage for a new era of wonder and amazement. His profound influence can be seen in the way modern magicians approach their art, embracing innovation while honoring the timeless traditions that Herrmann himself upheld. Through his enduring legacy, Alexander Herrmann continues to beckon aspiring magicians to dream big, think outside the box, and strive for excellence in every performance. Beyond his magical prowess, Herrmann's legacy also encompasses his philanthropic efforts, as he used his platform to bring joy and wonder to those in need. His contributions to society extended far beyond the stage, leaving a lasting impact on communities and individuals alike. Whether through charitable endeavors or awe-inspiring acts of magic, Herrmann's legacy serves as a testament to the power of using one's gifts for the betterment of others. As we explore the depths of Herrmann's legacy, it becomes clear that his influence reaches far beyond the confines of a performance hall. His mark on the world of magic remains indelible, serving as a guiding light for future generations of illusionists and enchanters. Through his enduring impact, Herrmann continues to redefine what it means to be a master magician, transcending mere trickery to evoke genuine emotions and spark unbridled imagination. With each new generation that embraces his teachings, Alexander Herrmann's legacy is perpetuated, ensuring that the magic he brought into the world will continue to inspire awe and wonder for years to come.

Setting the Stage for a Lifetime of Wonder

The stage held a promise, a glimpse into a world where reality blended with mystery. Alexander Herrmann's tremendous artistry was about to unfold, setting the scene for a lifetime of awe-inspiring wonder. As he stepped onto that hallowed platform, he bore not just the weight of anticipation but the fervent desire to transport his audience into realms unknown. In the flickering glow of the gaslights, a mere mortal would transcend to become a maestro of marvels. He had mastered more than sleight of hand; he had perfected the enigma of the human heart. Each prop, each gesture, and each gaze contained a fragment of his spirit, interwoven into an intricate tapestry that would enthrall generations. The stage was his canvas, and his magic was a symphony that whispered secrets and spun dreams. His dedication to his craft was palpable, as every meticulous detail became part of an immersive experience. It was not merely about the illusions but about the emotions they evoked, the spellbinding connection that transcended time and space. Traveling from city to city, he shared his bewitching creations, casting a spell that left audiences perpetually yearning for one more moment of enchantment. Behind the scenes, his relentless pursuit of perfection led him to evolve his performances continually. Through collaborations with artisans and inventors, he forged innovative feats that defied belief and redefined what it meant to be spellbound. The audience was not just a witness, but a vital participant in a grand narrative woven by his artistry. Amidst the applause and gasps of disbelief, he humbly sought to leave behind a legacy of inspiration. His devotion to sharing the wonder of his craft extended beyond his final act. It was a commitment to kindle the spark of imagination in the hearts of the young and reignite the sense of wonder in the souls of the jaded. Each meticulously choreographed show was a testament to his unwavering resolve to infuse the world with magic, creating a reservoir of memories that shimmered like precious jewels in the collective consciousness. The stage was not just a platform for illusion; it was a sanctum where miracles transpired, where belief triumphed, and where the wonder of existence unfolded. Alexander Herrmann's legacy was not merely etched in stone or ink; it lived on in the cherished recollections of those who had been touched by his ineffable artistry. And so, he set the stage, not just for himself, but for a perpetual panorama of mesmerizing wonder, blazing a trail through history and etching his name into the annals of immortality.

The Early Life of Alexander Herrmann

Introduction to the Early Years

Alexander Herrmann's formative years played a pivotal role in shaping the remarkable individual he would become. His family roots and heritage provided a rich tapestry of influences that left an indelible mark on his character and aspirations. Growing up in a nurturing environment infused with a deep appreciation for the arts, young Alexander was immersed in a world of creativity and wonder. His early experiences instilled within him a profound sense of curiosity and an unwavering passion for exploration. This insatiable thirst for knowledge and discovery became the cornerstone of his future endeavors. The supportive and encouraging atmosphere fostered by his family laid the groundwork for the emergence of his extraordinary talents. As a child, Alexander sought solace and inspiration in the enchanting stories and fables passed down through generations, each narrative steeped in tradition and history. These tales ignited his imagination and ignited a fervent desire to captivate and enthrall audiences with the magic they contained. He experienced firsthand the timeless allure of illusion and transformation, laying the foundation for his future as a masterful magician. Through the lens of his formative years, one can glimpse the budding ingenuity and boundless potential that would ultimately propel Alexander Herrmann onto the world stage. The amalgamation of his familial bonds, cultural heritage, and early exposure to the captivating art of magic coalesced to sculpt a young prodigy destined for greatness.

Family Roots and Heritage

The story of Alexander Herrmann's early years would be incomplete without delving into the rich tapestry of his family's roots and heritage. The Herrmann family hailed from a long line of performers, with a tradition steeped in the world of entertainment and magic. Tracing their lineage back through generations, it becomes evident that the love for spectacle and wonder was ingrained in their very DNA. Throughout history, the Herrmanns had been renowned for their contributions to the world of illusion and enchantment. Tales of their performances, handed down from one generation to the next, spoke of their ability to captivate audiences and weave spells of awe and amazement. Each new member of the family inherited not only a name but also a legacy of captivating hearts and minds through their magical prowess. Beyond their professional achievements, the Herrmann family prided itself on forging strong bonds with fellow magicians and performers, extending their influence beyond the stage. In numerous anecdotes and historical records, their unwavering camaraderie with others in the industry becomes apparent, highlighting the sense of community and shared passion that permeated their lives. This network of connections proved to be a wellspring of inspiration and support, fostering an environment where creativity could flourish and dreams could manifest into reality. The family's heritage was not solely defined by their professional pursuits. A deep appreciation for artistic expression, combined with a profound respect for the craft of magic, provided a solid foundation for each successive generation to build upon. From the early days of honing their skills in the art of prestidigitation to the sophisticated performances that would later establish their renown, the Herrmanns embodied a commitment to excellence that resonated with all who had the privilege of witnessing their acts. In unraveling the tapestry of the Herrmanns' heritage, one cannot ignore the impact of their cultural background on the development of their artistic identity. Their roots bore the marks of diverse influences and traditions, infusing their performances with a depth and complexity that transcended mere spectacle. It was this amalgamation of heritage, tradition, and innovation that set the stage for Alexander Herrmann's remarkable journey, laying the groundwork for the indelible mark he would etch upon the world of magic.

A Childhood of Wonder

Alexander Herrmann's childhood was filled with wonder and fascination, as he grew up in a world where magic seemed to be woven into the very fabric of his existence. From a young age, he displayed an insatiable curiosity about the mysteries of the world, often spending hours exploring the enchanted forests and picturesque landscapes that surrounded his family home. The vibrant colors of the changing seasons, the whispering of the wind through the trees, and the playful dance of sunlight on the water all seemed like magical phenomena to the young Alexander. His boundless imagination led him to observe and ponder the natural phenomena around him, eager to uncover the secrets behind the extraordinary. Every rainbow, every shooting star, and every blooming flower held a special significance for him, igniting a sense of awe and inspiration. His parents, recognizing his unique perspective on the world, nurtured his inquisitive nature, encouraging him to delve deeper into the mysteries that captivated his young mind. Throughout his childhood, Alexander found solace in the realm of enchantment, often losing himself in fantastical stories and tales of mythical creatures that stirred his imagination. His youthful spirit soared on the wings of fantasy, as he reveled in the magical realms described in fairy tales and folklore. These early experiences laid the foundation for his future endeavors as a magician, imbuing him with an unquenchable thirst for the extraordinary and the inexplicable. Moreover, his encounters with traveling entertainers and performers who would visit his small town left an indelible mark on him, sparking a profound fascination with the art of illusion and spectacle. He was enchanted by their incredible feats and mystifying performances, which seemed to defy the laws of reality. Each encounter left him spellbound, yearning to understand the secrets behind these captivating displays. Little did he know that these encounters would shape his destiny and chart a course for his illustrious career as a master magician. As he navigated the wondrous landscape of his formative years, Alexander Herrmann's deep connection with the extraordinary continued to blossom, laying the groundwork for the magical journey that awaited him. His childhood of wonder sculpted a soul brimming with curiosity, creativity, and an enduring love for the enchanting mysteries of the world.

Early Fascination with Magic

Alexander Herrmann's early fascination with magic began as a child, where he found himself captivated by the mystique and allure of illusions. From a tender age, he would eagerly watch traveling magicians perform at local fairs and village gatherings, his eyes wide with wonder and his mind full of curiosity. The display of skill and wonderment left an indelible mark on the young Alexander, igniting a passion within him that would shape the course of his life. It wasn't just the tricks and sleights that fascinated him; it was the sense of amazement and delight that these performances brought to the faces of the audience. He saw the potential for magic to bring joy and astonishment to people's lives, and this realization fueled his desire to become a master of the craft. As he immersed himself in the world of magic, he found solace and purpose in the art form, relishing the opportunity to transport others to a realm of enchantment and disbelief. His early experiences with magic became the foundation upon which he built his illustrious career, and the memories of those formative years remained etched in his heart throughout his life.

Influences and Inspirations

Alexander Herrmann's early fascination with magic was not only a result of his own innate curiosity, but also due to the numerous influences and inspirations that shaped his artistic development. His exposure to a diverse range of magical performances ignited a deep-seated passion within him. From witnessing local street performers to attending elaborate stage shows, young Alexander soaked up every aspect of these captivating displays, striving to understand the secrets behind each illusion. Moreover, within his own family, Herrmann found a wellspring of inspiration. His older brother, Carl Herrmann, who was already carving his path as a respected magician, served as both a mentor and an ideal to aspire to. Carl's mastery of the craft not only impressed Alexander but also instilled in him a fierce determination to excel in the same field. The brothers' shared love for magic became a source of camaraderie and competition, propelling Alexander to push the boundaries of his capabilities. Beyond his immediate family, Herrmann drew inspiration from renowned magicians and entertainers of his time. He eagerly studied the performances of figures like Robert-Houdin, Jean Eugène Robert-Houdin, borrowing elements from their acts while cultivating his unique style. By observing and immersing himself in the works of these legendary figures, Alexander cultivated a deep respect for the art of magic and an unyielding commitment to honing his own skills. In addition to professional influences, personal experiences and encounters played a pivotal role in shaping Alexander's early years. Chance encounters with traveling magicians and chance encounters with traveling magicians, awe-inspiring stories from his family's globetrotting adventures, and interactions with fellow enthusiasts further fueled his passion and emboldened him to pursue magic with unwavering dedication. These encounters would leave an indelible mark on his artistic journey, igniting an insatiable thirst for knowledge and excellence. As Alexander Herrmann's fascination with magic deepened, so too did his quest for originality and innovation. By drawing from the rich tapestry of influences and inspirations that permeated his formative years, he began to cultivate a vision that blended tradition with progressive flair, laying the groundwork for the extraordinary career that lay ahead.

The Family Dynamic

The family dynamic of the Herrmanns played an instrumental role in shaping Alexander Herrmann's early life and future career as a magician. Growing up in a household that fostered creativity, curiosity, and a love for the arts, Alexander was surrounded by the influences of his parents and siblings. His family's unwavering support and encouragement contributed significantly to his journey into the world of magic. The Herrmanns shared a deep passion for performance and showmanship, instilling in young Alexander an appreciation for captivating an audience. At the heart of the family dynamic was a sense of unity and collaboration. Despite the inevitable challenges and hardships that come with pursuing a career in the entertainment industry, the Herrmanns stood by each other, offering guidance, mentorship, and unconditional love. They functioned not only as a familial unit but also as a creative collective, inspiring one another to push boundaries and strive for excellence. Their shared experiences and shared values created a nurturing environment where Alexander could explore his talents and develop his unique magical style. Moreover, the family dynamic served as a platform for the exchange of ideas and techniques. The Herrmann siblings, including Alexander's older brother Compars Herrmann, who was also a renowned magician, engaged in continuous dialogue about their craft, exchanging insights and honing their skills. This collaborative spirit fueled the brothers' mutual growth, as they learned from each other's successes and failures. Together, they forged a bond based on respect, competition, and a mutual dedication to advancing the art of magic. Beyond the realm of magic, the family dynamic also encompassed various aspects of daily life. From managing finances to navigating personal relationships, the Herrmanns navigated the complexities of life as a close-knit unit.

This holistic approach equipped Alexander with not only practical life skills but also a profound understanding of the importance of emotional support and camaraderie. In essence, the family dynamic within the Herrmann household provided Alexander with the essential foundation for his magical journey. It imbued him with a sense of purpose, resilience, and an unwavering commitment to his craft. The invaluable lessons learned from his family would shape his character and drive, setting the stage for his remarkable ascent in the world of magic.

Brothers in Magic

Alexander Herrmann's early years were closely intertwined with his brother, Compars Herrmann, who played a central role in shaping his magical abilities. As siblings, they shared a deep bond that extended beyond familial ties and into the world of magic. Compars was not only an older brother to Alexander but also a mentor, confidant, and partner in the pursuit of their shared passion for enchantment. Together, they embarked on a journey that would leave an indelible mark on the history of magic. The brothers' camaraderie extended beyond their personal relationship and permeated their performances, where their seamless synchronization and mutual understanding captivated audiences worldwide. Their unique bond allowed them to synchronize their movements in ways that transcended the conventional boundaries of magic, creating an aura of mystique and wonder that entranced all who witnessed their performances. Through their collaboration, they pioneered innovative techniques and illusions that pushed the boundaries of traditional magic, setting new standards for the art form. Despite their deep connection, the relationship between the Herrmann brothers also bore the hallmarks of healthy competition, which spurred them to continually outdo one another in their craft, driving each to greater heights of artistic expression. This friendly rivalry fueled their growth as magicians, propelling them to constantly refine their skills and develop increasingly awe-inspiring acts. Their mutual respect and admiration for each other's talents served as a source of inspiration and motivation, elevating their shared pursuit of mastery in the enchanting world of magic. The impact of their collaborative synergy rippled through the annals of magic history, leaving an enduring legacy that continues to inspire and influence magicians to this day. Together, they exemplified the true essence of fraternity, harnessing their mutual love for the art of magic to transcend the ordinary and achieve the extraordinary.

A Glimpse into Herrmann's World

As a young boy growing up in Paris, Alexander Herrmann was surrounded by a world of wonder and enchantment. His family's home was a haven for creativity and imagination, with his parents fostering an environment that encouraged their children to explore their interests and develop their talents. The walls of the Herrmann household resonated with laughter, music, and the occasional burst of applause as the siblings entertained one another with their emerging magical skills. These early experiences served as the foundation for Alexander's lifelong passion for magic. Within the confines of his family abode, Alexander found solace in his burgeoning fascination with the art of illusion. His curious mind eagerly absorbed every trick, technique, and secret that came his way, whether through books, mentors, or chance encounters with traveling performers. He reveled in the excitement of uncovering the mysteries behind sleight of hand and the allure of mesmerizing an audience. At the heart of it all was a deep-seated desire to bring joy and astonishment to others through his performances. Amidst the hustle and bustle of Parisian life, Alexander sought refuge in secluded spaces where he could practice his burgeoning craft undisturbed. His makeshift workshop became a sanctuary of creativity, teeming with props, apparatus, and the precious tools of his trade. Here, he honed his skills, tirelessly perfecting his acts until each movement flowed seamlessly and every gesture exuded an air of mystery. It was within these walls that the young magician began to carve out his unique identity, laying the groundwork for the incredible feats that would define his legacy. The influence of his surroundings cannot be overstated, as the vibrant tapestry of Paris imprinted itself upon Alexander's artistic soul. The city's rich cultural tapestry, eclectic street performances, and captivating theater productions provided a backdrop against which his own talents flourished. Every cobblestone and every street corner held the potential for inspiration, fueling his boundless imagination and propelling him to new heights of creativity. Thus, as we peer into the formative years of Alexander Herrmann, we catch a glimpse of a world brimming with promise and potential. It is here, within the tapestry of youth and boundless imagination, that the enchanted journey of the Great Herrmann truly begins.

Nurturing a Gifted Child

As we delve into the early upbringing of Alexander Herrmann, it becomes evident that his parents played a crucial role in nurturing his burgeoning talents. From a tender age, Alexander exhibited a curiosity and fascination with the art of magic that set him apart from his peers. His parents, recognizing his innate giftedness, wholeheartedly supported and encouraged his passion for magic. Whether it was attending local magic shows or purchasing him his first deck of cards, they sought to foster his creativity and determination. They understood that a supportive environment was pivotal in allowing their son to flourish. Furthermore, they instilled in young Alexander a strong sense of discipline and perseverance, knowing that these qualities would serve him well on his path to greatness. Through their unwavering belief in his potential, his parents laid the foundation for what would later become an illustrious career in the world of magic. Additionally, they provided him with access to mentors and resources, ensuring that he received the necessary guidance to hone his skills. Their unwavering love and encouragement instilled in Alexander a profound sense of confidence and self-belief, essential attributes that propelled him towards achieving his dreams. Their commitment to nurturing his gift not only shaped his future but also left an indelible mark on the landscape of magic. The significance of parental influence cannot be overstated, and in the case of Alexander Herrmann, it was indeed foundational in shaping the trajectory of his life. The impact of such nurturing and support during his formative years is beautifully reflected in the enchanting performances that would later captivate audiences worldwide.

Setting the Stage for Greatness

Alexander Herrmann's early years were marked by an extraordinary combination of talent, curiosity, and an insatiable thirst for knowledge. From a young age, it was evident that he possessed a special flair for captivating audiences and an innate ability to connect with people through his performances. His family played a pivotal role in shaping and nurturing his talents, providing unwavering support and encouragement as he ventured into the world of magic. As the youngest member of a family deeply entrenched in the world of entertainment, Alexander found himself immersed in an environment where creativity and showmanship were valued above all else. His older brothers, Carl and Compars, themselves established magicians, served as both mentors and sources of inspiration for the budding prodigy. Under their guidance, Alexander honed his craft, constantly pushing the boundaries of what was possible in the realm of illusion. Beyond the confines of his family's influence, young Alexander sought knowledge and guidance from an array of mentors and masters of the craft. His voracious appetite for learning led him to study the works of renowned magicians and delve into the intricacies of ancient magical traditions. It was during this formative period that he began to develop his own unique style, blending traditional techniques with innovative approaches that would set him apart as a magician ahead of his time. While his peers were preoccupied with conventional pursuits, Alexander delved deeper into the history and philosophy of magic, immersing himself in its myriad forms to unearth its true essence. His unwavering dedication to his art, coupled with a genuine passion for enchanting and delighting audiences, set the stage for his meteoric rise to greatness. Throughout these foundational years, Alexander's profound understanding of the human psyche and his innate ability to evoke wonder and awe became the cornerstones of his magical prowess. He meticulously studied every nuance of performance, ensuring that each gesture, word, and expression resonated in perfect harmony with his audiences, captivating them in a symphony of mystery and delight. The nurturing and guidance he received during his early years imparted upon him not only a deep respect for the art of magic but also instilled in him an unyielding commitment to craftsmanship and authenticity. These values would come to define his illustrious career and establish him as one of the most revered and influential magicians of his era.

Humble Beginnings

Family Roots and Heritage

Alexander Herrmann, known to the world as 'Herrmann the Great,' emerged from a rich tapestry of cultural and historical influences that shaped his family's heritage. The Herrmann family could trace their roots back through generations of performers, artists, and artisans, whose collective experiences contributed to the magical legacy that would ultimately define Alexander's destiny. The Herrmanns' ancestral lineage was deeply intertwined with the vibrant world of performance arts, particularly within the realms of magic and illusion. In tracing back the family's history, one uncovers a fascinating chronicle of entertainers, magicians, and craftsmen who fascinated audiences across continents. This deep-rooted connection to the art of enchantment would eventually spark the young Alexander's early fascination with magic. From the humble beginnings of performing enchantments at local fairs to captivating audiences across the grand stages of Europe, the Herrmann name would become synonymous with wonder and awe. Within the context of the era, the family's heritage was also intricately woven into the fabric of social and cultural movements. As Alexander's ancestors navigated through the ever-changing landscapes of artistry, they bore witness to tumultuous times that sculpted their perspective on the world. Their experiences imbued in Alexander a profound sense of empathy, resilience, and a deep appreciation for the transformative power of magic. Moreover, the family heritage intersected with historical junctures, precipitating a unique fusion of traditions, folklore, and innovative approaches to stagecraft. Alexander's forebears were part of a lineage that was not only steeped in the mastery of illusions but also attuned to the spirit of their time. Through their performances, they sought to not only entertain but also to transport audiences to realms where wonder and fantasy reigned supreme. In exploring the cultural and historical frameworks that underpinned the Herrmann family's roots, one gains insight into the enduring values that served as the bedrock of Alexander's magical journey. As we delve deeper into this enthralling saga, it becomes evident that the tapestry of the Herrmann family's heritage played an instrumental role in shaping the remarkable trajectory of Alexander Herrmann, the prodigious magician who enchanted the world.

A Child's Curiosity in Magic

As Alexander Herrmann grew up, his fascination with magic continued to blossom. From a tender age, he had an insatiable curiosity about the art of illusion and sleight of hand. His young mind was captivated by the mystique and wonder that magic brought to the world. Whether watching street performers in Paris or sneaking into local theaters to witness magicians in action, Alexander was entranced by every aspect of magic. It was not merely the tricks themselves that captivated him, but also the reactions of the audience, the sense of awe and amazement that filled the air. This profound impact on both the performer and the spectators ignited a passion within him that would shape his entire life. As a child, he spent countless hours practicing simple tricks and experimenting with various sleights in an effort to unravel the secrets behind the illusions. The joy he felt when successfully executing a trick was immeasurable, and this early triumph motivated him to delve deeper into the art of magic. His inquisitive nature led him to seek out books and articles on magic, devouring every piece of information with relentless enthusiasm. As he honed his skills, his magical prowess began to draw attention from those around him. Family and friends marveled at his developing talent and encouraged him to pursue his passion with unwavering support. Little did they know that this young boy's fascination with magic would evolve into an extraordinary career that would leave a lasting legacy in the world of entertainment. Through Alexander Herrmann's childhood experiences, we witness the genesis of a remarkable journey that would propel him towards becoming one of the most celebrated magicians of all time.

Life in the Streets of Paris

The bustling streets of 19th-century Paris set the stage for young Alexander Herrmann's formative years. Nestled within the vibrant tapestry of the city, he found himself captivated by the endless array of sights, sounds, and experiences. From an early age, the rhythms of this enchanting metropolis became the backdrop for his burgeoning passion for magic. Wandering through the cobblestone pathways, he encountered a unique blend of characters - street performers, artisans, and fellow wide-eyed dreamers. Their collective energy left an indelible mark on his impressionable mind, fueling his burgeoning fascination for the art of illusion. Every corner held untold mysteries, every street performer seemed to wield a touch of magic. It was within this lively urban landscape that his innate curiosity intertwined with the allure of the unknown, sowing the seeds of his future greatness.

The Influence of a Magical Environment

Growing up in the vibrant streets of Paris, Alexander Herrmann was surrounded by an atmosphere teeming with art, culture, and enchantment. The pulsating heart of the performance arts world, the city provided a fertile ground for young Herrmann's burgeoning fascination with the realm of magic. Amidst the cobblestone alleys and bustling markets, he encountered a diverse tapestry of performers - from street magicians exerting their craft in captivating displays to grand theatrical productions showcasing the allure of illusion. These encounters ignited a spark within him, driving him to explore the mystical art forms that captivated his imagination. The magical environment enveloping Herrmann was not confined to mere entertainment; it embedded within him a profound appreciation for the transformative power of spectacle. The stories woven by these artists, both on stage and in the open air, spoke volumes to his tender heart, instilling in him a love for storytelling through the marvelous medium of magic. Each act witnessed on the busy streets left an indelible impression on the young dreamer, fueling his desire to someday cast spells of wonder and awe upon audiences far and wide. Furthermore, this early exposure to the world of magic within such a vivacious and culturally rich setting imbued Herrmann with an understanding of the interconnectedness between performance and society. The magic he beheld did not exist in isolation; it was a reflection of the hopes, dreams, and uncertainties shared by the people who gathered to witness its wonders. This realization kindled in him a sense of responsibility, recognizing the potential for magic to transcend mere trickery and resonate deeply with the human spirit. It laid the groundwork for his future as a magician who sought to not only dazzle, but also to touch the hearts and minds of those who experienced his performances. Ultimately, the influence of Paris's magical milieu fostered in Alexander Herrmann an unwavering belief in the power of wonder to uplift, inspire, and bridge the gaps between individuals. It was amidst the backdrop of this enchanting environment that he found the nurturing soil for his budding talents and aspirations, sowing the seeds for the remarkable journey that lay ahead.

Early Inspirations and Role Models

As Alexander Herrmann navigated his humble beginnings, he was surrounded by a bevy of inspirations and role models who played a significant part in shaping his magical journey. Growing up in an enchanting environment filled with the allure of mystique and wonder, young Herrmann found himself captivated by the performances of traveling magicians who visited his town. These mesmerizing displays of illusion ignited a spark within him from an early age, planting the seeds of curiosity and fascination.

Additionally, Herrmann discovered inspiration in the pages of spellbinding books and ancient texts that spoke of the art of magic, feeding his burgeoning passion for the craft. As he delved deeper into the world of magic, Herrmann found himself drawn to legendary performers who left an indelible mark on the magical landscape. He avidly studied their techniques, learning from their mastery and craftsmanship, and striving to imbue his own performances with the same captivating artistry. Among these luminaries, Herrmann found guidance and influence, forging a path that celebrated tradition while incorporating his unique flair. Moreover, his family members, particularly his older brother, served as role models and mentors, instilling in him invaluable wisdom and encouraging him to pursue his dreams relentlessly. Their unwavering support and belief in his potential became pillars of strength during the formative years of Herrmann's magical odyssey. Their encouragement propelled him forward, propelling him to defy the odds and embrace his calling with unyielding determination. It was from these early inspirations and influential figures that Alexander Herrmann drew the foundation of his magical identity, setting the stage for the extraordinary feats and sorcery that would later captivate audiences around the world.

Struggles and Challenges Faced

Alexander Herrmann's journey into the world of magic was not without its trials. As a young performer, he faced numerous challenges that tested his resolve and determination. One such obstacle was the skepticism and doubt from those around him. Many questioned his choice to pursue magic as a career, often dismissing it as frivolous or impractical. This lack of support could have easily discouraged him, but instead, it fueled his determination to prove his detractors wrong. Additionally, financial constraints presented a significant hurdle for Herrmann. Securing the resources needed to perfect his craft and establish himself in the competitive world of magic was no easy task. From procuring necessary props to securing performance opportunities, every step forward required immense dedication and sacrifice. Moreover, Herrmann encountered numerous setbacks in mastering certain magical techniques. He struggled with perfecting illusions and sleight of hand, often facing frustration and self-doubt along the way. Despite these challenges, he refused to be deterred and relentlessly pursued improvement. Beyond these personal struggles, external factors such as societal prejudices and the ever-changing landscape of entertainment added further complexity to his journey. Being a performer in a time when magic was not always respected as an art form placed additional pressure on Herrmann to prove the value and significance of his chosen vocation. Despite these barriers, he strived to create a space for himself and his art within the cultural landscape. Each hardship he faced served as a testament to his unwavering resilience and passion for magic. Through perseverance and unwavering dedication, Alexander Herrmann transformed these challenges into stepping stones towards his eventual success.

Developing an Unwavering Passion

At the heart of Alexander Herrmann's journey were the formative years that shaped his unyielding dedication to the art of magic. Despite facing numerous obstacles and hardships, his unwavering passion for magic continued to burn brightly, fueling his relentless pursuit of mastery. As a young boy in the vibrant streets of Paris, his fascination with the mysterious and enchanting world of magic took root. The exhilaration he felt each time he witnessed a dazzling illusion or sleight of hand performance was a spark that ignited a lifelong passion within him. It was during these impressionable years that his destiny intertwined with the captivating allure of magic, instilling in him an insatiable thirst for knowledge and a burning desire to learn the secrets behind every trick and illusion. The challenges he encountered only served to reinforce his determination, propelling him forward on a path illuminated by his fervent devotion to the craft. His commitment to magic became an intrinsic part of his identity, shaping his worldview and infusing every aspect of his life with the wonder and magic he sought to share with the world. Through each setback and triumph, his unwavering passion for magic remained steadfast, a beacon guiding him through the tumultuous waters of uncertainty and doubt. It was this indomitable spirit that fueled his tireless quest for excellence, driving him to push the boundaries of what was thought possible within the realm of magic. Amidst the trials and tribulations, his passion served as a source of inspiration, propelling him to overcome adversity and emerge as a visionary in the world of enchantment and wonder. As we delve into the depths of Alexander Herrmann's journey, we bear witness to the profound impact of an unwavering passion – a force that transcended barriers and ignited a legacy that would endure for generations to come.

Support from Family and Friends

The journey of a budding magician is often accompanied by numerous challenges and daunting obstacles. It is during these formative years that the unconditional support and encouragement of loved ones play an invaluable role in shaping the path towards success. For Alexander Herrmann, the unwavering faith and backing of his family and friends were instrumental in fostering his burgeoning love for magic. The genuine belief in his abilities and potential served as a wellspring of inspiration, propelling him to overcome adversity and pursue his passion with unwavering determination. Each step he took was bolstered by the knowledge that a steadfast network of support stood firmly behind him, ready to uplift and guide him through both triumphs and setbacks. Family, being the bedrock of his existence, provided a nurturing environment where his fervor for magic could flourish unhindered. Encouraged by their reassurance and pride in his aspirations, young

Alexander was emboldened to explore and experiment with the mystical arts, laying the groundwork for a remarkable future. Their understanding and willingness to embrace his unconventional pursuits created a sanctuary in which creativity and innovation thrived, allowing him to cultivate his talents and refine his artistry without inhibition. Each new trick mastered, each sleight of hand perfected, was celebrated with unmatched enthusiasm, fostering an environment teeming with positivity and affirmation. In addition to the unwavering support of his family, Herrmann was fortunate to be surrounded by a circle of friends whose belief in his potential was unwavering. Their camaraderie infused his journey with joy and resilience, providing avenues for collaboration, feedback, and mutual growth. Through shared experiences and mutual mentorship, they nurtured an environment conducive to learning and self-discovery, reinforcing each other's aspirations and ambitions. Their collective passion for magic formed the connective tissue of a fraternity bound by the pursuit of excellence, thereby fortifying Herrmann's resolve and fostering an indomitable spirit. Together, they weathered setbacks, celebrated victories, and enriched one another's lives through a shared commitment to the art of illusion. The influence of these friendships rippled through Herrmann's formative years, leaving an indelible mark on his journey toward becoming a master of magic.

First Steps into the World of Magic

As Alexander Herrmann ventured further into the world of magic, he found himself immersed in a mesmerizing realm where reality and illusion danced together. His early performances, often showcased to his close friends and family, became an embodiment of his unwavering dedication and an evolving artistry. With each trick, each sleight of hand, and each flourish of a wand, young Herrmann began to etch his name onto the canvas of magical history. Drawing inspiration from the enchanting streets of Paris and the bustling metropolitan life, Alexander Herrmann infused his acts with a deep understanding of human emotions and desires. He gradually discovered the profound delight in captivating an audience, in making them believe in the extraordinary, and in offering them moments of pure astonishment. Through these early experiences, Herrmann realized that his passion for magic was not just a fleeting interest but a calling that beckoned him to explore uncharted territories of wonderment and marvel. Eager to refine his craft, Alexander sought out every opportunity to learn from seasoned magicians and illusionists. He braved challenges, honed his skills, and relentlessly pursued excellence. These formative years laid the groundwork for his future brilliance, instilling in him a commitment to elevate the art of magic to new heights. By embracing the trials and triumphs of his journey, Herrmann garnered insights that would later set him apart as a trailblazer in the world of enchantment. Infused with an unyielding determination, Alexander Herrmann transitioned from an ambitious novice to an emerging luminary, leaving indelible impressions with every spellbinding performance. His relentless dedication and innate talent intertwined harmoniously, casting a spell on all those who had the privilege of witnessing his early feats. The applause, whispers of amazement, and undying sense of wonder in the eyes of his audience fueled his resolve to challenge the boundaries of what was deemed possible within the realm of magic. These initial steps into the world of magic were transformative for Alexander Herrmann, shaping his identity as a maestro of mystery and leaving an indelible mark on the captivating tapestry of his illustrious career.

Laying the Foundation for Greatness

Entering the enigmatic world of magic at such a tender age, Alexander Herrmann's journey was nothing short of extraordinary. As he took his first steps into this captivating realm, little did he know that he was laying the foundation for what would become an illustrious career. The early exposure to the art of illusion and wonderment sparked a fire within him, driving him to explore the depths of this mysterious craft with unwavering determination. With each new trick and sleight of hand, the young Herrmann was unknowingly setting the stage for greatness. His passion for magic blossomed, intertwining seamlessly with his innate talent and insatiable thirst for knowledge. Amidst the cobblestone streets and twinkling lights of Paris, Herrmann honed his skills, practicing tirelessly to perfect every nuance of his performance. It was here that he absorbed the essence of showmanship and charisma, traits that would later define his mesmerizing presence on stage. The bustling atmosphere of the city imbued in him a sense of tenacity, shaping his resilience in the face of adversity and instilling in him the courage to chase his dreams relentlessly. Throughout this formative period, Herrmann not only cultivated his dexterity and flair but also imbibed the captivating allure of mystery that magic effortlessly exudes. Every encounter with a new audience, every awe-struck expression in response to his tricks, fueled his pursuit of perfection and stoked the flames of his ambition. As he delved deeper into the world of illusions, Herrmann found himself surrounded by like-minded individuals, forging connections within a close-knit community of magicians and performers. These interactions, filled with shared secrets and boundless creativity, played an instrumental role in shaping his artistic vision. The collaborative spirit that permeated these circles nurtured his growth, offering invaluable insights and propelling him forward on his quest for mastery. Through collective experimentation and spirited discussions, he gleaned profound wisdom that would later set him apart as a master of his craft. The years spent in laying this foundation were pivotal, serving as the crucible where Herrmann's artistry was tempered and refined. It was during this period that he sowed the seeds of innovation, experimenting fearlessly with techniques and concepts that would ultimately elevate his performances to new heights. These early experiences, though fraught with challenges and setbacks, instilled in him a resolute spirit and an unwavering belief in the transformative power of magic. From these humble beginnings, a legend was set in motion—a legacy of wonder and enchantment that would endure through generations, leaving an indelible mark on the world of magic.

Training Under His Brother

Shared Dreams and Aspirations

From the earliest days of their childhood, Alexander and his brother shared an unspoken understanding, a deep connection woven by their mutual love for the art of magic. Their shared dreams and aspirations transcended the ordinary bounds of brotherhood, uniting them in a common pursuit of excellence. It was in the little moments, hidden from the world, that their bond blossomed – nights spent poring over magic books under dim lamplight, the thrill of unraveling new tricks together, and the unspoken promise to conquer the world with their art. Their mutual passion for magic was a flame that burned bright within each of them, igniting their ambitions and propelling them forward on a path carved by destiny. As they immersed themselves in the mesmerizing world of illusions and wonder, their shared experiences became the cornerstone of their unbreakable bond. Each victory achieved, each setback endured, only served to stoke the fire of their shared dreams, reinforcing their unyielding commitment to one another and to the art they held dear. In the quiet sanctuary of their shared workspace, they honed their skills and nurtured their imagination. Countless hours were devoted to perfecting their craft, relentlessly pushing the boundaries of what was possible. It was here that they silently vowed to elevate their performances beyond the realm of ordinary mortals. With every meticulously rehearsed routine and every whispered incantation, they etched their names into the annals of magic history. The aspiration to captivate audiences with their enchanting displays of skill and artistry bound them closer than blood ever could. Their dreams intertwined and weaved a tapestry of shared purpose, giving rise to a synergy that surpassed the sum of its parts. In each other, they found not only a confidant but also a kindred spirit, a companion in the relentless pursuit of perfection. Together, they solidified their resolve to leave an indelible mark on the world of magic, driven by an unwavering belief in each other's potential and fueled by an undying love for the magical arts. As destiny beckoned, casting its radiant light upon them, the brothers embraced the exhilarating journey that lay ahead, bound by an unshakable bond forged in the crucible of shared dreams and aspirations.

The Bond Between Brothers

The bond between Alexander Herrmann and his brother Carl was one woven with the threads of destiny, talent, and an unbreakable fraternal connection. From a young age, it was evident that the Herrmann brothers shared a deep understanding of one another's aspirations and dreams. Bound by their mutual love for magic and the yearning to dazzle audiences worldwide, they embarked on an extraordinary journey together. The unspoken understanding between them transcended mere words; it was an unbreakable link that solidified their partnership in both life and magic. As they navigated through the complexities of mastering the art of illusion, their bond soared to remarkable heights. The collaborative energy between the two brothers was palpable, fueling their relentless pursuit of perfection. They spurred each other on, offering unwavering support and encouragement, while also challenging each other to push the boundaries of their craft. Despite inevitable hurdles and setbacks, they remained steadfast, drawing strength from their shared ambitions. The echoes of their shared laughter reverberated through the walls of their practice space, punctuating the long hours of dedicated rehearsal. Their mutual enthusiasm for magic served as a binding force that cemented their sibling bond into an unshakable alliance. Together, they seamlessly amalgamated their distinct styles and techniques, creating a harmonious synergy that set the stage for their future triumphs. However, alongside their shared camaraderie, there existed a healthy sense of competition—a silent catalyst that propelled them to reach unprecedented artistic heights. The friendly rivalry between the brothers was underscored by a profound respect for each other's capabilities. This beautifully intricate relationship fostered an environment conducive to growth, innovation, and unparalleled synergy. During quieter moments, away from the dazzling lights of the stage, the brothers engaged in deep conversations about their visions and the legacy they hoped to leave behind. Through these discussions, they further solidified their intertwined destinies, forging a pact that transcended the bounds of time. Their bond weathered storms and celebrated triumphs, emerging as a testament to the unyielding power of brotherhood. In essence, the bond between Alexander and Carl Herrmann was a tapestry intricately woven with mutual admiration, relentless dedication, and an unspoken promise to elevate each other to greater heights. Their collaboration, underpinned by an unbreakable camaraderie, would lay the foundation for their indelible mark on the world of magic—the pinnacle of which was yet to come.

In the Shadow of Excellence

Growing up in the awe-inspiring presence of an accomplished magician like his brother, Alexander Herrmann found himself engulfed in the shadow of excellence from a young age. As he witnessed his brother's mesmerizing performances and the profound impact they had on audiences, a blend of admiration, inspiration, and aspiration took root in his impressionable heart. The example set by his brother became more than just a benchmark; it became a beacon guiding his own journey into the world of magic. Though daunting, this shadow was not one of overshadowing or obstructing, but rather one of illumination and enlightenment. It served as a constant reminder of the heights to which one could ascend with dedication and genuine passion. The ever-present specter of his brother's mastery was not a burden, but rather a source of motivation and determination. It instilled within Alexander a desire to carve his own path while upholding the legacy of his mentor and brother. Every accolade achieved by his brother served as a testament to what was attainable, spurring him to strive for greatness in his own right. However, residing in the cosmic glow of another's achievements also brought its share of challenges. It meant grappling with the weight of expectations, both self-imposed and external, and the inevitable comparisons that naturally arose. Yet, Alexander embraced these challenges as opportunities for growth and learning. Instead of being stifled, he sought to harness the energy of his brother's success and channel it into his own creative endeavors, always mindful of preserving his individuality and distinct style. In the shadow of his brother's illustrious career, Alexander Herrmann found not darkness, but a source of warmth and guidance, a symbol of what was possible, and a touchstone for his own aspirations. This nurturing environment paved the way for the emergence of a budding magician, who would later captivate audiences and etch his own name in the annals of magical history.

Endless Days of Practice

The pursuit of mastery in the art of magic demands unyielding dedication and unwavering perseverance. This holds especially true for Alexander Herrmann as he embarked on his journey under the guidance of his elder brother. Each day dawned with a singular focus – to hone his craft through relentless practice. There were no shortcuts, no substitutes for the painstaking hours spent perfecting every nuance of his performances. Despite the grueling nature of the daily regimen, Alexander approached it with an earnest and resolute spirit. The dusty halls of their practice studio bore witness to countless trials and errors, as he meticulously polished each sleight of hand and maneuvered through intricate illusions. His commitment knew no bounds, often pushing the boundaries of physical and mental endurance. The sound of cards shuffling and coins clinking became a familiar symphony, echoing through the hallowed walls as he labored tirelessly, refining his techniques. Even the most seemingly mundane gestures held profound significance, each movement contributing to the seamless execution of his illusions. The long hours dissolved into the ether, overshadowed by the sheer determination that fueled Alexander's pursuit of perfection. As the days blurred into nights and then seamlessly transitioned into the next day, the lines between practice and life itself began to fade. Magic ceased to be a mere craft; it became an inseparable part of his essence, shaping his very being. His unrelenting dedication burgeoned into a testament to an unwavering commitment, a narrative etched in the annals of the history of magic. Amidst these endless days of practice, there lay a transformation – a metamorphosis wrought through sheer persistence and an unshakeable passion. Every fumble and stumble served as yet another lesson learned, reinforcing his resolve to transcend mediocrity. It was through these arduous endeavors that his skills ascended beyond the realms of commonplace, marking the emergence of a prodigious talent destined to leave an indelible mark on the world of magic.

Learning Through Observation

Observation is a powerful tool, an art in itself that young Alexander Herrmann took to heart during his formative years under the guidance of his talented older brother. Rather than simply being told what to do, Alexander absorbed the intricacies of magic through keen observation of his brother's performances and practice sessions. This immersive approach allowed him to internalize the nuances of sleight of hand, the precise timing of illusions, and the captivating stage presence required to hold an audience spellbound. Each movement, each expression, and each flourish became etched in his mind as he strove to understand not just the 'how' but also the 'why' behind every maneuver. It was through this dedicated observation that Alexander began to develop his own unique style, drawing inspiration from his brother's mastery while simultaneously forging his own path in the world of magic. Beyond the technical aspects, Alexander also learned the importance of connecting with the audience on an emotional level. He witnessed firsthand how his brother used subtle gestures and expressions to elicit wonder, joy, and amazement from the spectators. These valuable lessons extended beyond the realm of magic, shaping Alexander into a more empathetic and perceptive individual. As he honed his craft, the influence of his brother's mentorship became intertwined with his own burgeoning creativity, resulting in a harmonious blend of tradition and innovation. This chapter of Alexander's journey serves as a testament to the profound impact that genuine observation can have on one's growth and development. It laid the groundwork for the evolution of a magician who not only dazzled the world with his extraordinary feats but also touched hearts and inspired minds through the sheer power of his art.

Embracing Guidance and Critique

Embracing guidance and critique was a pivotal aspect of Alexander Herrmann's journey to mastering the art of magic. Under the tutelage of his elder brother Carl, Alexander demonstrated an eagerness to absorb all aspects of the craft. Carl's mentorship extended beyond traditional teaching as he provided valuable constructive criticism and insightful feedback. This nurturing environment allowed Alexander to flourish and deepened his understanding of the nuances of magic. Instead of shying away from critique, Alexander embraced it, recognizing that it was an integral part of his growth as a magician. His resilience in the face of criticism became a defining trait, shaping his commitment to excellence. Every performance became an opportunity to learn and refine his skills. The bond between the brothers provided a safe space for honest, candid feedback that propelled Alexander's evolution as a magician. Their shared passion for magic fueled a mutual desire for continuous improvement, fostering an environment where honest critique was regarded as a gift rather than a burden. Through this process, Alexander developed a profound respect for the art form and a true appreciation for the power of constructive critique. Beyond skill development, embracing guidance and critique also solidified the bond between the brothers, creating a foundation of trust and support that would endure throughout their careers. As Alexander navigated the complexities of the magical world, Carl's wisdom and insight served as a beacon, guiding him through challenges and triumphs alike. The experiences forged a lasting bond predicated on mutual respect and a genuine love for the art of magic. This interplay of mentorship and receptiveness to critique laid the groundwork for Alexander's future success, instilling in him a deep understanding of the transformative power of constructive feedback.

Fostering a Deep Love for Magic

Alexander Herrmann's deep love for magic was nurtured from a young age, stemming from moments of wonder and awe that captured his imagination. It was in the gentle guidance of his brother that this passion was shaped and cultivated into an unwavering commitment to the art of illusion. Every feat of magic, every delicate sleight of hand, and every captivating performance echoed the undying affection he held for the craft. In the quiet hours of their shared space, the brothers would immerse themselves in the world of magic, meticulously studying ancient texts and practicing time-honored techniques passed down through generations. The mystical allure of conjuring illusions exuded a profound sense of joy and fulfillment that resonated deep within Alexander's spirit, driving him to pursue mastery with unyielding dedication. Beyond the confines of practice sessions, Alexander's love for magic extended to the communities he encountered during his travels. His sincere desire to evoke astonishment and joy propelled him to tirelessly refine his art, injecting every performance with a genuine sense of wonder and enchantment. Countless hours were devoted to perfecting each trick, each flourish, and each intonation, an endeavor fueled by a pure love for the magic that transcended the stage. His fervor for the art form shone through in every interaction, as Alexander sought to inspire others with the same reverence and passion that had ignited his own journey. Whether entertaining royalty or captivating humble audiences, his genuine appreciation for the transformative power of magic endeared him to all who witnessed his extraordinary feats. It was this inherent love for magic that allowed him to transcend the mere role of performer, becoming a custodian of wonder and an ambassador for the timeless allure of illusion. Through trials and triumphs, doubts and daring endeavors, the fire of Alexander's love for magic burned unwaveringly bright, illuminating the path towards a legacy that would endure for generations to come.

Lessons in Perseverance

In the journey of mastering the art of magic, perseverance stands as a cornerstone that shapes the character and determination of an individual. The path to mastery is lined with hurdles, setbacks, and moments of self-doubt. It is within these tempests that aspiring magicians truly discover the depth of their grit and strive for excellence. Alexander Herrmann's unwavering commitment to his craft serves as a testament to the invaluable lessons one can glean from perseverance. Through countless hours of tireless practice and unyielding dedication, he honed his skills, each setback igniting a fiercer resolve to succeed. The essence of perseverance transcends the realms of the magical arts, extending its reach into the tapestry of everyday life. It cultivates resilience, fostering the ability to weather storms and emerge stronger, armed with the wisdom gained from navigating adversity. Aspiring magicians often find themselves confronted with tricks that seem insurmountable, illusions that elude mastery, and performances that fall short of expectations. Yet, in embracing these challenges and persisting with indomitable fortitude, they imbue their craft with an unstoppable spirit. Perseverance also intertwines with the pursuit of creativity, pushing individuals to transcend the boundaries of tradition and chart new paths. Alexander Herrmann's determination to carve out a unique style within the realm of magic epitomizes this union of resilience and innovation. His relentless pursuit of groundbreaking illusions and distinctive performances exemplifies the transformative power of steadfast perseverance. Each trial metamorphoses into an opportunity for growth, propelling individuals to surpass their previous limitations and redefine the scope of their potential. Furthermore, the art of magic often demands patience and unwavering dedication, with the realization that the fruits of labor may not manifest immediately. The journey from novice to virtuoso requires the endurance to endure the plateau periods, where progress appears stagnant. In these moments, perseverance acts as an unwavering beacon, guiding individuals through the wilderness of doubts and discouragement, towards the eventual summit of triumph. Embracing the process becomes an act of faith, a testament to the profound belief in the intrinsic value of persistent effort and unwavering resolve. The tapestry of Alexander Herrmann's life serves as a vivid canvas depicting the symbiotic relationship between perseverance and attainment. Through his unwavering perseverance, Herrmann etched his name in the annals of magic, leaving an indelible mark on the art form. The tale of perseverance woven within his journey serves as both an inspiration and a guiding light, illuminating the transformative power embedded within the depths of unwavering determination.

Crafting a Unique Style

Alexander Herrmann's journey of training under his brother was not only a process of learning magic tricks but also of crafting a unique style that would set him apart in the world of illusion. While perseverance and dedication formed the backbone of his training, it was during this crucial phase that Alexander began to realize the importance of infusing his performances with individuality and flair. Instead of merely emulating his brother's techniques, he sought to develop his own distinctive approach to magic. This transition from an apprentice to a visionary artist was marked by countless hours of introspection and experimentation. It involved pushing beyond the boundaries of traditional magic and exploring uncharted territories of creativity. Alexander deeply understood that his ability to captivate and enthrall audiences lay in his capacity to offer something truly original and authentic. His quest for uniqueness led him to draw inspiration from various sources, including art, literature, and even everyday experiences. He meticulously absorbed the essence of these influences and translated them into mesmerizing acts that would become his signature. Thus, his performances exuded a charm that was distinctly his own, captivating spectators with an enchanting blend of elegance, mystery, and theatrical brilliance. It was through harnessing his innate talents and infusing them with personal touches that Alexander Herrmann cultivated a style that transcended mere trickery and elevated magic into an artistic expression of profound beauty. His commitment to creating a unique magical identity not only propelled him to stardom but also left an indelible mark on the history of conjuring. Crafted with passion and honed with relentless dedication, Alexander's singular style became a hallmark of his artistry, ensuring that his legacy as a pioneering magician would endure throughout the ages.

A Brother, A Mentor, A Friend

Within the intricate world of magic, the significance of familial bonds and mentorship cannot be overstated. For Alexander Herrmann, his older brother was more than just a sibling; he was a guiding force, a source of wisdom, and a confidant on this extraordinary journey. Their relationship transcended the conventional roles of brothers, evolving into a partnership that fueled the flames of creativity and excellence. Through the kaleidoscope of experiences they shared, Alexander found not only a mentor in magic but also a friend whose support and encouragement were unwavering. As an aspiring magician, Alexander looked up to his brother with reverence, recognizing the depth of his knowledge and the finesse with which he executed illusions. His brother's mastery of the craft became a wellspring of inspiration, igniting a passion within Alexander to carve his unique niche in the world of magic. Beyond just imparting technical expertise, his brother became a compass, steering him towards innovation and a deeper understanding of the art form. In the quiet hours of practice, there existed a camaraderie that went beyond the confines of traditional tutelage. It was a bond forged by shared aspirations and mutual respect. Their exchanges were not merely about honing the technical intricacies of magic; they delved into the philosophy behind the illusions, the artistry of performance, and the emotional resonance it could evoke in audiences. In these moments, Alexander cherished not only the guidance but also the genuine friendship that blossomed between them. Amidst the challenges and triumphs, the bond between the brothers remained a steadfast anchor in a sea of uncertainty. Whether navigating uncharted territories of experimentation or finding solace in each other's company during periods of self-doubt, their partnership embodied the essence of camaraderie and support. The strength of their bond was such that it transcended professional realms, fostering an environment of trust and collaboration that enriched their craft. Beyond the realm of stage performances, their bond ventured into personal realms, where conversations encompassed dreams, fears, and the pursuit of happiness. In his brother, Alexander found a confidant who understood not only the magician but also the person behind the illusion. Their relationship traversed the spectrum of emotions, embracing each other's vulnerabilities and celebrating victories as one. The legacy of their partnership reverberates through the annals of magic history, a testament to the profound impact of fraternity and mentorship. As Alexander Herrmann carved his own path to greatness, he stood on the shoulders of a brother who was not only a mentor but also a lifelong friend. Theirs was a bond that illuminated the transformative power of kinship and guidance, exemplifying the timeless adage that behind every great magician, there is often a brother – a mentor, and above all, a friend.

The Rise of Herrmann the Great

Encounters with Early Success

Alexander's move towards a promising future in magic began with notable small victories. His early performances, although modest in scale, captivated audiences and earned him a loyal following. As a young performer, he exhibited an innate talent for captivating the imagination of his spectators, drawing them into a world of wonder and enchantment. Each successful trick or illusion reinforced Alexander's belief in his chosen path, igniting a passion that would drive him to achieve greater feats and make a lasting mark on the world of magic. The recognition from these early achievements spurred him on, demonstrating that his pursuit of excellence was not in vain. Through dedication and unwavering determination, Alexander Herrmann laid the foundation for his future prominence in the world of magic. It was during this time that he honed his skills, tirelessly perfecting each act and infusing it with his own unique charm and flair. Despite the challenges that inevitably arose, his resolve remained unshaken, fuelled by a deep-seated desire to share the marvels of magic with the world. These formative experiences provided Alexander with invaluable insights and lessons, shaping him into a consummate showman and magician. His encounters with early success, while humble in nature, sowed the seeds for the extraordinary journey that lay ahead, defining him as a name synonymous with greatness in the realm of magic.

A Pivotal Performance

Amidst the backdrop of uncertainty and skepticism, Alexander Herrmann embarked on a transformative journey that would elevate his status as a master magician. It was during one fateful evening in Paris, under the shimmering glow of ornate chandeliers at the renowned Théâtre du Palais-Royal, where Herrmann was poised to stage a performance that would forever alter the course of his career. The air crackled with anticipation as the audience collectively held their breath, eagerly awaiting the spectacle that was about to unfold before their incredulous eyes. As the curtains parted, revealing Herrmann's poised form amidst an ethereal mist, the theater was enveloped in an electrifying atmosphere. With calculated precision, he unleashed a mesmerizing display of illusions and sleight of hand, seamlessly intertwining undeniable skill with an enigmatic allure that left spectators spellbound. Each flick of the wrist and flourish of his cape wove an enchanting narrative, transcending the confines of mere entertainment and delving into the realm of artistry. It was not merely a succession of tricks; it was a meticulously choreographed symphony that unfolded with breathtaking fluidity. As gasps of amazement and thunderous applause reverberated through the hallowed halls, Herrmann's unwavering dedication to his craft became palpable. This performance was not simply a spectacle, but a testament to his unyielding passion and unwavering commitment to his art. Beyond the mystique and grandeur, this pivotal performance symbolized a profound turning point for Herrmann. It marked the moment his name was etched into the annals of magic history, solidifying his status as a luminary whose influence would endure for generations to come. His artistry transcended cultural barriers, captivating the hearts and minds of audiences worldwide, and igniting a renaissance in the world of magic. In the aftermath of this transformative evening, critics and patrons alike sang praises of Herrmann's unparalleled virtuosity, hailing him as a visionary whose mastery knew no bounds. The pulsating energy of that night lingered long after the final curtain fell, casting an indelible imprint on the landscape of magic and elevating Herrmann to the revered status of an icon. As the audience dispersed into the Parisian night, whispers of Herrmann's extraordinary feat permeated the city, kindling a fervor that would propel him towards unparalleled heights of acclaim and adulation. A precedent had been set, and from that moment onward, the world bore witness to the ascension of a maestro whose influence resonated far beyond the confines of the stage.

Carving a Place in Magic History

Alexander Herrmann's journey to carving a place in magic history was marked by both triumphs and challenges, all of which ultimately contributed to his lasting impact on the world of magic. His unwavering dedication to his craft set him apart, as he tirelessly sought to perfect his art and leave an indelible mark on audiences across the globe. Herrmann's performances were not merely displays of skill and showmanship; they were profound expressions of his deep-seated passion for magic and illusion. Each routine, each sleight of hand, and each carefully choreographed act was a testament to his relentless pursuit of excellence. As he continued to refine his repertoire of illusions, Herrmann simultaneously embarked on a mission to elevate the status of magic as an esteemed art form. Through his innovative performances and unwavering commitment to the craft, he sought to shift perceptions and demonstrate the profound impact that magic could have on the hearts and minds of spectators. By doing so, he sought to empower aspiring magicians and inspire a new generation of performers to carry the torch forward, ensuring that the timeless art of magic would endure for generations to come. Herrmann's determination to carve a place in magic history was paralleled by his genuine desire to connect with audiences on a deeply personal level. Beyond the spectacle and grandeur of his performances, he strived to forge meaningful connections with those who witnessed his magic, knowing that these interactions held the potential to transcend the boundaries of language and culture. His ability to weave a sense of wonder and awe into every performance established him as a transcendent figure in the realm of magic, leaving an indelible mark on the hearts and minds of countless individuals worldwide. Moreover, Herrmann's enduring influence extended far beyond the stage, as he dedicated himself to mentoring and nurturing the talents of aspiring magicians. His mentorship and guidance served as a beacon of inspiration for emerging artists, imparting invaluable wisdom and encouragement to those who sought to follow in his footsteps. This legacy of mentorship and support solidified his position as a visionary leader within the magical community and ensured that his impact would be felt for years to come. The legacy of Alexander Herrmann's remarkable journey is one that continues to resonate within the annals of magic history, forever etching his name alongside the great masters of the craft. His unwavering dedication, steadfast commitment to excellence, and profound impact on the world of magic serve as an enduring testament to the transformative power of the human spirit.

An Artisan's Dedication

Dedication is the bedrock of greatness. For Alexander Herrmann, his pursuit of perfection in the art of magic was fueled by an unwavering dedication to his craft. Every waking moment was consumed by his passion for magic, and he dedicated himself wholeheartedly to mastering every nuance of this mesmerizing art. His relentless pursuit of excellence became the hallmark of his career, setting him apart as a true artisan of magic. Herrmann's dedication extended far beyond the confines of the stage. Countless hours were spent honing his skills, perfecting each illusion, and refining every aspect of his performances. He spared no effort in seeking out new techniques, pushing the boundaries of what was possible, and pioneering innovations that would wow audiences around the world. His dedication was not solely for personal gain, but rather a commitment to elevating the art of magic itself. Throughout his journey, Herrmann faced numerous obstacles and setbacks, yet his dedication remained unyielding. He embraced challenges as opportunities for growth, continuously striving to surpass his own limitations. Whether it was mastering a new sleight of hand or devising groundbreaking illusions, Herrmann's dedication knew no bounds. The intricacies of Herrmann's dedication permeated every facet of his life. His attention to detail was unparalleled, evident in meticulously crafted props, flawless execution of illusions, and captivating storytelling woven into each performance. This dedication led to an indelible mark on the world of magic, as Herrmann's innovative techniques and magical prowess captivated audiences across continents. At the heart of Herrmann's dedication lay a genuine love for the art form. He recognized the transformative power of magic, understanding that a well-executed performance could inspire wonder and awe in even the most skeptical of hearts. His dedication to sharing this enchantment with the world became a driving force that propelled him to international acclaim. As we unravel the layers of Herrmann's remarkable journey, it becomes evident that his legacy is intricately intertwined with the unwavering dedication he exhibited throughout his career. It is this dedication that elevated him from a mere performer to a maestro of magic, leaving an indelible imprint on the annals of magical history.

Facing Initial Challenges

As Alexander Herrmann embarked on his journey to become one of the greatest magicians, he encountered numerous challenges that tested his determination and resolve. The transition from an aspiring magician to a renowned figure in the world of magic was not without its hurdles. Dealing with the initial challenges required both a resilient spirit and an unwavering passion for the art of magic. Herrmann had to navigate through a myriad of obstacles, each presenting its own unique set of difficulties. In the early stages of his career, financial constraints often posed a significant challenge. Funding his performances, procuring the necessary tools and equipment, and maintaining a sense of stability proved to be daunting tasks. However, such adversity only fueled Herrmann's dedication to his craft. Apart from financial constraints, securing opportunities to showcase his talents and gain exposure also proved to be a formidable obstacle. The bustling world of entertainment already had established stars, making it difficult for a young Herrmann to carve out his place in the industry. Countless rejections and disappointments marked this phase of his journey, testing his resolve and pushing him to redefine his approach towards gaining recognition. Furthermore, skepticism and doubt from audiences and critics added an extra layer of complexity to Herrmann's initiation into the world of magic. His unconventional style and innovative techniques were met with skepticism, and many questioned his ability to make a lasting impression in the magical realm. However, rather than succumbing to the pressures and doubts, Herrmann channeled these challenges as opportunities for growth and learning. Overcoming these initial challenges required steadfast determination, unyielding perseverance, and an unshakable belief in his own potential. It was during these trying times that Herrmann honed not only his magical skills but also his character, fortifying himself to emerge as a force to be reckoned with in the world of magic.

Earning Recognition

Earning recognition in the world of magic is a journey fraught with challenges and triumphs. For Alexander Herrmann, this path was no different. As he navigated the tumultuous waters of the entertainment industry, he faced numerous obstacles that tested his resolve and determination. One of the pivotal moments that contributed to Herrmann's recognition was his unwavering commitment to perfecting his craft. Despite facing initial skepticism and doubt, he remained steadfast in his dedication to magic, honing his skills with unwavering persistence. This relentless pursuit of excellence set him apart and began to draw attention from audience members and critics alike. Herrmann's performances exuded an unmatched fervor and passion, captivating audiences and leaving a lasting impression on all who had the privilege of witnessing his magic. The ripple effect of his awe-inspiring shows echoed through the corridors of the entertainment world, solidifying his reputation as a premier magician. As Herrmann continued to showcase his unparalleled talents, invitations to perform at illustrious venues and prestigious events began to pour in, further cementing his status as a formidable magician. His remarkable ability to weave wonder and intrigue into every act earned him the respect and admiration of his peers, elevating him to the echelons of magical stardom. It was during this period that Herrmann's name became synonymous with enchantment and mystique, marking the culmination of his tireless efforts to earn recognition. Despite the arduous nature of the journey, Herrmann's unwavering commitment to his artistry and his steadfast determination had finally borne fruit, propelling him into the hallowed realms of magical acclaim. Earning recognition was not merely a milestone for Herrmann; it was a testament to his unwavering spirit and unyielding pursuit of excellence. His ascent to prominence serves as a testament to the adage that perseverance, dedication, and an unwavering focus on one's passion can pave the way for enduring success.

Building a Reputation

With talent and perseverance, Alexander Herrmann continued to build a reputation as a captivating magician. His dedication to the craft was unwavering, and audiences began to take notice of his unparalleled skill and showmanship. Herrmann's performances were not mere displays of magic; they were experiences that left spectators in awe. Through his mastery of illusion, he transported his audiences to a realm where the impossible became plausible, enchanting all who bore witness to his artistry. As word spread of his remarkable abilities, people from far and wide sought out the opportunity to witness the magic of Herrmann. His growing reputation drew attention from not only magic enthusiasts but also prominent figures of the time, solidifying his status as a preeminent entertainer. Each show added another layer to his illustrious reputation, firmly establishing him as a magician of unparalleled caliber. The connection Herrmann forged with his audience further propelled his acclaim. His performances went beyond mere entertainment; they resonated deeply with those who experienced them, leaving an indelible mark on their hearts and minds. This deep emotional impact solidified Herrmann's eminence within the world of magic. Notably, it was not only his technical prowess that contributed to his acclaim, but also his charismatic stage presence and genuine connections with his spectators. His reputation spread like wildfire across continents, marking him as a magician without equal. In every performance, Herrmann demonstrated an unwavering commitment to delivering the extraordinary, setting him apart from his contemporaries. The unmistakable essence of his shows, characterized by elegance, mystery, and pure wonder, became synonymous with his name, further enhancing his reputation. It was during this period that Herrmann's legendary status began to take root, laying the foundation for his enduring legacy.

Establishing a Unique Style

Alexander Herrmann's journey to becoming one of the most renowned magicians of his time was not solely attributed to his breathtaking performances or his mastery of illusion. It was, in a large part, due to his unrivaled ability to create and establish a truly unique style that set him apart from his contemporaries. Throughout his career, Herrmann demonstrated a commitment to innovation and creativity, constantly pushing the boundaries of conventional magic. He wasn't content with simply mastering existing tricks; he sought to breathe new life into the art form, infusing it with his own unmistakable flair. This dedication to originality and invention became the hallmark of his performances and solidified his position as a trailblazer in the world of magic. What truly distinguished Herrmann was his adept blending of theatricality and magical skill. With a refined sense of showmanship and an understanding of the power of storytelling, Herrmann transformed his illusions into captivating tales, drawing audiences into his intricate narratives. His keen awareness of the emotional impact of his magic allowed him to craft experiences that transcended mere spectacle, leaving a lasting impression on all who witnessed his shows. The use of elaborate props and stage effects further contributed to the grandeur of his performances, creating an immersive and unforgettable experience for his spectators. Herrmann's attention to detail extended beyond his acts, encompassing every aspect of his public persona. From his distinctive attire to his charismatic stage presence, he carefully cultivated an enigmatic allure that captivated audiences worldwide. Moreover, his commitment to perfection and his relentless pursuit of excellence manifested in every facet of his art, from the precision of his movements to the seamless execution of his illusions. This unwavering dedication, coupled with his distinctive style, elevated Herrmann to unparalleled heights within the magical community. By continually reinventing himself and his craft, Herrmann secured his legacy as a true innovator, influencing generations of magicians to come. As we delve deeper into the evolution of Herrmann's illustrious career, it becomes evident that his unique style was not only a defining characteristic but also a testament to his visionary approach and unwavering passion.

Gaining the Moniker: Herrmann the Great

In the world of magic, reputations are often built on a foundation of excellence and innovation. For Alexander Herrmann, achieving the status of 'Herrmann the Great' was not simply a matter of gaining popularity, but rather a testament to his unwavering commitment to his craft. As he continued to captivate audiences with his dazzling performances and unparalleled showmanship, whispers of admiration soon transformed into resounding praise. It was through his tireless dedication and relentless pursuit of perfection that he earned the illustrious moniker that would forever become synonymous with his name. The title 'Herrmann the Great' was not bestowed upon him lightly; it was a recognition of his extraordinary skill, boundless creativity, and unyielding passion for magic. With each mesmerizing illusion and every masterful sleight of hand, Herrmann solidified his reputation as a magician of unparalleled prowess, leaving audiences in awe and earning their unwavering adulation. His ascent to greatness was marked by an unwavering dedication to pushing the boundaries of what was thought possible, continually striving to outdo himself with unprecedented feats of magic. Throughout his journey, Herrmann remained humble, always attributing his success to the support of his fans and the unwavering guidance of his mentors. The title 'Herrmann the Great' became a symbol of inspiration for aspiring magicians around the world, spurring them to reach for new heights in their own artistic endeavors. Beyond just a name, it embodied a legacy of excellence, a standard against which all future magicians would be measured. As he embraced the mantle of 'Herrmann the Great', Alexander Herrmann ushered in a new era of magic, one defined by innovation, artistry, and a steadfast commitment to enchanting audiences. It was a title that signified not just his individual triumph, but also the enduring impact he had on the realm of magic, forever altering its course and elevating it to unprecedented heights.

A New Era Begins

The attainment of the title 'Herrmann the Great' marked a turning point in Alexander Herrmann's magical journey. It came with immense responsibility and the weight of expectation. As he embraced this moniker, a newfound sense of purpose coursed through him. A heightened determination to push the boundaries of magic enveloped his being, and he set out to embark on a new era that would redefine the landscape of illusion and wonder. This period signified a pivotal moment in Herrmann's career, where innovation took center stage. With his reputation preceding him, audiences anticipated performances that exceeded all previous conceptions of magic. Taking to the stage with unparalleled fervor and creativity, Herrmann presented spellbinding acts that left spectators in awe and disbelief. The air crackled with anticipation each time he graced the limelight, as people clamored to witness the marvels he had in store. Amidst this transformative phase, Herrmann's artistic vision evolved, steering him towards uncharted territories of ingenuity. His relentless pursuit of perfection drove him to push the limits of what was perceived as possible. He sought to fuse traditional techniques with innovative concepts, thereby sculpting a neo-classical approach to magic that was both captivating and revolutionary. Moreover, 'Herrmann the Great' became more than just a name; it symbolized a standard of excellence that he zealously upheld. His commitment to leaving an indelible mark on the world of magic fueled a relentless dedication to his craft. Every trick, every flourish, and every interaction with his audience was infused with a sincere desire to foster an unforgettable experience, transcending mere entertainment to leave an enduring imprint on the hearts and minds of those who bore witness. As Herrmann stepped into this new epoch, his influence resonated far beyond the confines of the stage. He became a beacon of inspiration for aspiring magicians, igniting a spark of creativity that reverberated throughout the magical community. His legacy began to take root, weaving its narrative into the fabric of the art form, and setting the stage for future generations to follow in his profound footsteps. Herrmann's aspiration to usher in a new era was not merely confined to the realms of magic; it extended into the broader scope of human connection and wonder. His performances were not simply displays of skill and dexterity, but rather conduits for evoking emotions, sparking imagination, and transmuting disbelief into belief. Through his art, he sought to kindle a sense of childlike wonder in all who beheld his illusions, ensuring that the enchantment of his craft transcended time and space, bridging eras and cultures in a symphony of universal admiration.

From Apprentice to Master

A Young Talent Emerges

Alexander's early promise as a magician set the stage for his future successes. From a young age, Alexander Herrmann displayed a remarkable aptitude for magic, captivating those around him with his natural talent for sleight of hand and illusion. His parents, themselves amateur magicians, recognized his potential and nurtured his fascination with the art form. With their encouragement, Alexander's passion for magic flourished, becoming an integral part of his identity. He devoured every book on magic that he could find and avidly attended any performances by visiting magicians. This insatiable thirst for knowledge and exposure allowed him to absorb the secrets of the trade and develop an understanding of the intricacies involved. As he honed his skills, it became apparent that Alexander was destined for greatness in the world of magic. His dedication and unwavering commitment to his craft set him apart from his peers and foreshadowed the extraordinary feats he would later accomplish. Even in these formative years, Alexander's performances held an air of sophistication and confidence beyond his years, drawing acclaim from audiences who were in awe of his prodigious abilities. His innate charisma and magnetic stage presence made it evident that he was meant to share his gifts with the world. Throughout this period, Alexander remained humble and eager to learn, seeking guidance from experienced magicians while simultaneously offering his fresh perspective and ideas. This harmonious balance of reverence for tradition and eagerness to innovate would become a hallmark of his distinguished career. As he matured, his determination solidified, fueling his inexorable drive to achieve mastery in the art of magic. A young talent had indeed emerged, and the world would soon bear witness to the extraordinary journey that lay ahead for Alexander Herrmann.

Following in Family Footsteps

Alexander Herrmann's journey into the world of magic was heavily influenced by his family's rich magical heritage. Born into a family of magicians, Alexander was surrounded by the mystique of magic from a very young age. His father, Samuel Herrmann, was an accomplished magician known for his mesmerizing stage presence and innovative illusions. From the moment Alexander could walk, he was captivated by the art of magic, watching his father perform and eagerly absorbing every trick and technique. It was clear to all who knew the Herrmann family that Alexander possessed a natural talent and an insatiable passion for magic. Samuel recognized this potential early on and took Alexander under his wing, nurturing and honing his budding skills. The bond between father and son grew stronger as they worked together, with Samuel imparting invaluable wisdom and expertise. As Alexander matured, the family dynamic evolved into a mentorship, laying the groundwork for his future success. Heeding his father's guidance, Alexander diligently studied the classic principles of magic, mastering foundational techniques and developing a deep understanding of its complexities. Under the watchful eye of Samuel, Alexander flourished, cultivating a profound respect for the art form and its traditions. Influenced by his father's unwavering dedication, Alexander internalized the values of discipline and commitment that would shape his magical journey. Through the guidance of his family, Alexander not only inherited the secrets of centuries-old illusions but also imbibed the philosophy that magic is not just a performance, but a profound expression of wonder and enchantment. Every step of Alexander's magical odyssey echoed the legacy of his family, affirming his destiny to follow in their illustrious footsteps and leave an indelible mark on the world of magic.

Embracing the Stage

From a young age, Alexander Herrmann demonstrated an unyielding passion for magic. This unwavering devotion led him to embrace the stage as a platform to exhibit his innate talents and unleash his creative energies. As he stepped into the limelight, there was a palpable sensation of anticipation and excitement in the air, signaling that a star was on the rise. The stage became a realm where Herrmann found liberation—an arena where he could bewitch audiences with his unmatched skills and captivate them with his enigmatic charisma. Embracing the stage was not merely about performing; it was about creating an experience that transcended the boundaries of imagination and reality. Every step onto the stage was a testament to his commitment to enchanting and inspiring all who bore witness to his extraordinary craft. It was where he felt most alive, and his vibrant energy radiated through every dazzling performance. As he immersed himself in the mesmerizing world of illusions, the stage became a canvas upon which he painted tales of wonder and astonishment. Herrmann's dedication to the art of magic was reflected in every seamless movement and every spellbinding gesture. The stage, with its velvet curtains and gleaming spotlights, became his sanctuary—a place where dreams materialized and fantasies took flight. With each performance, Herrmann's connection with the stage deepened, evolving into a bond forged by shared moments of disbelief and applause. His love for the stage was evident in the meticulous attention to detail that characterized every aspect of his showmanship. It was here that he found solace, purpose, and an unwavering sense of belonging. Embracing the stage meant assuming the role of a storyteller, using illusions as the medium through which narratives of mystery and awe unfolded. It was a responsibility that Herrmann embraced wholeheartedly, infusing each performance with a touch of magic that left an indelible mark on the hearts of all who watched. The stage provided Herrmann with an unparalleled canvas to communicate his innermost emotions, share his insights, and spark joy in the hearts of spectators. Every moment spent in the spotlight was an opportunity to weave a tapestry of enchantment and wonder, leaving an enduring legacy that would transcend generations.

Lessons from the Masters

As Alexander Herrmann embraced the stage and began his journey towards mastering the art of magic, he sought out opportunities to learn from the established masters of the craft. It was during this pivotal phase that Herrmann encountered a diverse array of mentors who would guide him in honing his skills and understanding the intricacies of illusion and performance. One of the first influential figures in Herrmann's life was his older brother, Carl. A seasoned magician in his own right, Carl served as both a mentor and role model to the aspiring young talent. Under Carl's tutelage, Alexander absorbed invaluable insights into the psychology of audience engagement and the technical precision required for executing seamless illusions. Their shared experiences not only cultivated a deep bond between the brothers but also instilled in Alexander a profound respect for the time-honored traditions of magic. Beyond his familial guidance, Herrmann actively sought out opportunities to learn from renowned magicians of the era. He traveled across continents, attending performances and seeking private audiences with esteemed practitioners. Each encounter presented an invaluable opportunity for Herrmann to glean wisdom from the masters, whether it was the finesse of manipulating objects or the mesmerizing allure of storytelling through sleight of hand. In addition to acquiring technical expertise, Herrmann also imbibed the philosophical underpinnings of magic as imparted by these mentors. They emphasized the importance of creating an emotional connection with the audience, urging him to view magic not merely as a series of tricks, but as a transformative experience that transcended entertainment. Such profound insights reshaped

Herrmann's approach to magic, urging him to align his aspirations with a deeper purpose—using his craft to evoke wonder, awe, and joy in those who witnessed his performances. The lessons learned from these masters were not confined to the realm of magic; they extended to encompass life itself. Through their teachings, Herrmann imbibed valuable principles of discipline, dedication, and resilience—qualities that would serve as the bedrock of his illustrious career. As he internalized these teachings, Alexander Herrmann underwent a metamorphosis, evolving from a promising apprentice into a maestro in the making—a transformation that would redefine the landscape of magic for generations to come.

Refining His Craft

Alexander Herrmann's journey from apprentice to master was marked by a relentless pursuit of excellence and an unwavering commitment to refining his craft. As he absorbed the lessons from the masters before him, he recognized the significance of constant refinement, understanding that growth and evolution were essential for any artist seeking to leave an indelible mark on the world. With a dedication bordering on obsession, he embraced every opportunity to hone his skills, constantly pushing the boundaries of what was deemed possible. In his quest for perfection, Alexander immersed himself in the intricacies of the art. Every movement, every gesture, and every expression became a canvas upon which he painted the tapestry of his enchanting performances. He delved deep into the psychology of magic, recognizing that true mastery lay not only in the execution of tricks but also in the profound emotional impact they could create. The process of refinement was not without its challenges. Countless hours were spent in solitary practice, tirelessly perfecting each sleight of hand and nuance of performance. The endless rehearsals and tireless experimentation demanded unyielding patience and an unwavering belief in his vision. Yet, amidst the struggle, there was an undeniable sense of joy—a joy born from witnessing his artistry evolve and flourish with each passing day. Furthermore, the refinement of his craft extended beyond the confines of the stage. Alexander fervently studied the works of other artists, drawing inspiration from diverse disciplines to infuse fresh perspectives into his own repertoire. He sought out mentors, engaged in spirited discussions, and eagerly soaked up the wisdom of fellow magicians and performers, recognizing that true growth stemmed from a willingness to learn from those who had walked the path before him. His pursuit of perfection was not merely a personal endeavor; it was a testament to his unwavering passion for the art of magic. Through the relentless pursuit of refinement, Alexander Herrmann transformed himself from a promising apprentice into a master whose name would resonate through the annals of history.

Challenges and Triumphs

As Alexander Herrmann continued to refine his craft, he faced numerous challenges that tested his dedication and resilience. The path to mastery was fraught with obstacles, from mastering complex illusions to winning over skeptical audiences. Despite these hurdles, Herrmann's unwavering passion and determination propelled him forward. He continually sought out new techniques and methods, pushing the boundaries of what was thought possible in the world of magic. His relentless pursuit of perfection often led to moments of frustration and self-doubt, but each setback only fueled his desire to overcome and succeed. Through tireless practice and unwavering commitment, Herrmann conquered these challenges and emerged stronger and more accomplished. Each triumph, whether big or small, served as a testament to his unyielding spirit. One of his most significant triumphs came in the form of a groundbreaking performance that captivated both critics and audiences alike. It was a turning point in Herrmann's career, marking his ascent to prominence within the magic community. This pivotal moment not only solidified his reputation as a master illusionist but also opened the door to a world of endless possibilities. Throughout this journey, Herrmann's unwavering dedication and perseverance in the face of adversity became an inspiring example for aspiring magicians and performers around the world. His challenges and triumphs serve as a reminder that success is not merely achieved through skill, but through resilience and tenacity in the face of adversity.

Developing a Unique Style

As Alexander Herrmann continued on his magical journey, he realized the importance of developing a unique style that would set him apart from other magicians of his time. This was no easy feat, as the world of magic was filled with talented performers, each offering their own brand of illusion and spectacle. Herrmann spent countless hours experimenting with different techniques, honing his persona, and crafting an image that would capture the imagination of his audience. His efforts were marked by a relentless pursuit of originality, a quest to infuse his performances with a touch of something truly exceptional. Drawing inspiration from various sources, including his mentors and the vibrant tapestry of the stage, Herrmann began to weave together a style that seamlessly blended grandeur with intimacy. He understood that a truly memorable magician needed to evoke both awe and connection; to be larger than life yet relatable. This duality became a hallmark of his performances, captivating audiences and leaving them spellbound. His journey toward a unique style was not without its challenges. There were moments of doubt, where he questioned if his vision was too ambitious or if he was drifting too far from convention. Yet, with unwavering determination, Herrmann pushed forward, fueled by a deep-seated belief in his artistic vision. It was this resilience that allowed him to transcend mediocrity and step into the realm of greatness. What truly set Herrmann's style apart was his ability to blend traditional magic with modern innovation. He sought to honor the classical roots of his craft while introducing contemporary elements that kept his performances fresh and relevant. This harmonious fusion resonated with audiences across cultural and generational boundaries, earning Herrmann a reputation as a visionary in the world of magic. In the end, Herrmann's unique style was not merely a product of his technical skill or showmanship; it was a reflection of his undying passion for the art of magic. Every gesture, every word, and every illusion spoke volumes about his love for the craft. It was this authenticity, this genuine adoration for what he did, that made his performances transcend mere entertainment and become moments of pure enchantment. And so, as he continued to refine his unique style, Alexander Herrmann unwittingly etched his name into the annals of magical history, leaving a legacy that continues to inspire and delight to this day.

The Turning Point

As Alexander Herrmann honed his craft and developed his unique style, he reached a pivotal moment in his career—an event that would come to be known as the turning point. After years of dedicated practice and relentless pursuit of perfection, Herrmann's performances began to captivate audiences in ways never seen before. His innovative approach to magic, coupled with an unwavering commitment to showmanship, set him apart from his contemporaries. The turning point came during a landmark performance at a prestigious theater in Paris. As Herrmann took the stage, there was an air of anticipation and excitement among the audience. With a sense of confidence and grace, he demonstrated a series of illusions that left onlookers spellbound. The energy in the room crackled with awe and wonder, and it was clear that something extraordinary was happening. This performance marked a significant shift in Herrmann's career, propelling him into the spotlight as a master magician. Not only did the Parisian audience respond with resounding applause, but esteemed figures within the world of magic began to take notice. Critics lauded Herrmann's virtuosity, praising his seamless execution and remarkable creativity. Peers and mentors alike hailed the performance as a defining moment in magic history. Herrmann had not only demonstrated technical prowess but had also infused his illusions with a captivating narrative, drawing spectators into a world of enchantment and mystery. The turning point didn't just signify a personal victory for Herrmann; it signaled a shift in the very landscape of magic itself. Suddenly, the art form was elevated to new heights, inspiring a generation of aspiring magicians and redefining the expectations of what was possible on stage. Magicians worldwide sought to emulate Herrmann's style, and his influence reverberated across continents, igniting a wave of innovation and reinvention. The impact of this turning point was far-reaching, shaping the future of magic for decades to come. Herrmann's name became synonymous with excellence, and his legacy as a trailblazer was secured. From that moment onward, he was recognized as a luminary in the world of magic, wielding a profound influence that transcended geographical and cultural boundaries. The turning point was not just a singular event in Herrmann's career; it was a testament to the transformative power of artistic vision and unwavering dedication.

Recognition by Peers

Alexander Herrmann's exceptional talent and dedication did not go unnoticed within the tight-knit community of magicians and illusionists. As he approached the pivotal stage in his career where he was no longer just an apprentice but on the verge of ascending to mastery, Herrmann began to enjoy a surge in recognition from his peers. This acknowledgment stemmed from his unwavering commitment to honing his craft and pushing the boundaries of traditional magic. Throughout his journey, Herrmann fostered strong relationships with fellow magicians, exchanging knowledge and techniques, and earning their respect through his innovative approaches. One significant form of recognition came from invitations to exclusive gatherings and performances among esteemed magicians, where Herrmann had the opportunity to showcase his evolving skills and receive valuable feedback. These experiences further fueled his determination to perfect his art and earn a place among the greats of his time. The affirmation he received from esteemed colleagues during this phase of his career served as both validation and motivation. It solidified Herrmann's belief in his abilities and cemented his aspiration to fully realize his potential as a master magician. The encouragement and support from the magical community provided him with the confidence to take bold creative risks and experiment with new illusions, ultimately setting him on a trajectory toward unmatched artistry and prominence in the world of magic. As Herrmann's reputation continued to flourish, peers and mentors alike hailed his artistry and commitment to preserving the integrity of magic as an esteemed form of entertainment. Their acknowledgment bore testament to his unyielding devotion to the craft and the impact his work had on advancing the art of magic. Each commendation and gesture of solidarity inspired Herrmann to strive for excellence and distinction, propelling him ever closer to the pinnacle of the magical world. In reflection, the recognition bestowed upon Alexander Herrmann by his peers not only affirmed his remarkable progress but also underscored the bonds of mutual respect and camaraderie that thrive among dedicated practitioners of this captivating art form.

Ascending to Mastery

After years of dedication and hard work, Alexander Herrmann found himself on the cusp of mastering the art of magic. The recognition from his peers was a validation of his relentless pursuit of excellence. As he ascended to this new level, he was acutely aware of the responsibility that came with it. Mastery wasn't just about skill and technique; it required a deep understanding of the history and traditions of magic, as well as a commitment to innovation and growth. As Herrmann delved deeper into his craft, he sought inspiration not only from the great magicians of the past but also from other art forms. He studied the works of renowned painters, musicians, and writers, recognizing that true mastery extended beyond the boundaries of any single discipline. This holistic approach allowed him to infuse his performances with a richness and depth that set him apart from his contemporaries. The turning point in Herrmann's journey to mastery came when he realized that true greatness was achieved not through individual achievement, but through the elevation of the entire magical community. He became a mentor to aspiring magicians, sharing his knowledge and experiences generously. By nurturing the next generation of performers, Herrmann ensured that the legacy of magic would continue to thrive long after he was gone. Throughout this period of ascent, Herrmann faced numerous challenges and setbacks. Each obstacle served as a test of his resolve, pushing him to refine his skills and deepen his understanding of the craft. His unwavering determination, coupled with a genuine love for the art of magic, fueled his continuous growth. At last, Alexander Herrmann stood at the pinnacle of mastery, not as a solitary figure basking in his own accomplishments, but as a towering presence within the magical community. His influence was felt far and wide, transcending geographical borders and cultural differences. With humility and grace, he embraced the title of master, recognizing that it was not an endpoint but a new beginning—the beginning of a legacy that would inspire generations to come.

Touring Europe

Setting the Stage for European Tours

Europe has long held a deep fascination with the art of magic, entwined with its rich tapestry of history, folklore, and mystique. From the medieval court magicians of kings and queens to the street performers weaving spells of wonder, Europe's love affair with magic has endured through the ages. It is against this timeless backdrop that Alexander Herrmann ventured into the continent, carrying his passion and prodigious talent with him. As he crossed the borders into this land steeped in enchantment, Herrmann stepped into a world where magic was not just a spectacle, but an integral part of the cultural fabric. The cobblestone streets of ancient cities, the opulent theatres adorned with velvet curtains, and the whispers of legends and myths all contributed to Europe's allure for Herrmann, who yearned to weave his own magic into this enduring legacy. Each country he visited bore its own unique blend of traditions and magical folklore, from the grand illusionists of France to the enigmatic sorcerers of Italy. The very air crackled with anticipation as Herrmann began his journey, poised to add his own chapter to the spellbinding narrative of European magic. As he prepared to unveil his remarkable talents to audiences across the continent, Herrmann found himself captivated by the reverence and appreciation for magic that permeated every corner of Europe. It was in this environment of deep-rooted magic traditions that Herrmann first felt the weight of his responsibility as a maestro of illusion. His footsteps echoed through historic landscapes, following in the shadows of the great magicians before him, and as he cast his own spell on the stage, he knew that he was participating in a lineage that transcended time itself. The prospect of sharing his art with such a storied audience filled him with a profound sense of purpose and awakened a fervent desire to honor the traditions of each country he visited. Setting foot on the soil of Europe was not merely a journey for Herrmann; it was a pilgrimage to immerse himself in the rich history of magic and to inscribe his indelible mark upon its legacy.

Herrmann's First Steps in Europe

Upon arriving in Europe, Alexander Herrmann embarked on a journey that would shape the trajectory of his magical career. Immersing himself in the rich tapestry of European culture, Herrmann eagerly embraced the opportunity to share his art with diverse audiences and convey the universal language of magic. His initial performances captivated and enthralled spectators, marking the beginning of an extraordinary chapter in his illustrious career. Known for his charismatic stage presence and spellbinding illusions, Herrmann quickly gained recognition as a trailblazer in the realm of magic, captivating the hearts and minds of audiences across varied European landscapes. Each new city presented Herrmann with an opportunity to showcase his talents and connect with individuals from all walks of life. From the bustling streets of Paris to the enchanting alleyways of Rome, Herrmann's performances transcended linguistic barriers, eliciting awe and wonder from spectators of every background. As he traversed the continent, Herrmann remained unwavering in his dedication to preserving the integrity and allure of magic, paying homage to the rich cultural heritage that permeated each majestic European city. Stepping into this unfamiliar yet exhilarating territory, Herrmann's passion for his craft illuminated every corner of Europe, establishing a legacy that would endure the test of time. Beyond the applause and acclaim, Herrmann found solace in the shared moments of disbelief and sheer delight that his performances ignited. It was amidst these humble exchanges that the true impact of his artistry was felt, weaving a tapestry of magic that mirrored the beauty and diversity of the European landscape itself. Subsequent to his inaugural ventures, Herrmann's reputation blossomed, attracting devoted fans and esteemed patrons who eagerly awaited his mesmerizing displays of skill and artistry. From enchanting palaces to intimate theaters, Herrmann's presence graced historic venues, leaving an indelible impression upon the cultural fabric of each European destination. Undeterred by the challenges of traveling and performing in foreign lands, Herrmann's resilience and passion propelled him to conquer the European stage with an unwavering sense of purpose and dedication. As Herrmann's influence continued to burgeon, his European tours not only elevated the status of magic but also reinforced the timeless allure of wonder and enchantment, evoking an enduring sense of unity and marvel among spectators from all corners of the continent. The confluence of cultures and experiences became pivotal in shaping Herrmann's artistic vision, infusing each performance with an ineffable charm and splendor that transcended geographical boundaries. Through his exceptional artistry and unwavering spirit, Herrmann's first steps in Europe set the stage for an enchanted journey that would etch his name into the annals of magical history.

Navigating Cultural Differences

During his early European tours, Alexander Herrmann encountered a rich tapestry of cultures, each with its own traditions, customs, and languages. Navigating these cultural differences was both challenging and enriching for Herrmann. He showed a genuine respect for the diverse communities he encountered, taking the time to learn about local customs and etiquette. By doing so, he endeared himself to audiences across Europe, creating a lasting impact. Herrmann understood that magic transcends language barriers, and as such, he took great care to tailor his performances to resonate with each unique audience. Whether in Vienna, Paris, London, or Rome, he tactfully incorporated cultural elements into his shows, earning admiration and applause from spectators of all backgrounds. Beyond the stage, Herrmann immersed himself in the local way of life, embracing new experiences and establishing meaningful connections with people from various walks of life. Through this immersion, he gained a deeper understanding of the human experience, broadening his perspective and ultimately enhancing his magical artistry. This chapter highlights the profound impact of cultural exchange on Herrmann's journey, showcasing his ability to bridge divides and foster unity through the universal language of magic. It is a testament to his sincere appreciation for the diversity of European cultures and his unwavering commitment to connecting with people on a profound, human level.

Performing in Iconic Venues

Performing in iconic venues across Europe was an experience unlike any other for Alexander Herrmann. These grand and historic theaters, opera houses, and palaces provided the perfect backdrop to showcase his astonishing magic and captivate audiences of all backgrounds. From the opulent Royal Opera House in London to the enchanting Théâtre du Palais-Royal in Paris, each venue held centuries of history and culture within its walls. Each performance felt like a historical moment in itself, with the echoes of legendary artists and performers fueling Herrmann's ambition to leave his own legacy in these hallowed halls. The sights and sounds of these iconic venues became a source of inspiration for Herrmann, driving him to push the boundaries of his craft and deliver unforgettable experiences to his spectators. Every venue presented its unique challenges, from the acoustics of the grand concert halls to the logistics of staging elaborate illusions within the confines of historic stages. Herrmann navigated these obstacles with grace and innovation, earning the admiration of both audiences and fellow performers. The prestige of these venues also brought increased pressure, as Herrmann understood the weight of the legacies he was following and the expectations of the discerning European audiences. However, this pressure served as a catalyst for Herrmann, urging him to elevate his performances to even greater heights and solidify his reputation as a master magician. Moreover, performing in such iconic venues allowed Herrmann to connect with the heart and soul of each city, leaving an indelible mark on the cultural fabric of Europe. The stories and legends tied to these locations intertwined with Herrmann's own narrative, creating a rich tapestry of magic, history, and artistry. In many ways, these performances were not just entertainment but a celebration of the enduring spirit of magic and the power of human imagination. They represented a convergence of talent, tradition, and innovation, demonstrating the universal language of wonder that transcends borders and unites people from all walks of life. For Alexander Herrmann, every performance in these iconic venues was an opportunity to weave his magic into the very fabric of European culture and contribute to the ongoing legacy of artistic excellence.

Stories from the Road

Touring Europe was not just about performing in iconic venues; it was also about experiencing the richness of each country's culture. As Alexander Herrmann journeyed through the cobblestone streets and bustling cities, he encountered a myriad of fascinating stories that left an indelible mark on his magical journey. One particularly memorable tale took place in the heart of Paris. Herrmann found himself strolling along the Seine River, enchanted by the romantic allure of the city. In a quaint cafe nestled in a charming corner, he struck up a conversation with a local artist who shared captivating anecdotes of Parisian lore. This encounter sparked inspiration for one of Herrmann's most beloved illusions, rooted in the enchanting narratives he had heard. Amidst the picturesque settings of Italy, Herrmann encountered a group of passionate storytellers who regaled him with ancient fables passed down through generations. Immersed in the warmth of their tradition, Herrmann gleaned invaluable insight into the art of captivating an audience—a skill that would later shape his performances in immeasurable ways. The roads of Europe were not always adorned with splendor; they also posed unforeseen challenges. In the rugged terrains of the Alps, Herrmann faced treacherous weather that tested his resilience. Yet, these trials served as profound lessons, forging an unwavering determination that would define his illustrious career. Further east, in the mystical lands of Eastern Europe, Herrmann encountered mystical tales steeped in folklore and mysticism. Discussions with local shamans and wise elders provided glimpses into a world beyond the ordinary, offering a treasure trove of inspiration for new illusions that captivated audiences with their otherworldly charm. These stories from the road underscored the profound impact of cultural immersion on Herrmann's magical artistry. Each encounter, whether joyous or challenging, wove an intricate tapestry of experiences that enriched his performances with layers of emotional depth and authenticity. Such was the transformative power of his travels—a testament to the enduring legacy of a magician who sought not only to dazzle, but also to connect hearts and minds through the universal language of wonder.

The Challenges of Travel

Traveling as a magician in the late 19th century presented numerous challenges that tested the resolve and adaptability of performers like Alexander Herrmann. The logistics of moving equipment, costumes, and props from one city to the next were formidable, especially given the limited transportation options available at the time. Herrmann and his troupe often found themselves navigating long and arduous journeys by train, carriage, or even by boat, each mode of transport presenting its own set of obstacles. In addition to the physical strain of constant travel, there were also language barriers and cultural differences to contend with. As they crossed borders and performed in various countries across Europe, Herrmann and his team had to quickly adjust to new customs, etiquette, and audience expectations. This demanded not only linguistic dexterity but also a deep understanding of the nuances of different societies. Furthermore, the unpredictable nature of travel meant that performances were sometimes jeopardized by unforeseen delays, inclement weather, or other unexpected circumstances. Despite meticulous planning, the relentless pace of touring often resulted in fatigue, illness, and emotional strain for the performers. Yet, amidst these trials, the magic of Alexander Herrmann continued to captivate audiences, showcasing his unwavering dedication to his craft. Amidst the adversities of travel, Herrmann's resilience shone brightest, as he sought to bring joy and wonder to audiences throughout Europe despite the myriad challenges that stood in his way.

Meeting the Masters of Europe

Throughout Alexander Herrmann's European tours, he had the honor of meeting and collaborating with some of the most renowned masters of magic across the continent. These encounters not only enriched Herrmann's own repertoire but also fostered a sense of unity and camaraderie among magicians. One particularly memorable meeting took place in Paris, where Herrmann crossed paths with the esteemed French illusionist, Jean Eugène Robert-Houdin. Their exchange of ideas and techniques left an indelible mark on Herrmann, who embraced the opportunity to learn from the wisdom and experience of his fellow magician. In London, Herrmann was awestruck by the mesmerizing performances of John Nevil Maskelyne and George Alfred Cooke at the Egyptian Hall. Engaging in discussions with these celebrated illusionists opened Herrmann's eyes to diverse performance styles and innovative staging, igniting his own creative spark. The mutual respect and admiration exchanged during these encounters transcended language barriers and cultural differences, serving as a testament to the universal language of magic. Herrmann's journey also led him to encounter the enigmatic Austrian magician Ludwig Döbler in Vienna. Their collaboration resulted in a groundbreaking fusion of traditional and contemporary magic, captivating audiences with unparalleled artistry and showmanship. The spirit of collaboration and mutual inspiration among these luminaries contributed to the evolution of magic as an esteemed and respected art form throughout Europe. Another influential figure Herrmann encountered on his travels was the Italian conjurer Eusapia Palladino. Her expertise in mentalism and psychic phenomena broadened Herrmann's understanding of the intricacies of perception and audience interaction, prompting him to incorporate new elements into his own performances that continued to captivate and astound spectators. Each meeting with these masters of magic not only expanded Herrmann's technical prowess but also enriched his artistic sensibilities, instilling in him a deep appreciation for the diversity and depth of magical expression. These encounters served as more than mere professional exchanges; they forged lasting bonds and enduring legacies, shaping the landscape of magic in Europe and beyond.

Adapting to Diverse Audiences

One of the most remarkable aspects of Alexander Herrmann's European tours was his ability to adapt to diverse audiences. As he traveled from one country to another, he encountered a wide array of cultural norms, expectations, and attitudes towards magic. Instead of trying to impose a singular style or performance, Herrmann recognized the importance of understanding and respecting each audience's unique perspective. This ethos became ingrained in his approach to every show, and it played a pivotal role in his success across the continent. In countries like France, Italy, and Spain, known for their passionate and expressive nature, Herrmann would infuse an extra touch of theatrical flair into his acts. He understood that these audiences appreciated grand gestures and emotional storytelling, so he tailored his performances accordingly. On the other hand, in more reserved settings such as those in Germany and Austria, Herrmann exhibited a sense of precision and elegance, captivating audiences with his meticulous sleight of hand and refined demeanor. Moreover, in each new city or town, Herrmann made an effort to learn about local traditions and customs. By incorporating elements of regional folklore, history, or beliefs into his magic, he created a sense of connection that transcended language barriers. Whether performing in a prestigious theater or an intimate salon, he adeptly bridged the gap between his artistry and the cultural tapestry of his audience. Beyond cultural nuances, Herrmann's adaptation extended to the social dynamics of his audiences. From royal courts to working-class taverns, he effortlessly adjusted his performance to resonate with people from all walks of life. His ability to engage with, entertain, and leave a lasting impact on everyone who gathered to witness his magic truly distinguished him as a master of universal appeal. Adapting to diverse audiences wasn't merely a strategic tool for Herrmann; it embodied his genuine respect and empathy towards the people he encountered on his journey. By embracing the differences and celebrating the similarities, he not only won over hearts but also broadened the reach of magic as an art form, leaving an indelible mark on the history of European entertainment.

Memorable Performances and Receptions

During his tours across Europe, Alexander Herrmann delivered countless memorable performances and experienced remarkable receptions from audiences of all walks of life. His unparalleled skill and captivating stage presence left lasting impressions that reverberated throughout the continent. In the grand theaters and intimate venues where he showcased his talents, Herrmann's magical feats mesmerized and enchanted spectators, transcending language barriers and cultural differences. The applause and awe that greeted him at the culmination of each performance were a testament to the indelible impact he had on everyone fortunate enough to witness his artistry. Each show became a treasured memory for those in attendance, as they cherished the moments when reality seemed suspended, and the impossible became possible through Herrmann's mastery. His ability to evoke wonder and astonishment turned each performance into an unforgettable event. Beyond the stage, Herrmann's receptions were equally unforgettable. He was renowned for his graciousness and warmth, endearing himself to hosts, patrons, and fellow performers alike. His genuine appreciation for the support and admiration extended to him was evident in his interactions with all who crossed his path. Whether in opulent ballrooms or humble gathering places, Herrmann's personal charm and humility left a lasting impression on those he encountered. Guests felt genuinely acknowledged and valued in his presence, fostering a sense of camaraderie and mutual respect. The memories of these receptions, sprinkled with anecdotes and shared laughter, forged lasting connections that extended far beyond the confines of the performance space. These experiences not only enriched Herrmann's journey but also left an enduring legacy that resonated with both colleagues and admirers. The impact of these memorable performances and receptions during his European tours would continue to shape Herrmann's career and influence the landscape of magic for years to come.

Reflecting on the Impact of European Tours

Touring Europe had a profound impact on Alexander Herrmann's career, shaping him into the internationally renowned magician he was known as. The experiences garnered from performing in various European countries not only elevated his artistry but also broadened his understanding of the world and its diverse cultures. As Herrmann reflects on the impact of these tours, it becomes evident that each stop along the European journey left an indelible mark on both his craft and personal development. The

European tours allowed Herrmann to immerse himself in different cultural landscapes, exposing him to a rich tapestry of traditions, beliefs, and artistic expressions. This exposure provided him with a deeper appreciation for the human experience and influenced the evolution of his magical performances. Engaging with audiences from different backgrounds encouraged Herrmann to tailor his acts to resonate with diverse sensibilities, thereby honing his ability to connect with people at a universal level. Furthermore, the European tours presented Herrmann with the opportunity to collaborate and learn from some of the most revered magicians and performers of the time. Interactions with these masters enabled him to exchange ideas, refine his techniques, and expand his repertoire of illusions, ultimately contributing to the innovation and sophistication of his shows. The invaluable mentorship and camaraderie fostered during these tours laid the groundwork for Herrmann's future success and cemented his status as a trailblazer in the world of magic. Beyond the realm of magic, the impact of European tours extended to Herrmann's personal growth. Navigating the trials and triumphs of travel instilled in him a resilience that transcended the stage, serving as a constant reminder of the power of perseverance and adaptability. These experiences cultivated a spirit of curiosity and open-mindedness, characteristics that would define Herrmann's approach to both his craft and life. Ultimately, as Alexander Herrmann reflects on the profound impact of his European tours, he acknowledges the pivotal role they played in shaping the legacy he would leave behind. The lessons learned, friendships forged, and audiences inspired during this transformative period contributed immeasurably to the remarkable journey of a magician who captivated the hearts and minds of people around the world.

Sleight of Hand: The Art of Deception

The Essence of Illusion

Illusions are the enchanting fabric that weaves through the tapestry of magic, captivating audiences with their sense of wonder and mystery. At their core, illusions hinge upon the suspension of disbelief, drawing spectators into a realm of fascination where the impossible becomes possible. The art of illusion involves transcending the boundaries of reality, enveloping observers in a wondrous spectacle that defies logical explanation. What sets illusions apart is their ability to elicit profound emotional responses from individuals. As spectators behold a remarkable feat, whether it's an object defying gravity or vanishing into thin air, they experience an intoxicating blend of astonishment, curiosity, and awe. It's this deep emotional connection that lures them in, leaving an indelible impression on their minds and hearts long after the performance concludes. Moreover, the essence of illusion lies in its capacity to ignite the imagination. By presenting a scenario beyond the realms of the ordinary, magicians invite their audience to stretch their thoughts and question their understanding of the world. This act of mental gymnastics not only entertains but also stimulates cognitive engagement, inspiring viewers to view the world through a lens of endless possibilities. A pivotal aspect of the allure of illusions is the element of surprise. From daring escapes to mind-bending transformations, illusions command attention by subverting expectations and delivering unforeseen outcomes. This element of unpredictability infuses performances with an exhilarating energy, ensuring that every moment holds the promise of astonishment. Ultimately, the essence of illusion encompasses the seamless blending of technical prowess with storytelling finesse. It bridges the gap between the seen and the unseen, inviting audiences to embark on a journey where reality intertwines with fantasy. Through the delicate interplay of skill and showmanship, illusions not only entertain but also kindle the flames of wonder, leaving an enduring mark on all who bear witness to their mesmerizing charm.

Understanding the Audience's Perspective

Understanding the audience's perspective is pivotal in the realm of magic and illusion. It encompasses a profound comprehension of human perception, psychology, and emotion. As magicians, we are not only creators of wonder and amazement but also orchestrators of storytelling and intrigue. We must delve deep into the minds and hearts of our spectators, understanding their desires for mystery, their thirst for awe, and their yearning for enchantment. To truly connect with our audience, we must empathize with their curiosity and skepticism alike, appreciating the intricate dance between belief and disbelief that accompanies every magical performance. We become custodians of trust, responsible for nurturing an environment where astonishment thrives yet respects the integrity of genuine wonder. By acknowledging and respecting the audience's perspectives, we enhance the depth and authenticity of the mystical experience we offer. Moreover, understanding the audience's perspective extends beyond the actual performance. It encompasses the anticipation and excitement leading up to the show, the moments of disbelief and bewilderment during the act, and the lingering sense of fascination and contemplation afterward. As magicians, we are cognizant of the emotional journey our audience embarks upon from the first glimpse of a poster to the final bow. We strive to craft an immersive voyage into the unknown, one that leaves an indelible mark on the hearts and minds of those who witness our art. We recognize that our audience members arrive with differing backgrounds, experiences, and beliefs. Their unique perspectives enrich the tapestry of reactions and interpretations woven during our performances. As such, we embrace the diversity of viewpoints as a source of inspiration, challenging us to continually innovate and adapt our craft to resonate with a spectrum of individuals. The more we comprehend the kaleidoscope of perspectives within our audience, the deeper our connection becomes, enabling us to weave narratives that transcend barriers and unite us in shared amazement.

Historical Roots of Sleight of Hand

Sleight of hand, the art of skillful deception through manual dexterity, has a rich and captivating history that dates back centuries. Its origins can be traced to ancient civilizations where it was used not only for entertainment but also as a means of mysticism and storytelling. In ancient Egypt, talented performers used sleight of hand techniques to captivate audiences with seemingly magical feats, weaving tales of gods and legends into their performances. The Persian Empire also embraced the art of sleight of hand, incorporating it into elaborate displays of illusion and wonder. These early instances of sleight of hand laid the groundwork for its evolution into the mesmerizing form of entertainment we recognize today. Moving forward in time, sleight of hand continued to flourish during the Renaissance period. Visionaries such as Leonardo da Vinci and Giovanni Battista della Porta explored the realms of optical illusions and visual trickery, paving the way for the advancements that shaped modern sleight of hand. As society progressed, the allure of sleight of hand transcended borders, captivating audiences across Europe and beyond. During the 18th and 19th centuries, the burgeoning field of magic saw the rise of daring performers who honed their craft, bringing forth a new era of innovation and spectacle. From the opulent theaters of Paris to the bustling streets of London, sleight of hand became an integral part of the cultural tapestry, enchanting spectators from all walks of life. Through the ages, influential magicians and illusionists have contributed to the development of sleight of hand, each leaving an indelible mark on the art form. Their ingenuity and dedication have elevated sleight of hand into a timeless vehicle of enchantment.

Today, the historical roots of sleight of hand continue to inspire contemporary magicians as they perpetuate the legacy of this extraordinary art. By delving into its compelling past, we gain a profound appreciation for the enduring allure and significance of sleight of hand.

Famous Techniques and Their Origins

Sleight of hand, the magical art of dexterity and deception, has captivated audiences for centuries. Within this extraordinary craft, there lies a rich tapestry of famous techniques that have left indelible marks on the world of magic. Each technique carries its own unique history and significance, representing the endless innovation and creativity within the realm of illusion. Let us embark on a journey through time and explore the origins of some of the most renowned sleights of hand in magical history. The venerable Coin Palm, dating back to ancient China, is hailed as one of the earliest recorded sleights in magical performance. Its elegant execution and seamless concealment of a coin within the palm have mesmerized audiences for generations. Drawing inspiration from this ancient technique, many modern magicians continue to astound spectators with their adroit manipulation of currency. Another celebrated technique, the French Drop, traces its roots to 18th century Europe. Magicians adeptly employ this sleight to simulate the vanishing of an object, leaving audiences spellbound by the seemingly inexplicable disappearance. This timeless technique embodies a legacy of mystique and intrigue, embodying the essence of wonder that defines the art of deception. Moreover, the iconic Cups and Balls routine, an enduring staple of magic performances, boasts a history that spans across cultures and civilizations. With origins that can be traced back to ancient Egypt and Rome, this mesmerizing display of skill and subterfuge continues to enthrall audiences worldwide. The seamless choreography between the cups and the deft movements of the magician demonstrate a harmonious fusion of technique and showmanship, creating an enchanting spectacle that transcends time. In addition, the ambitious Card Control technique, a cornerstone of card manipulation, evolved from its early inception in gambling parlors to become a cornerstone of prestidigitation. Originating from the clandestine world of cardsharps, this intricate technique epitomizes the intersection of skill and finesse, transforming the humble deck of cards into a canvas for bewitching displays of legerdemain. Lastly, the age-old Trick Coin, a fascinating artifact with origins shrouded in mystery, has been wielded by countless magicians to confound their audiences. Through ingenious design and masterful execution, this deceptive prop has enraptured spectators with its bewildering effects, serving as a testament to the enduring allure of magical artifice. Each of these illustrious techniques weaves a narrative of ingenuity and artistry, enriching the vibrant tapestry of sleight of hand. As we delve into their origins, we gain a profound appreciation for the heritage and evolution of these enduring marvels, perpetuating the legacy of astonishment that embodies the timeless allure of magic.

Psychology Behind Deception

Understanding the intricate psychology behind deception delves into the depths of human perception and cognition. The art of illusion and sleight of hand is more than just captivating tricks; it's a profound manipulation of the human mind. By comprehending the subtle nuances of the human psyche, magicians are able to create awe-inspiring moments that defy logic and leave audiences spellbound. At its core, the psychology behind deception revolves around the fundamental concepts of attention, misdirection, and cognitive bias. Magicians harness these principles to craft illusions that challenge our understanding of reality. One key aspect of this psychology is the management of attention. Magicians understand that human attention is limited, and by skillfully directing it, they can control what the audience perceives. This manipulation allows them to conceal their actions in plain sight, creating an environment ripe for astonishment. Additionally, misdirection plays a pivotal role in the art of deception. By diverting attention away from the crucial moves, magicians exploit the inherent flaws in human attention to produce seemingly impossible feats. Through careful choreography and timing, they orchestrate an intricate dance of visual stimuli, leading spectators down paths of wonder and disbelief. Moreover, the psychology behind deception encompasses the exploration of cognitive bias. Human minds tend to follow predictable patterns and make assumptions based on previous experiences. Magicians leverage these biases to introduce deliberate contradictions and logical deviations that confound the audience's expectations. This strategic manipulation of mental frameworks creates fertile ground for extraordinary illusions to flourish and mesmerize. In essence, unveiling the psychology behind deception illuminates the profound connection between artistry and human cognition. Understanding the innate susceptibilities of perception allows magicians to craft experiences that transcend the boundaries of rationality, instilling a sense of wonder and enchantment. It's a fusion of calculated precision and empathetic awareness, creating a narrative that captivates and inspires. Delving into this intricate psychology unveils the art of magic as a profound exploration of human nature, as magicians wield the power of mystery to provoke introspection and craft moments of pure magic.

Skills: Practice and Precision

Skills: Practice and Precision The art of sleight of hand requires an unwavering dedication to practice and precision. It is not merely about mastering a few clever movements; it demands a commitment to honing one's craft to achieve seamless and undetectable manipulation. Through hours of relentless practice, magicians develop the nimbleness and dexterity required to execute their illusions with flawless finesse. Every subtle gesture, every swift movement, and every fleeting moment must be executed with utmost precision, making the seemingly impossible appear effortless to the audience. Precision is the cornerstone of deception, allowing magicians to weave spells of wonder and disbelief. Achieving such precision is no easy feat; it demands an unyielding resolve to tirelessly refine each maneuver until it becomes second nature. The precision of sleight of hand lies not only in the physical execution but also in the mental discipline required to maintain focus and composure amid the most intricate maneuvers. Magicians engage in endless repetition, ensuring that every motion is executed flawlessly, without the slightest hint of artifice. This relentless pursuit of perfection demands unwavering dedication and a profound respect for the art form. Without these attributes, the illusion would crumble, leaving the audience disillusioned. Beyond precision, practice plays a pivotal role in refining the subtleties of sleight of hand. Repetition breeds familiarity, transforming complex manipulations into instinctive movements. Furthermore, practice serves as a gateway to innovation, empowering magicians to push the boundaries of their artistry. It is through tireless practice that magicians lay the foundation for their most captivating performances, infusing creativity and ingenuity into every illusion. The path towards mastery is paved with countless setbacks and failures, yet it is through these challenges that true growth occurs. Magicians embrace each stumble as an opportunity to strengthen their resolve and deepen their understanding of their craft. Through this continuous process of skill refinement and precision enhancement, they elevate their performances to astonishing heights, captivating audiences with the seamless execution of their illusions. Ultimately, the pursuit of excellence through practice and precision is the hallmark of a dedicated magician committed to upholding the tradition of the mystifying art of sleight of hand.

Blending Artistry with Technique

In the realm of magic, the seamless fusion of artistry and technique is what sets the remarkable apart from the ordinary. It is within this delicate balance that the true essence of wonderment reveals itself. The magician's canvas is not one of paint or clay but rather that of time and space, where illusions are crafted to defy the laws of reality. Blending artistry with technique involves not only mastering sleight of hand but also infusing each movement with a sense of elegance and grace. Every gesture, every flourish must convey a story—a narrative that captivates the audience and draws them into a world where the impossible becomes possible. The artistry lies in the subtlety of the performance, in the way the magician uses misdirection to guide the audience's focus where it needs to be while gracefully executing the sleights that defy logic and belief. A skilled magician understands the symbiotic relationship between technique and showmanship, seamlessly intertwining the two to create an experience that transcends mere entertainment—an experience that leaves an indelible impression on the hearts and minds of those who bear witness. Moreover, blending artistry with technique demands an unwavering dedication to the craft. Hours upon hours are spent honing these skills, refining each movement, perfecting every nuance until it becomes second nature. It requires a profound understanding of the psychology behind deception, an awareness of how the mind interprets and processes sensory information, and the ability to exploit these cognitive mechanisms to elevate the performance to a level of pure enchantment. This amalgamation of meticulous practice and artistic insight yields a performance that is not just magical; it is transformative. Furthermore, the interplay between artistry and technique is deeply rooted in history, stemming from the ancient traditions of mysticism and wonder. Throughout the ages, masterful illusionists have elevated magic to an art form—an expression of creativity and ingenuity that resonates across cultures and generations. By studying the techniques and storytelling prowess of iconic performers from the past, modern magicians can continue to push the boundaries of what is conceivable, infusing new life into age-old wonders. In doing so, they pay homage to the timeless allure of magic while propelling it into the future. Ultimately, the seamless blend of artistry and technique defines the very soul of magic, weaving together the threads of creativity, skill, and passion to create an enchanting tapestry of wonders. It is a testament to the enduring allure of the unseen, the unexplained, and the extraordinary—a testament that speaks to the eternal fascination with that which defies logic and reason. This harmonious union invites audiences to suspend their disbelief and embrace the enchantment that unfolds before their eyes, sparking a sense of childlike wonder and delight that transcends language, culture, and time.

Iconic Performers and Their Influence

The world of magic has been graced with an array of iconic performers who have left an indelible mark on the art form. Each of these magicians brought their unique style, innovation, and charisma to the stage, captivating audiences with their spellbinding acts of illusion and sleight of hand. Hailing from diverse backgrounds and eras, these legendary figures not only shaped the evolution of magic but also inspired countless aspiring magicians to pursue their dreams. One such luminary is the enigmatic Harry Houdini, whose daring escapades and unparalleled showmanship revolutionized the realm of magic. Houdini's death-defying stunts, such as his infamous water torture cell act, earned him international acclaim and cemented his legacy as one of history's most celebrated magicians. His tireless commitment to pushing the boundaries of what was deemed possible in the world of magic continues to inspire magicians to this day. Similarly, the elegant performances of Dai Vernon, known as

Challenges of Maintaining Mystery

Maintaining mystery in the world of magic is an intricate and demanding task, often requiring a delicate balance between tradition and innovation. As iconic performers continue to push the boundaries of what is possible, they face the challenge of preserving the enigma that lies at the heart of their craft. The relentless pursuit of originality must coexist with the need to protect the secrets that captivate audiences worldwide. This delicate dance embodies the paradox of magic—a constant quest for novelty while safeguarding timeless allure. Keeping the sense of wonder alive necessitates a deep understanding of the ever-evolving expectations of spectators. Magicians must navigate the fine line between familiarity and astonishment, presenting illusions that honor the classics while delivering fresh marvels. Alongside technical expertise, they must master the art of emotional storytelling, weaving narratives that enhance the mysterious aura surrounding their performances. Moreover, in an era defined by technological advancement and information accessibility, magicians encounter the additional hurdle of combating exposure. Striking a balance between sharing insight into their craft and shielding its mystique poses an ongoing challenge. The rise of social media and digital platforms has intensified this struggle, compelling magicians to adapt their strategies for preserving the sanctity of their art in an age of unprecedented transparency. Furthermore, global interconnectedness has led to diverse cultural influences converging within the realm of magic, necessitating a nuanced approach to crafting illusions that resonate across borders and beliefs. Successfully maintaining mystery demands unwavering dedication to the preservation of wonder, coupled with an unyielding commitment to uplifting and inspiring audiences. Magic, in its essence, thrives on the intangible—on the immersive experience of disbelief and astonishment. Overcoming the challenges of upholding the enigmatic nature of magic requires a profound appreciation for its history, an acute awareness of contemporary dynamics, and an unwavering passion for pushing the boundaries of imagination. Navigating these complexities with grace and integrity remains essential as magicians strive to perpetuate the timeless allure of the art of deception.

Reflecting on the Journey of Innovation

As we reflect on the journey of innovation in the world of magic, it becomes evident that the art of deception has continuously evolved to captivate and mesmerize audiences. From the earliest documented performances to the modern-day spectacles, the essence of innovation has been at the core of magical endeavors. Innovation within the realm of sleight of hand has not only presented magicians with new creative opportunities but has also posed unique challenges that have fueled the pursuit of excellence. The ability to maintain mystery and astonish viewers while embracing innovation is a testament to the enduring allure of magic. Throughout history, master illusionists have leveraged innovation to push the boundaries of what is possible, redefining the art form and leaving an indelible mark on the world of entertainment. In looking back on the milestones of innovation, one cannot overlook the pivotal role of technological advancements. The integration of state-of-the-art equipment and digital effects has revolutionized magic, enabling performers to craft unprecedented illusions that transcend conventional limitations. This harmonious marriage of tradition and innovation has ushered in an era of enchantment that continues to captivate global audiences. Moreover, the advent of social media and digital platforms has provided magicians with new avenues to showcase their innovative prowess, connecting them with enthusiasts worldwide. By embracing these advancements, today's magicians are perpetuating the legacy of innovation and ensuring the perpetuity of the enchanting craft. Furthermore, as the journey of innovation unfolds, it is essential to acknowledge the profound impact of cross-cultural exchange and collaboration. The fusion of diverse magical traditions and techniques from across the globe has infused the art form with newfound dynamism and diversity, enriching its tapestry. Through cultural exchange, magicians have broadened their creative horizons, drawing inspiration from a myriad of sources and infusing their performances with a multifaceted vibrancy. This collaborative spirit of innovation has not only invigorated the magical landscape but has also fostered an inclusive environment where fresh ideas flourish and traditions harmoniously interweave. Embracing this collective creativity, magicians continue to elevate the art of deception, sparking wonder and enchantment in every corner of the world. In conclusion, the journey of innovation within the realm of magic mirrors the timeless quest for transcendence and wonder. It is a testament to the ingenuity, resilience, and unyielding creativity of the human spirit. As the next chapters of magical evolution unfold, the spirit of innovation will undoubtedly continue to propel the art of sleight of hand to unparalleled heights, enthralling audiences and shaping the captivating vistas of illusion for generations to come.

Mastering Sleight of Hand

The Essence of Sleight of Hand

Sleight of hand, often regarded as the cornerstone of magic, embodies a delicate balance of artistry and skill. It is an intricate dance between the magician's dexterity and the seamless execution of maneuvers that deceive and astonish audiences. At its essence, sleight of hand involves the masterful manipulation of objects in a manner that defies perception, leaving spectators in awe of the seemingly impossible. This craft requires unparalleled dedication, precision, and an unwavering commitment to the art form. As magicians delve into the world of sleight of hand, they encounter a myriad of key techniques that form the very foundation of their craft. From classic palm transfers and fluid card controls to the expert management of props, each technique serves as a vital building block in creating illusions that transcend the boundaries of reality. Understanding the nuances of these techniques is not merely about mastering their execution, but also appreciating the rhythm and flow that bestows an air of mesmerizing elegance upon the performance. Furthermore, the essence of sleight of hand extends beyond mere technical proficiency. It encompasses an intuitive understanding of timing, movement, and psychology, as well as an acute awareness of misdirection. The magician treads the fine line between captivating an audience through seamless manipulation and holding them spellbound with the magic of their presence. Through the art of subtlety and nuance, the magician breathes life into seemingly ordinary acts, transforming mundane gestures into captivating moments of wonder. Ultimately, sleight of hand represents a fusion of tradition and innovation. While it pays homage to time-honored techniques passed down through generations of magicians, it also evolves through the infusion of contemporary flair and creativity. Magicians strive not only to uphold the revered legacy of their predecessors, but to push the boundaries of what is conceivable, pioneering new pathways in the realm of illusion. Embracing the essence of sleight of hand is more than a pursuit of technical prowess; it is an ongoing dialogue between the past, present, and future of magic. In delving into the heart of sleight of hand, magicians embark on a profound journey of self-discovery and artistic expression. It is a disciplined practice that demands unwavering dedication and persistence, yet rewards with the sheer marvel of transcending the ordinary to craft moments of pure enchantment.

Building the Foundation: Key Techniques

Mastering sleight of hand is an art form that demands dedication, precision, and an unwavering commitment to honing one's skills. To achieve proficiency in this intricate craft, it is essential to lay a solid foundation built upon key techniques that serve as the pillars of expertise. These fundamental techniques form the basis for all manner of illusions, enabling magicians to captivate audiences with seamless and mesmerizing performances. Whether it's the deft manipulation of cards, the nimble movements of the hands, or the subtle misdirection of attention, mastering sleight of hand requires a deep understanding of each technique's nuances and the ability to execute them flawlessly under the scrutiny of keen spectators. Embracing the foundational strategies of sleight of hand empowers magicians to create moments of wonder and disbelief that linger in the hearts and minds of their audience long after the performance has concluded. Among the pivotal techniques that form the bedrock of sleight of hand mastery are palming, the pass, false shuffles, and the double lift. Each of these techniques demands painstaking practice and unwavering focus, as they are the building blocks upon which the entire tapestry of illusion is woven. Palming, for instance, involves concealing an object in the palm of the hand without arousing any suspicion, often forming the basis for vanishing acts and miraculous productions. The pass, meanwhile, allows for the seamless exchange of cards in a manner imperceptible to the human eye, laying the groundwork for astonishing transpositions and transformations. False shuffles, on the other hand, enable magicians to maintain the order of a deck while creating the illusion of thorough mixing, providing the groundwork for mind-bending revelations and impossible card location routines. Lastly, the double lift serves as a primary tool for creating illusions that hinge on manipulating the perception of successive cards, allowing for astonishing revelations and confounding sequences. Mastering these key techniques is a rite of passage for any aspiring magician, requiring countless hours of dedicated practice, unwavering perseverance, and a passion for the art of illusion. By delving into the intricacies of these foundational techniques, magicians lay the groundwork for awe-inspiring performances that defy explanation and leave audiences spellbound.

The Journey of Practice and Patience

A mastery of sleight of hand is not an art that can be rushed or forced. Instead, it is a journey that requires unwavering dedication, patience, and relentless practice. Every magician who aspires to achieve excellence in this craft must understand that the path to proficiency is paved with countless hours of diligent training and an unyielding commitment to improvement. The journey begins with a humble acceptance of one's current skills, acknowledging both strengths and weaknesses. It entails a constant pursuit of refinement, a relentless drive to perfect every movement and gesture. Through patient repetition of techniques and an unrelenting drive to better oneself, the journey of practice becomes a transformative process that shapes not only one's technical prowess but also cultivates discipline and resilience. Patience is the cornerstone of this journey; it allows the magician to embrace setbacks and failures as opportunities for growth rather than deterrents.In the pursuit of mastering sleight of hand, patience becomes an invaluable companion, tempering the impatience that often accompanies the desire for instant gratification. Without it, frustration might set in, leading to a stagnation of progress. Yet, with patience, every repetition becomes a step forward, every mistake a lesson learned. The journey of practice and patience is, in essence, a deeply personal odyssey that tests not just one's technical abilities but also fortitude of character. In the face of adversity and challenges, it is this resilience and determination honed through patient practice that allows a magician to remain steadfast on their path to mastery. Each hour invested in refining techniques is a testament to one's unwavering dedication, and each setback overcome is a triumph of perseverance. Ultimately, the journey of practice and patience is a lifelong commitment, an ongoing quest for excellence that demands humility, persistence, and an enduring love for the art of deception and wonder.

The Role of Dexterity and Misdirection

Sleight of hand, as a form of stage magic, relies heavily on the art of misdirection and the dexterity of the performer. These two elements are integral to creating the illusion that captivates and mystifies audiences around the world. Dexterity, or the skilled use of hands, forms the foundation of many sleight of hand techniques. It involves meticulous practice to achieve seamless movements that appear effortless to the observer. The magician must master the control and precision of their hand movements to execute tricks with finesse, leaving spectators spellbound. This level of mastery can take years of dedicated training and relentless perseverance. Each gesture, each subtle maneuver, contributes to the overall deceptiveness of the performance, all hinging on the magician's nimble dexterity. Equally crucial is the concept of misdirection, a fundamental principle in the magician's arsenal. Misdirection involves diverting the audience's attention away from the actual method of the trick, ensuring that they focus on a strategic aspect of the performance. Whether it's a compelling story, an engaging gesture, or an intricate prop, misdirection compels the audience to look where the magician wants them to, concealing the true mechanics of the illusion. It's an exquisite dance between the performer and the audience, guiding their perception towards the magical spectacle while skillfully obscuring the mechanics at work. Mastering the interplay of dexterity and misdirection demands an immense understanding of human psychology and a deep empathy for the audience's perspective. It requires a profound appreciation for the art of storytelling through intricate gestures and an ability to manipulate attention seamlessly. The success of a sleight of hand performance hinges on the seamless coordination of these elements, weaving an enchanting tapestry of deception and wonder. In the hands of a skilled practitioner, the fusion of dexterity and misdirection transcends mere trickery and ascends to an art form, captivating hearts and minds alike. These two timeless pillars of magic continue to shape and define the craft, offering endless opportunities for innovation and creativity while honoring the rich traditions of illusion. As we delve further into the intricacies of sleight of hand, we unravel the deep significance of these essential elements, celebrating the dedication and ingenuity required to master this awe-inspiring discipline.

Lessons from the Masters

As we delve into the intricate world of sleight of hand, it is essential to recognize the invaluable wisdom passed down through generations of masters in the art of illusion. These revered figures have not only honed their technical skills over years of dedication but have also cultivated an unparalleled understanding of the psychology behind magic. By observing their performances and deconstructing their methods, aspiring magicians gain insights that transcend mere technique. The true essence lies in comprehending the nuances of misdirection, showmanship, and audience engagement. Masters of sleight of hand understand the significance of creating an emotional connection with their spectators, a skill refined through countless performances. Through their experiences, they impart lessons on anticipation, timing, and the seamless integration of storytelling with prestidigitation. Embracing these teachings allows emerging magicians to transition from skilled technicians to captivating performers capable of weaving enchantment around every movement. Furthermore, these learned masters emphasize the importance of embracing innovation while upholding traditional values in magic. By studying the evolution of sleight of hand throughout history, one can draw inspiration from the past while embracing contemporary advancements. This harmonious blend fosters creativity and ensures that the timeless allure of magic remains dynamic and relevant in the modern age. Every gesture, every glance, and every whispered incantation work in harmony to perpetuate the legacy of the art form. With profound respect for the contributions of these masters, we acknowledge that their enduring influence continues to shape the future of magic, instilling a sense of responsibility in the next generation to carry forth the torch of wonder and mystery.

Integrating Innovation with Tradition

In the world of magic, the integration of innovation with tradition is a delicate and pivotal balance that separates the ordinary from the extraordinary. It is a harmonious dance between paying homage to the roots of the art while continually pushing the boundaries to create new wonders. As magicians, we stand on the shoulders of those who came before us, drawing inspiration from timeless classics and age-old techniques that have transcended generations. Yet, it is an inherent desire to carve our own path and leave our mark on the world of magic that drives us to explore innovative approaches and daring feats. This delicate interplay between tradition and innovation is at the heart of mastering sleight of hand. It is the seamless fusion of classic maneuvers with modern flair that captivates audiences and leaves them in awe. Embracing tradition means understanding the foundational principles that have stood the test of time, and respecting the craftsmanship and dedication that have preserved these timeless secrets. However, it is the spirit of innovation that breathes new life into these age-old techniques, infusing them with creativity, unpredictability, and a touch of personal artistry. While the fundamentals of sleight of hand lay the groundwork for mastery, it is the willingness to innovate and evolve that elevates a magician from proficient to exceptional. This evolution goes beyond technical prowess; it embraces the development of unique gestures, narrative-driven performances, and a deep connection with the audience. By infusing traditional acts with innovative storytelling, unexpected twists, and interactive elements, magicians can transport their spectators into a realm where reality blurs with illusion, creating an unforgettable experience. The beauty of integrating innovation with tradition lies in its ability to sustain the allure of classic illusions while breathing new life into age-old marvels. This synergy allows magicians to pay homage to the greats who paved the way while forging their own legacy through the art of sleight of hand. It is a testament to our commitment to preserving the mystique of magic while embracing the ever-changing landscape of entertainment. As we bridge the gap between tradition and innovation, we honor the past, celebrate the present, and pave the way for enchanting wonders yet to come.

Stories from the Workshop

In the workshop, where the art of magic comes to life, countless stories unfold within the walls that bear witness to relentless dedication and unwavering passion. Here, beginners step into a world of endless possibilities, embracing the intricacies of manipulation and the beauty of deception. As the air fills with the scent of polished wood and echoing laughter, seasoned magicians act as mentors, imparting wisdom gleaned from years of honing their craft. Each tool, from the humble deck of cards to the delicate coins, holds the potential to captivate and mystify audiences, and it is in this hallowed space that aspiring illusionists learn to harness such power. From the first tentative attempts at sleight of hand to the triumphant mastery of complex maneuvers, every magician's journey is rife with challenges and triumphs, all woven into the very fabric of the workshop. The room pulsates with the energy of unyielding determination and unspoken camaraderie as practitioners share their experiences, exchanging insights and techniques that transcend language barriers. Echoes of applause reverberate in these walls, serving as a constant reminder of the profound impact that their art has on those who behold it. Each spilled drop of sweat and every missed beat during practice sessions serve as testaments to the unwavering commitment that fuels their aspirations. Amidst the trials and tribulations, seeds of creativity take root, yielding new and innovative illusions that push the boundaries of what is deemed possible. It's here, in this crucible of creativity and resilience, that magicians forge not only their technical skills but also their characters, cultivating virtues such as patience, perseverance, and an unyielding pursuit of excellence. These stories from the workshop stand as a testament to the enduring spirit of magic, reminding us that behind every spellbinding performance lies a tale of dedication, sacrifice, and unbridled passion for the mesmerizing art of illusion.

Facing Challenges Along the Way

Mastering sleight of hand is no easy feat; it demands unwavering dedication and an unyielding commitment to overcoming the numerous challenges that present themselves along the way. Aspiring magicians often encounter a variety of obstacles, both internal and external, as they navigate this intricate craft. One of the most prevalent challenges is the daunting task of perfecting each movement and gesture to execute seemingly effortless illusions. This requires countless hours of repetitive practice, honing skills to achieve seamless fluidity in performance. Additionally, performers must wrestle with their own doubts and frustrations, as the pursuit of perfection can be both mentally and emotionally taxing. Moreover, there's the constant pressure to innovate and push the boundaries of traditional techniques while maintaining the integrity of classic illusions. This delicate balance between novelty and authenticity presents a formidable trial for even the most seasoned practitioners. Furthermore, the challenge extends beyond technical mastery to include the art of misdirection, a crucial component of sleight of hand. Participants must learn to divert attention subtly and effectively, heightening the mystique of each illusion. This skill is cultivated through persistent experimentation and adaptation, requiring nimble adaptability to suit various settings and audiences. The journey is not without its share of setbacks, rejections, and moments of self-doubt. Magicians often face skepticism from critics and must confront the arduous task of gaining recognition and acceptance within a competitive industry. Each setback provides an opportunity for growth and learning, strengthening the resolve of those dedicated to mastering the craft. Despite these challenges, the sheer perseverance and passion exhibited by practitioners attest to the profound allure and enduring magic of sleight of hand. Every obstacle serves as an invitation for personal and artistic development, fostering a resilience that is fundamental to the evolution of this revered art form.

Reflecting on Progress and Growth

Reflecting on progress and growth in the art of sleight of hand is a deeply personal and enlightening journey. It's a process that allows a magician to look back at their humble beginnings and acknowledge how far they have come. Every successful sleight, every mesmerizing act of illusion, and every perfected movement marks an important milestone in their growth. It's an opportunity to celebrate the dedication, perseverance, and creativity that have shaped their craft. This period of reflection also provides insight into the evolution of their technique and performance style. Magicians often find that their strategies, subtleties, and nuances have matured over time, resulting in a more refined and captivating showcase of skill. Through introspection, they recognize the impact of experience and wisdom on their ability to captivate audiences with seamless and bewildering illusions. Additionally, it prompts them to appreciate the supportive network of mentors and fellow magicians who have contributed to their development. These connections have played an instrumental role in nurturing their talent and guiding them through the challenges of mastering sleight of hand. Moreover, reflecting on progress and growth serves as a reminder of the importance of continuous learning and adaptation. Magicians acknowledge the ever-changing landscape of magic and recognize the value of staying abreast of modern techniques and trends. This self-awareness fosters a mindset that is open to experimentation and innovation, enabling them to enhance their repertoire with fresh ideas and approaches. They embrace the fact that progression in the art of sleight of hand is not just about refining existing skills but also about embracing new possibilities and pushing the boundaries of traditional magic. Finally, this process allows magicians to recognize the profound effect their craft has had on their own personal growth. The dedication, discipline, and resilience demanded by the pursuit of mastery have undoubtedly permeated other aspects of their lives. They develop a sense of self-belief and determination that extends beyond the realm of magic, empowering them to overcome obstacles in various domains. As they reflect on their progress, they become acutely aware of the transformative power of their art, not only as entertainers but also as individuals who have evolved through their passion and dedication.

Looking Ahead: The Future of Illusion

As we stand at the precipice of the future, it is crucial to contemplate the trajectory of illusion and magic. The art form has evolved significantly over the years, embracing modern technology while still honoring its rich traditional roots. Looking ahead, it's evident that illusion will continue to captivate and mesmerize audiences across the globe. One of the most intriguing aspects is the integration of virtual and augmented reality into magic performances. Imagine a world where illusions are not confined to physical spaces but transcend into a digital realm, blurring the lines between reality and fantasy. This melding of technological innovation with classic sleight of hand presents an exciting frontier for magicians to explore. Furthermore, the future of illusion holds immense potential for cross-disciplinary collaborations. Magicians working in tandem with artists, engineers, and psychologists can add new layers of depth and complexity to their performances, creating immersive experiences that defy expectations and spark wonder. Another area worth pondering is the role of storytelling within magic. We anticipate a shift towards narrative-driven illusions that immerse audiences in compelling stories, leaving a lasting impact far beyond the spectacle itself. When magic becomes a vehicle for storytelling, it transcends mere entertainment and becomes a profound emotional journey. Moreover, the global reach of magic is poised to expand even further, transcending geographical boundaries through digital platforms and live streaming. This accessibility has the potential to cultivate a new generation of aspiring magicians from diverse backgrounds, fostering a rich tapestry of perspectives and styles within the art. With these innovative advancements on the horizon, it's crucial to uphold the core principles of authenticity and artistry in magic. While technology may usher in groundbreaking possibilities, the essence of human connection and genuine astonishment must remain at the forefront. As we navigate the ever-changing landscape of illusion, let us embrace the evolution while preserving the timeless allure that has enchanted generations before us.

The Influence of Magic Manuals

A Luminous Guide: The Role of Magic Manuals

Magic manuals are not merely instruction books; they represent a gateway to an enchanting realm where secrets are unveiled and the extraordinary becomes possible. Within these treasured tomes lie the accumulated wisdom of generations of illusionists, each page bearing the imprint of countless hours of dedication, experimentation, and revelation. The significance of magic manuals as guiding lights in the journey to mastery cannot be overstated. They serve as companions to aspiring magicians, offering invaluable insights, techniques, and inspiration to aid them on their quest for artistic excellence. These venerable texts, often passed down from one magician to another, forge a connection between past and present, allowing practitioners to tap into the timeless expertise of their predecessors. As novices immerse themselves in the pages of these manuals, they encounter a wealth of knowledge that serves as a foundation for their understanding of the art form. Every turn of the page reveals new perspectives, shedding light on the mechanics of illusions and the intricacies of performance. However, the true significance of magic manuals lies not solely in the acquisition of technical skills, but in the cultivation of a deeper appreciation for the art of magic. These works provide a glimpse into the creative processes and influences that have shaped the evolution of magic, fostering an understanding of the rich heritage that underpins the craft. As readers delve into the narratives woven within these guides, they gain an intimate understanding of the challenges, innovations, and triumphs that have defined the magical landscape. Furthermore, magic manuals play a pivotal role in preserving the traditions and customs of the magical community, safeguarding its heritage for future generations. Through these written works, the ethos and ethos and ethics of the art are imparted, instilling aspirants with a reverence for the principles that uphold the practice of magic. In essence, magic manuals serve as beacons, illuminating the path to mastery and offering indispensable guidance to those who seek to navigate the ethereal realms of wonder and illusion.

Treasured Tomes of Illusionists

The world of magic is enriched with a wealth of treasured tomes, each serving as an invaluable repository of the secrets and wisdom of illusionists through the ages. These esteemed volumes are not merely books; they are conduits of arcane knowledge, passing down the intricate and mesmerizing art of magic from one generation to the next. With every delicate turn of the page, readers enter a realm where reality blurs and the impossible becomes tantalizingly within reach. It is within these books that the true essence of magic resides, waiting to be unearthed by those with the courage and dedication to pursue its mysteries. These treasured tomes are akin to precious artifacts, carefully preserved by practitioners and enthusiasts alike. Within their hallowed pages lie the blueprints for wondrous illusions and the keys to unmasking the riddles of enchantment. Aspiring magicians delve into these texts with unwavering reverence, understanding that each word carries the weight of centuries of magical tradition and innovation. The respect accorded to these volumes is not only a testament to their profound influence, but also a reflection of the boundless admiration and adoration inspired by the art of magic. Beyond their value as educational resources, these tomes serve as portals to the minds of the illustrious conjurors whose names have become synonymous with greatness. From Houdini to Herrmann, from Wonder to Thurston, the stories and incantations contained within these books illuminate the storied journeys of the master magicians who have carved their indelible mark upon the annals of magic history. Each volume is a treasure trove of anecdotes and revelations, allowing readers to form an intimate connection with the luminaries who have shaped the very fabric of this captivating craft with their brilliance and innovation. Moreover, these tomes stand as testaments to the diversity and depth of magical expression. They encompass a spectrum of styles and approaches, catering to the varied inclinations and aspirations of budding magicians. Whether one's passion lies in the realm of escapology, mentalism, or grand illusion, there exists a cherished manual that holds the keys to unlocking and mastering the chosen discipline. These books bridge the chasm between ambition and accomplishment, allowing fledgling magicians to amplify their understanding and refine their artistry under the guidance of venerable mentors. In conclusion, the treasured tomes of illusionists are not mere repositories of magical knowledge; they are living embodiments of the enduring spirit of magic. These revered volumes transcend time and space, fostering a profound and ever-evolving kinship between magicians across generations. Their presence sustains the never-ending dance of inspiration and ingenuity, ensuring that the luminous flame of magic continues to burn brightly, illuminating the path for all who dare to embrace its mystique.

Turning Pages into Practice

The knowledge encapsulated within the pages of magic manuals is not solely for perusal, but rather a gateway to practical application. As readers delve into the intricacies of each illusion, they embark on a journey that transforms theoretical understanding into tangible expertise. Turning pages becomes a ritualistic process as aspiring magicians absorb the nuances of each technique, honing their skills with every read. The magic that transpires from these pages transcends the mere act of reading; it is an alchemical process that transmutes words into wonders. It is amidst this transformation that individuals evolve from mere enthusiasts to adept practitioners of the mystical arts. Furthermore, embracing the wisdom inscribed within these manuals fosters a profound connection between the magician and the mentor, bridging the chasm between theoretical musings and impactful execution. Each turn of the page brings the aspirant closer to mastery, instilling a sense of purpose and dedication which permeates every aspect of their magical pursuits. Moreover, the process of turning pages into practice engenders a deep-rooted respect for the art, allowing practitioners to uphold the time-honored traditions while simultaneously fostering innovation and personal growth. Through this harmonious fusion of tradition and individual expression, the magic within these manuals breathes new life and relevance into age-old illusions. As the pages are turned and intricate details absorbed, the magician internalizes the ethos of their craft, gaining intimate familiarity with the foundational principles that underpin their performances. This metamorphosis from reader to practitioner marks the commencement of an enchanting odyssey wherein the written words leap off the page and manifest as bewitching displays of prowess. Ultimately, the process of turning pages into practice is a transformative experience that imbues aspiring magicians with the confidence, skill, and reverence necessary to command the stage with awe-inspiring performances.

Wisdom from the Wise: Historical Insights

Magic, in its many forms, has a rich and storied history that spans centuries and crosses cultural boundaries. Throughout this expansive tapestry, magicians have left behind invaluable insights, teachings, and wisdom that continue to influence and inspire practitioners today. The historical journey of magic manuals reveals not only the methods and techniques employed by magicians of yore, but also their innovative thinking, creativity, and dedication to the craft. These manual's pages are imbued with profound historical insights, presenting a fascinating glimpse into the evolution of magic as an art form. Delving into these historical texts offers a rare opportunity to connect directly with the minds and perspectives of past masters. We gain access to the inner workings of their illusions, the nuances of their performances, and the challenges they faced in an era vastly different from our own. Through their writings, we find timeless lessons on performance, presentation, misdirection, and the enduring power of magic to captivate and mystify. Furthermore, these manuals provide a window into the social and cultural milieus in which these magicians operated. They offer a unique lens through which to observe the shifting perceptions of magic, the changing tastes of audiences, and the ever-evolving societal roles of magicians. By tracing the lineage of magical knowledge through the ages, we come to appreciate the resilience and adaptability of the art of magic, as it has persisted and thrived amidst the ebb and flow of history. Additionally, historical magic manuals serve as reservoirs of creativity and ingenuity. Within their pages, we uncover the seeds of novel concepts, the genesis of iconic routines, and the origins of timeless illusions. Each text represents a treasure trove of inspiration for contemporary magicians, as they seek to honor tradition while infusing their performances with innovative flair. Lastly, through studying these historical insights, we recognize the essential role of continuity in magic. As we absorb the accumulated knowledge and experiences of the past, we become custodians of a living tradition, entrusted with the responsibility to preserve, reinterpret, and expand upon the wisdom of our magical forebears. In embracing this legacy, we pay homage to the enduring spirit of magic, bridging the chasm of time to uphold the enchantment and wonder that has enthralled audiences across generations.

Tools of Transformation: A Deeper Comprehension

In the realm of magic, every aspiring magician encounters a profound realization - that the enigma lies not only in the execution of tricks, but also in the understanding of the art's underlying principles. This chapter delves into the tools that serve as gateways to a deeper comprehension of magic. The pages of magic manuals unfold like treasure maps, guiding enthusiasts through the labyrinth of secrets hidden within illusions. The significance of these 'tools of transformation' cannot be overstated. Not merely instruction manuals, they are repositories of insights gathered through generations of magicians, each contributing their own unique perspective on an ancient and revered craft. Within their pages lie the building blocks of astonishment, waiting to be harnessed by those who seek to master the art. By immersing oneself in the contents of these invaluable tomes, a deeper appreciation for the intricacies of magic is gradually gained. Techniques such as misdirection, sleight of hand, and psychological manipulation are dissected with painstaking detail, offering readers a comprehensive understanding of the mechanics behind the mysteries. It is in this comprehension that true mastery is born, transforming fledgling performers into maestros of marvel. Moreover, these manuals serve as repositories of wisdom passed down from illustrious predecessors, offering a glimpse into the methods and philosophies of legendary magicians. They provide a link to the past, illuminating the evolution of magic while honoring the legacies of those who paved the way for future generations. As new generations absorb the knowledge contained within these volumes, they contribute to the continual evolution of the art, keeping its flame burning brightly. Within the covers of these manuals, one finds not just technical guidance, but an entryway into the rich tapestry of magical history. From stories of triumph to accounts of innovation and discovery, the narrative that emerges is one of dedication, resilience, and unwavering passion. Readers are immersed in a world where impossible feats become conceivable, and miracles are confined not to the realms of myth, but to the stage that exists between reality and illusion. As the journey through these texts unfolds, it becomes increasingly apparent that they are not mere guides, but companions on the road to enlightenment. They offer encouragement, advice, and the collective wisdom of the ages. They instill in the reader an understanding that magic is more than just a performance; it is a legacy to be nurtured and expanded upon, where illusion gives way to inspiration, and wonder becomes an enduring legacy.

Illuminating the Path to Mastery

On the journey to become a master magician, one must navigate a complex and intricate path that demands dedication, perseverance, and an unwavering commitment to the craft. No mere sleight of hand or illusion can define the mastery sought by Alexander Herrmann and countless others who have pursued perfection in the art of magic. True mastery is born from a profound understanding of the essence of magic, an ability to connect with audiences on emotional and intellectual levels, and a relentless pursuit of creative and technical excellence. The illumination of this path to mastery begins not with grand spectacles or dazzling displays, but with an ardent reverence for the subtle nuances and foundational principles that underpin the art of magic. It starts with recognizing that the true magic lies not in the tricks themselves, but in the artistry, storytelling, and connection that they facilitate. This understanding fosters a deep respect for the traditions and history of magic, serving as the guiding light that leads aspirants toward authenticity and proficiency. Moreover, the path to mastery necessitates an appreciation for innovation and adaptation while preserving the sanctity of time-honored techniques. It involves daring to seek new horizons without forsaking the wisdom of those who have come before. Visualize a path interwoven with threads of tradition and innovation, where the wisdom of ancient conjurors intermingles with the groundbreaking techniques of contemporary visionaries. The aspiring magician is not merely a student of magic, but also a custodian of its timeless legacy, entrusted with expanding, enriching, and perpetuating the boundless possibilities inherent in the art. Every step along this path offers an opportunity to absorb, internalize, and ultimately transcend existing paradigms. Mastery arises from the fusion of accumulated knowledge, the alchemical blending of conventional practices and progressive methods, and the meticulous honing of one's craft. However, it is not a solitary endeavor, for the path to mastery invites collaboration, mentorship, and the embrace of diverse perspectives. The luminaries of the past serve as invaluable guides, their wisdom immortalized in texts, treatises, and manuscripts that illuminate the way forward. Yet, equally important are the contemporary mentors and collaborators who impart fresh insights, challenge preconceived notions, and inspire continual growth. Every encounter, every exchange enriches and expands the comprehension of magic, propelling aspirants towards ever greater heights of artistry and skill. Ultimately, the enlightenment that accompanies the pursuit of mastery transcends the realm of mere technique, delving into the profound realms of creativity, empathy, and human connection. Aspiring magicians discover that the path to mastery is a profound metamorphosis, a transformative odyssey that shapes not only their art, but also their very essence. Through unwavering commitment, unwavering resilience, and an unyielding passion for the craft, they kindle the sparks of inspiration, innovation, and enchantment, casting a radiant glow upon the hallowed path that leads to mastery.

Tradition and Innovation Hand in Hand

Magic, as an art form steeped in tradition, has always embraced innovation. Throughout history, magicians have sought to build upon the teachings of their predecessors while also pushing the boundaries of what is possible. This delicate balance between honoring time-honored practices and embracing new techniques lies at the heart of magical evolution. In the world of magic, traditional methods serve as the foundation upon which contemporary illusions are built. The age-old principles of misdirection, sleight of hand, and showmanship continue to form the bedrock of magical performances. Yet, within this framework, magicians also strive to introduce fresh ideas and concepts that captivate modern audiences. The harmonious amalgamation of tradition and innovation can be observed across various facets of magical expression. From stage design and props to scripting and presentation, each element of a performance represents an opportunity to blend the old with the new. By paying homage to classic routines and effects while infusing them with modern flair, magicians create experiences that resonate with diverse audiences. Moreover, the relationship between tradition and innovation extends beyond individual performances. In the realm of magical instruction, seasoned magicians pass down their knowledge and expertise, upholding cherished traditions while imparting contemporary insights. This transfer of wisdom ensures that foundational techniques remain relevant even as new methodologies emerge, thereby forging a continuum of magical excellence. At its core, the marriage of tradition and innovation reflects a deep reverence for the rich tapestry of magical heritage, ensuring that time-honored techniques retain their allure even amidst a landscape of ever-evolving entertainment. Through this fusion, magicians pay homage to their predecessors while simultaneously crafting an enchanting future for the art of magic.

Foundations for Fleeting Marvels

Magic, at its core, is an art of fleeting marvels that captivate and astonish. Yet, behind every spellbinding performance lies a foundation built on unwavering dedication, relentless practice, and the deep wisdom distilled within magic manuals. These venerable tomes serve as guiding lights, illuminating the path for aspiring magicians and seasoned performers alike. Within their pages dwell secrets, techniques, and insights that form the bedrock of magical craftsmanship. The foundations for fleeting marvels are laid upon the timeless principles enshrined in these manuals. They provide not just instructions, but also a roadmap for understanding the intricate dance between tradition and innovation. Aspiring magicians learn from the ancient wisdom passed down through generations, while also embracing the ever-evolving landscape of the magical arts. It is within this delicate balance that the true essence of magic flourishes, weaving together the old and the new into mesmerizing performances that transcend time. From the graceful sleight of hand to the grand illusions that leave audiences breathless, the teachings found within these manuals nurture the seeds of creativity and ingenuity. They encourage magicians to explore uncharted territories, daring them to push the boundaries of what was once thought impossible. The foundational knowledge gleaned from these texts empowers magicians to breathe life into their acts, infusing each movement with a sense of wonder and enchantment. Moreover, the manuals act as repositories of historical significance, preserving the lineage of magical feats and the indelible mark left by influential figures in the world of illusion. Delving into their pages, one finds narratives of masterful performances and anecdotes that unveil the trials and triumphs of those who paved the way for future generations. In retracing this rich tapestry of magical heritage, magicians gain not only technical prowess but also a profound appreciation for the art form's enduring legacy. As we delve into the foundations for fleeting marvels, we must recognize that these manuals are not mere instructional texts; they are living testaments to the passion and dedication of countless magicians who have poured their hearts and souls into the pursuit of wondrous spectacle. Each turn of the page reveals a treasure trove of knowledge waiting to be unearthed, offering a glimpse into the profound artistry that has enthralled audiences for centuries.

Mentors on the Page: Influential Authors

In the annals of magic, certain authors have carved their names in history as beacons of knowledge and inspiration. Their written works extend beyond mere instructional manuals; they are testament to the artistry, wisdom, and dedication of these influential individuals. The pages they penned are not just repositories of tricks and techniques, but portals into the minds and experiences of master illusionists. One such luminary is Jean Eugène Robert-Houdin, often hailed as the father of modern magic. His seminal book, 'The Secrets of Conjuring and Magic,' stands as a cornerstone of magical literature, offering profound insights into the psychology of deception and performance. Each word penned by Robert-Houdin resonates with timeless wisdom, weaving a narrative that transcends generations and continues to shape the practice of magic today. Equally revered is Harry Houdini, whose impact on the world of magic extends far beyond his groundbreaking illusions and daring feats. Houdini's literary contributions, particularly 'The Unmasking of Robert-Houdin,' provide a captivating glimpse into the rich tapestry of magical history while debunking myths and illuminating the evolution of the art. Through his writings, Houdini imparted a sense of reverence for tradition and an unyielding quest for authenticity—a legacy embraced by contemporary magicians seeking to honor the craft while pushing its boundaries. Further enriching the magical canon is the towering figure of Roberto Giobbi, whose monumental work, 'Card College,' has become the go-to resource for aspiring card magicians worldwide. Giobbi's meticulous attention to detail, coupled with his lucid prose, fosters a deep understanding of the nuances of sleight of hand and the psychology of misdirection. By distilling his decades of expertise onto the page, Giobbi empowers readers to navigate the intricate realm of card magic with confidence and finesse, becoming torchbearers of an enduring tradition. These luminaries and many others have not only chronicled the secrets of their craft but have also instilled a sense of kinship and camaraderie within the magical community. Their writings serve as bridges connecting past, present, and future practitioners, fostering a continuum of learning, growth, and innovation. As aspiring magicians delve into these literary treasures, they embark on a transformative journey guided by the wisdom and mentorship of these revered authors, kindling a flame of passion and excellence that will illuminate the stages of tomorrow.

Continuing the Legacy: Passing Down Knowledge

Passing down knowledge holds a profound significance in the realm of magic, where each generation has a duty to preserve and perpetuate the art form's rich traditions. As prized mentors impart their wisdom upon eager apprentices, they play an integral role in sustaining the magical heritage. Through the diligent guidance of experienced masters, aspiring illusionists are empowered to not only learn the technical aspects of magic, but also to comprehend its deeper essence. The act of passing down knowledge is a sacred duty that connects magicians across time, transcending generations and weaving a tapestry of shared wisdom. From the handoff of intricate techniques to the imparting of invaluable performance insights, this transfer of knowledge ensures that the secrets of the craft remain alive and vibrant. Every gesture, every nuance, and every whispered tip becomes a link in this unbroken chain of magical expertise. In honoring the legacy of influential authors, contemporary magicians find themselves embracing the responsibility to safeguard and add to the treasure trove of magical knowledge. It is through this continuous propagation that timeless wonders are kept vital and relevant. As modern magicians absorb, refine, and expand upon the teachings of their predecessors, they inject newfound vitality into classic illusions, thus ensuring that the spirit of innovation thrives alongside tradition. Furthermore, this succession of wisdom fosters a sense of community within the magical fraternity, fostering connections that transcend eras and geographies. By cherishing and sharing the inheritance of magical knowledge, magicians recognize their place in a lineage of greatness, and in turn, inspire others to carry the torch forward. The collective collaboration between past and present luminaries serves to elevate the art of magic ever higher, ensuring a flourishing evolution that remains rooted in historical reverence. As aspiring magicians pay homage to the founding principles and time-honored techniques, they infuse their performances with a unique blend of veneration and innovation. In this way, the spirit of magic lives on, continually enriched by an unceasing flow of insight, creativity, and dedication. With each apprentice turned mentor, the magic community perpetuates an unbroken tradition, thus cementing enchantment as an enduring legacy to be revered and preserved.

Magic on the World Stage

A New Era for Magic

The transition of magic from local performances to a global phenomenon marks a captivating evolution in the history of this mystical art. As magicians honed their skills and developed new illusions, the allure of their craft transcended geographical boundaries, captivating imaginations across the world. Through the centuries, magic has undergone a remarkable transformation, finding its way into diverse cultures and societies, intertwining with the fabric of humanity. This era of magical globalization mirrors the interconnectedness of our modern world, showcasing how an age-old art form could capture the hearts and minds of people from all walks of life. The magic of a magician no longer remained confined to the streets or stages of their hometowns; instead, it embarked on a journey that would see it embraced by audiences from distant lands. The catalyst for this global expansion can be credited to the advent of mass media and transportation. With the rise of print media, magic secrets could be disseminated far and wide, inspiring budding magicians and enchanting readers with tales of extraordinary feats. As travel became more accessible, renowned magicians ventured beyond their homelands to showcase their talents to audiences in far-flung regions, building bridges through the universal language of wonder and illusion. Their performances sparked a newfound fascination for magic, igniting a passion for the mysterious and the inexplicable in every corner of the globe. Moreover, the era of magic's global reach also saw a beautiful exchange of cultural influences. As magicians shared their artistry with diverse communities, they absorbed the rich tapestry of traditions and beliefs they encountered, infusing their performances with a depth and resonance that resonated with audiences around the world. Techniques, props, and storytelling methods from different cultures began to intermingle, giving rise to a fusion of magical styles that celebrated the beauty of diversity. In turn, this cross-pollination of ideas enriched the magical landscape, bringing forth a renaissance that celebrated the uniqueness of each culture while fostering a sense of unity through the shared love for enchantment and mystery. The new era for magic not only witnessed its spread but also illuminated the universal threads that bind humanity. This unifying power of magic transcended language barriers and surpassed political divides, allowing people to embrace the astonishing and embrace the impossible as one global community. As we delve further into the global impact of magic, we find ourselves immersed in a world where wonder knows no borders—a world where the ancient art of magic continues to weave its spellbinding narrative across the tapestry of human experience.

Spreading Beyond Borders

Magic, in its essence, transcends cultural boundaries and geographical divides, weaving a tapestry that unites people from all corners of the globe. As the art of magic evolves, it continues to captivate the hearts and minds of individuals beyond borders, becoming a cherished form of entertainment that knows no limits. The profound allure of magic has propelled it to spread across the world, enchanting audiences with its enigmatic charm and universal appeal. From the bustling streets of metropolitan cities to the serene landscapes of remote villages, magic's enchanting presence knows no bounds, leaving an indelible mark on diverse communities. The global dissemination of magic has not only brought joy and wonder to spectators but has also fostered a deeper understanding and appreciation of various cultural traditions. As magicians showcase their craft in foreign lands, they often infuse their performances with elements unique to each region, seamlessly integrating local customs and folklore into their acts. This amalgamation of cultural influences enhances the richness of magical performances, creating an immersive experience that resonates with audiences on a profoundly emotional level. It is through this harmonious interplay of diverse influences that magic becomes a conduit for cultural exchange and mutual understanding, transcending linguistic barriers to evoke shared moments of awe and inspiration. Moreover, the proliferation of digital platforms and social media has played an instrumental role in propelling magic across international boundaries. Magicians now have the ability to showcase their mesmerizing feats to a global audience at the click of a button, instantly connecting with individuals from varying backgrounds, beliefs, and customs. Through these digital channels, magic transcends physical limitations, fostering a sense of unity and camaraderie among viewers who are captivated by the artistry and creativity of these performances. The accessibility of magic through digital mediums has further contributed to its widespread appeal, igniting a collective fascination that transcends geographical distances and cultural disparities. In essence, as magic continues to traverse the world, it stands as a testament to the enduring power of human imagination and the universal language of wonder. Its ability to transcend borders and unify individuals from diverse cultures reaffirms its status as a timeless art form that harmonizes the tapestry of humanity. With each spellbinding performance, magic reinforces the interconnectedness of our global community, offering a testament to the enduring spirit of enchantment that binds us all together.

Captivating Global Audiences

Magic has an incredible power to captivate and enthrall audiences around the world. As magical performances began to spread beyond borders, they found a universal appeal that transcended cultural differences. Magicians like Alexander Herrmann charmed audiences in distant lands, leaving everyone spellbound with their astonishing feats of illusion. The allure of magic knows no boundaries and transcends language and traditional barriers. Whether it's a grand stage production in Paris or an intimate performance in Tokyo, the wonders of magic have always been able to mesmerize audiences from all walks of life. The artistry and skill of magicians have brought people together, fostering a sense of unity and wonder across diverse societies. Magic, in its purest form, is a celebration of creativity, imagination, and the unexplainable, resonating deeply with individuals regardless of their background or beliefs. It's a testament to the universal human fascination with the extraordinary and the inexplicable. Traveling magicians and illusionists became cultural ambassadors, sharing not only their craft but also the spirit of wonder and awe with every new audience they encountered. Through their performances, they opened doors to understanding and appreciation, bringing people closer through shared experiences of sheer wonder and delight. In turn, audiences embraced these magical moments as cherished memories, carrying the enchantment of the performances with them long after the final curtain fell. The global reach of magic also enriched local cultures, influencing art, literature, and popular entertainment across continents. As magic reached new corners of the world, it ignited imaginations, inspired creativity, and sparked renewed interest in the age-old fascination with the impossible. From the bustling streets of New York to the serene villages of India, the impact of magic on global audiences has been profound, uniting people in joy and astonishment. Every clap and gasp of amazement echoed a shared appreciation for the extraordinary, forging connections that transcended geographical distances. The ability of magic to resonate with diverse audiences worldwide is a testament to its enduring power and universal appeal.

Cultural Exchange of Mysteries

Magic, with its universal appeal, has served as a powerful tool for cultural exchange and mutual understanding among diverse societies. Throughout history, the practice of magic has transcended language barriers and geographical boundaries, uniting people in wonder and amazement. As magicians have traveled the world, their performances have become bridges that connect different cultures, sparking curiosity and fascination. These encounters have facilitated the exchange of not only magical techniques but also cultural traditions, beliefs, and values. The fusion of these elements has enriched the art of magic and contributed to a deeper appreciation of global diversity. One of the most remarkable aspects of magical performances as a means of cultural exchange is that they often incorporate local customs and folklore into the acts. Magicians, recognizing the importance of respecting and embracing the traditions of the places they visit, infuse their illusions with elements specific to each culture, creating a unique blend of mystery and familiarity. This approach allows audiences to experience magic in a context that resonates with their own cultural background, fostering a sense of connection and shared humanity. Moreover, the cultural exchange facilitated by magic extends beyond the stage, as magicians engage with local communities, learn about their customs, and share their own experiences. This interaction cultivates mutual respect and empathy, breaking down barriers and promoting harmony between different cultures. Whether performing at grand theaters or intimate gatherings, magicians have the opportunity to leave a lasting impression that goes beyond the spectacle of their illusions. In turn, this cultural exchange has influenced the evolution of magic itself, inspiring magicians to innovate and adapt their performances to embrace the rich tapestry of global traditions. It has led to the creation of acts that not only entertain but also educate, providing audiences with insights into the beauty and diversity of the world. Through the exchange of mysteries, magic becomes a medium for celebrating the cultural heritage of nations while igniting curiosity and appreciation for the unfamiliar. Ultimately, the cultural exchange of mysteries through magic serves as a testament to the unifying power of the art form. It transcends political and social differences, fostering an environment where individuals can come together to celebrate the wonders of the world. As we continue to witness the magic of cultural exchange, we are reminded of the profound impact that this art form has on shaping our interconnected global community.

The Role of Technology in Magic's Spread

Magic has always been intricately linked with the art of illusion and wonder, captivating audiences across generations. However, its evolution in the modern era is significantly influenced by advancements in technology. The integration of technology has revolutionized the way magic is perceived and experienced, allowing magicians to reach a wider global audience and push the boundaries of what was once thought impossible. One of the most noticeable impacts of technology on magic is the use of digital media platforms for performances and exposure. Magicians are now able to showcase their acts to millions of viewers through online streaming services, social media, and video-sharing platforms. This instant accessibility has not only expanded the reach of magic but has also transformed the art form into a more inclusive and interactive experience, breaking geographical barriers and uniting diverse audiences in awe and amazement. In addition to the dissemination of performances, technology has enabled magicians to incorporate cutting-edge equipment and special effects into their acts. From augmented reality to holographic displays, the use of advanced technologies has elevated the visual spectacle of magic, offering audiences an immersive and unforgettable encounter with the impossible. Furthermore, the development of digital illusions and innovative props has brought a new dimension to traditional magic tricks, blurring the line between reality and fantasy. Moreover, the influence of technology extends to the realm of magic education and training. Online tutorials, virtual workshops, and interactive learning platforms have provided aspiring magicians with unprecedented access to knowledge and mentorship from seasoned professionals worldwide. As a result, the art of magic continues to evolve and flourish, as fresh talents emerge and contribute to the rich tapestry of magical performance and innovation. Despite these remarkable advancements, the integration of technology in magic has also posed challenges. With the proliferation of digital editing tools and visual effects software, maintaining the authenticity and integrity of live performances has become a critical concern. The need to strike a balance between technological enhancements and preserving the essence of live magic has become an ongoing discourse within the magician community. As magic continues to embrace technology, it is essential for practitioners to uphold the core principles of the craft – to inspire wonder, ignite imagination, and uphold the tradition of secrecy and mystery. By leveraging technology responsibly, magicians can continue to enchant global audiences while preserving the timeless allure and enigma that define the art of magic.

Challenges on the Global Stage

Performing magic on a global stage presents an array of unique challenges that magicians must navigate with agility and sensitivity. The diversity of cultures, beliefs, and traditions across different regions demands an acute understanding of local sensibilities to ensure that performances are respectful and well-received. Magicians face the task of transcending language barriers to effectively communicate their artistry in a way that resonates with audiences from various backgrounds. This requires meticulous attention to non-verbal cues, universal symbols, and emotive expressions, allowing magic to transcend linguistic constraints and connect on a profound, emotional level. Moreover, the logistics of international travel and performances present their own set of obstacles. From navigating complex visa requirements to adapting to unfamiliar performance spaces, magicians must exhibit adaptability and resourcefulness to ensure that their shows run seamlessly. Cultural nuances also play a significant role in the presentation of magic. What may be perceived as awe-inspiring in one culture could be met with skepticism or even offense in another. Respectfully integrating and celebrating diverse cultural elements while retaining the integrity of the performance is a delicate balancing act that demands meticulous research, collaboration with local experts, and a deep appreciation for the subtleties of each region's heritage. Additionally, the ethical dimensions of performing on a global scale cannot be overlooked. Magicians must adhere to stringent ethical standards while working across different countries and respecting the boundaries of cultural propriety. Sensitivity and mindfulness are paramount when crafting performances that honor the rich tapestry of global cultures without imposing Western ideals or overshadowing local traditions. Furthermore, the global stage brings increased scrutiny and accountability. Magicians are under pressure to uphold the highest standards of practice while navigating legal and regulatory frameworks that may differ significantly from those in their home countries. This demands a thorough understanding of international laws and ethical guidelines, ensuring that performances adhere to the legal and moral expectations of each country visited. Despite these challenges, the global stage offers unparalleled opportunities for cultural exchange, collaboration, and the unifying power of magic as a universal language. By embracing these complexities with humility, respect, and an unwavering commitment to cultural appreciation, magicians can create transformative, inclusive experiences that transcend boundaries and celebrate the wonder of our shared humanity.

Connecting with Diverse Cultures

Magic has a unique ability to transcend cultural boundaries and connect with diverse audiences around the world. As magicians like Alexander Herrmann took their acts to international stages, they encountered a rich tapestry of customs, beliefs, and traditions. One of the most fascinating aspects of this global journey was the opportunity to engage with diverse cultures and forge meaningful connections through the universal language of wonder and illusion. In each new location, Herrmann and his contemporaries sought to understand and appreciate the local customs, incorporating elements of these traditions into their performances as a gesture of respect and unity. This cultural sensitivity not only enhanced the impact of their shows but also fostered an atmosphere of mutual understanding and appreciation. The magic became a bridge between different ways of life, serving as a catalyst for shared experiences and moments of awe. It allowed audiences to not only witness extraordinary feats but also to feel a sense of kinship with the performers and the broader global community of magic enthusiasts. Beyond the stage, interactions with local communities provided magicians with profound insights into the human experience across varied societies. Through meaningful exchanges and collaborations, magicians were able to showcase the universality of magic while honoring the unique characteristics of each culture. In doing so, they celebrated diversity and promoted cross-cultural dialogue, reinforcing the idea that wonder knows no borders. As a result, the art of magic became a powerful tool for fostering empathy, breaking down stereotypes, and igniting curiosity about the world's rich tapestry of traditions. This genuine appreciation for diverse cultures became an integral part of the magical experience, enriching both the performers and the audiences. Ultimately, the global reach of magic not only entertained but also enlightened, leaving a lasting impression on all who were touched by its enchanting allure.

Impact on Local Traditions

Magic has not only captivated global audiences, but it has also made a profound impact on local traditions around the world. As magicians traveled to new lands, they encountered diverse cultural practices and beliefs. The interaction between magic and these local traditions created a fascinating blend of artistry and heritage. In some cases, magic performances incorporated elements specific to the culture in which they were presented, fostering a sense of unity and shared experience. This exchange of magical techniques and cultural influences enriched the art form and contributed to a deeper understanding among different communities. Furthermore, the presence of magic in various cultural settings served as a bridge, connecting people through wonder and entertainment. Magicians respected and honored local customs, often incorporating them into their acts with great reverence. This approach not only showcased the beauty of different traditions but also fostered mutual respect and appreciation. As a result, magic became a universal language that transcended borders and language barriers, binding people together through shared moments of astonishment and joy. On the other hand, the introduction of magic to local traditions sparked conversations about the role of innovation in preserving cultural heritage. While some welcomed the fusion of magic with traditional practices as a way to keep them relevant and engaging for newer generations, others raised concerns about potential dilution of authenticity. This dialogue highlighted the delicate balance between preserving traditions and embracing progress. Moreover, it encouraged open discussions on the evolution of cultural expressions and how they can adapt to a changing world while maintaining their essence. Despite these challenges, the overall impact of magic on local traditions has been remarkable. As magicians showcased their art in various cultural settings, they not only entertained but also left an indelible mark on the fabric of local communities. Through respectful engagement and collaboration, magic became an integral part of many traditions, evolving alongside them and creating enduring connections between the past and the present. This harmonious integration of magic into local customs has not only preserved cultural practices but also breathed new life into them, ensuring that they continue to be cherished and celebrated. It is a testament to the power of magic to transcend boundaries and unite people in appreciation of the rich tapestry of human creativity and expression.

Stories of Unforgettable Performances

Throughout his illustrious career, Alexander Herrmann regaled audiences around the world with unforgettable performances that left a lasting impression on all who witnessed his magical artistry. One such performance took place in the grand theaters of Paris, where Herrmann mesmerized the audience with his remarkable illusions and charming stage presence. As the curtains rose, he transported the crowd into a world of wonder, weaving together mystifying acts of levitation, mind-reading, and daring escapes that defied rational explanation. The energy in the theater crackled with excitement as gasps and applause echoed through the hall, testament to the profound impact of Herrmann's craft. His skillful manipulation of cards and coins as they danced between his nimble fingers left spectators in awe, while his ability to materialize objects out of thin air left them questioning the very fabric of reality. In another instance, at a prestigious venue in London, Herrmann captivated an audience representing a myriad of cultural backgrounds, effortlessly breaking down language barriers with his universal language of magic. His undeniable charisma and showmanship transcended borders and united people in a shared sense of wonder and enchantment, showcasing the unifying power of magic on a global scale. Beyond Europe, Herrmann ventured across the vast expanse of the United States, leaving an indelible mark on cities from New York to San Francisco. His performances in venues such as Broadway theaters and opulent ballrooms captured the hearts and imaginations of Americans from all walks of life, solidifying his reputation as a master showman with an unparalleled ability to evoke emotions and stir the imagination. Whether performing for aristocrats or common folk, Alexander Herrmann's magic spoke to the universal human desire for mystery and marvel, resonating deeply with each person in the audience. These stories of unforgettable performances stand as testaments to the enduring legacy of a man whose artistry transcended cultural boundaries, bringing joy and wonder to all corners of the globe. Each chapter added to the rich tapestry of his magical journey, leaving an indelible imprint on the history of magic and inspiring future generations to continue pushing the boundaries of the impossible.

Reflections on Magic's Global Influence

Magic's global influence has been nothing short of remarkable, transcending cultural boundaries and captivating audiences all around the world. Reflecting on this widespread impact, it becomes evident that magic has served as a universal language, uniting people from various backgrounds through the shared awe and wonder it inspires. The ability of magic to transcend language barriers and connect with individuals on an emotional level is truly unparalleled. As magicians have taken their craft to different corners of the globe, they have not merely entertained, but also acted as cultural ambassadors, bridging gaps between diverse societies. Through their performances, magicians have facilitated an exchange of ideas and experiences, fostering greater understanding and appreciation for different traditions and beliefs. This cultural exchange has enriched the art of magic, infusing it with a tapestry of influences and expanding its repertoire of illusions and storytelling. The global stage has provided a platform for magic to evolve and adapt, incorporating elements from various cultures into its performances. This fusion of diverse influences has contributed to the richness and diversity of magical techniques and styles seen today. From the mysticism of the East to the grandeur of Western theater, magic has absorbed a multitude of influences, resulting in a truly global tapestry of wonder and intrigue. While celebrating the universal appeal of magic, it is important to recognize the challenges that arise when performing across different cultural contexts. Sensitivity to local customs and traditions is crucial, and magicians must navigate these nuances with respect and understanding. By approaching each performance with cultural sensitivity, magicians can ensure that their art continues to inspire and delight audiences without causing offense or misunderstanding. Moreover, the global influence of magic has extended beyond the realm of entertainment, leaving an indelible mark on popular culture and shaping perceptions of wonder and possibility. Magic has fueled imagination and curiosity on a worldwide scale, encouraging individuals to embrace the unknown and marvel at the inexplicable. Its influence can be observed in literature, cinema, and even scientific innovation, where the spirit of magic has inspired breakthroughs and imaginative thinking. In exploring the reflections on magic's global influence, it is clear that the art form has transcended geographical boundaries to become a unifying force that ignites fascination and sparks joy across the world. As we continue to appreciate the beauty of magic's global journey, let us cherish the profound connections it has fostered and the enduring sense of wonder it continues to evoke in the hearts of all who experience it.

International Fame

The Path to Global Recognition

Alexander Herrmann's journey to international fame was not a quick or easy one. It was a culmination of dedication, talent, and an unyielding passion for magic that propelled him onto the global stage. His quest for recognition beyond his homeland of Germany began with a burning desire to share his craft with audiences around the world. Embracing the challenge of breaking through cultural and linguistic barriers, Herrmann tirelessly honed his magical skills to captivate and astonish audiences across different continents. As he embarked on his early international ventures, Herrmann was met with skepticism and uncertainty. However, his unwavering determination coupled with his charismatic stage presence gradually won over even the most discerning audiences. Through meticulous planning and an acute understanding of the nuances of performance in varied settings, Herrmann tailored his acts to resonate with international spectators. His ability to weave a universal appeal into his illusions bridged diverse cultures and languages, forging an unspoken connection with each and every observer. Herrmann's journey to global recognition was marked by a relentless quest for perfection and an unwavering commitment to his art. As he navigated through unfamiliar territories and encountered multifaceted challenges, he remained steadfast in his pursuit of excellence. Each performance served as a stepping stone, paving the way for him to leave an indelible mark on the global magic community. This remarkable trajectory sowed the seeds for a legacy that continues to inspire magicians and enthusiasts worldwide. The path to global recognition for Alexander Herrmann was not just a personal odyssey; it was a testament to the transcendent power of magic to bridge divides and unite people from all walks of life in shared wonder and delight.

Breaking Boundaries

Alexander Herrmann's journey to international fame was not without its challenges, but his relentless pursuit of excellence and his unwavering passion for magic propelled him to break through cultural and geographical boundaries. As he ventured beyond his native land, Herrmann faced the daunting task of introducing his art to unfamiliar audiences with diverse customs and traditions. His commitment to his craft enabled him to connect with people from all walks of life, transcending language barriers and uniting them through the universal language of astonishment and wonder. Breaking boundaries became more than just a professional ambition; it became a personal mission for Herrmann. His dedication to understanding and respecting the cultures he encountered endeared him to countless individuals, fostering a deep sense of mutual appreciation and respect. Through his performances, Herrmann not only showcased his extraordinary magical prowess but also bridged gaps between nations, fostering a spirit of unity and harmony. The impact of his efforts was profound, as he shattered stereotypes and misconceptions, paving the way for greater cultural exchange and understanding. Embracing the unfamiliar with humility and reverence, Herrmann demonstrated the transformative power of art to create meaningful connections that transcended borders. His ability to inspire awe and captivate hearts transcended geographical confines, leaving an indelible mark on every corner of the globe he touched. Breaking boundaries was not merely about conquering new territories; it was about building bridges built on mutual respect, curiosity, and empathy. The legacy of Alexander Herrmann's remarkable journey serves as a testament to the enduring power of the human spirit and the unifying force of magic.

First International Tour

Alexander Herrmann embarked on his first international tour with a blend of excitement and trepidation. As he ventured beyond familiar shores, the prospect of showcasing his art to diverse audiences filled him with both anticipation and uncertainty. The allure of performing on international stages was undeniable, but it also presented a new set of challenges. The logistical complexities of organizing performances in foreign lands, navigating cultural nuances, and captivating spectators from unfamiliar territories weighed heavily on his mind. Despite these concerns, Herrmann's determination to share his passion for magic with the world propelled him forward. The itinerary of his international tour was meticulously planned, with stops in major cities across Europe and beyond. From London to Paris, Berlin to St. Petersburg, Herrmann's enthralling performances left audiences spellbound at every venue. His mastery of illusion and sleight of hand transcended language barriers, captivating onlookers from diverse backgrounds. Each show became a testament to the universal appeal of magic, uniting people in awe and wonder regardless of their origins. Amidst the challenges of touring in unfamiliar lands, Herrmann found himself embracing the opportunity to immerse himself in new cultures. Engaging with local communities, sampling exotic cuisines, and exploring historic landmarks enriched his perspective and infused his performances with an authentic sense of connection. Through these interactions, Herrmann discovered that magic served as a unifying force, bridging gaps and fostering shared moments of astonishment and joy. The success of his international tour not only bolstered Herrmann's reputation as a preeminent magician but also laid the foundation for enduring global acclaim. Audiences across continents were captivated by his artistry, and the resounding praise that followed echoed far and wide. His first foray into international territories marked the beginning of a remarkable journey towards becoming a revered figure in the realm of magic on a global scale, solidifying his position as a trailblazer who deftly traversed borders and kindled a profound appreciation for the enchanting world of magic.

The Audience's Reception

From the opulent theaters of Paris to the bustling streets of London, Alexander Herrmann's international tours captivated audiences from all walks of life. The reception he received was nothing short of remarkable, an affirmation of his unparalleled talent and charisma. As he stepped onto the world stage, audiences marveled at his spellbinding performances, welcoming him with open arms and enthusiastic applause. Their fervent admiration fueled his passion for magic, propelling him to new heights of global stardom. The response to Herrmann's shows varied across different countries, each audience bringing its own unique energy and appreciation for his artistry. In Europe, where Herrmann initially gained traction, the crowds were awe-inspired by his mastery of illusion and impeccable showmanship. His performances in the majestic theaters of Vienna and Berlin left spectators spellbound, stirring whispers of his extraordinary talents throughout the continent. Venturing further into the heart of Asia, Herrmann encountered diverse cultures and traditions that enriched his magical journey. With reverence and humility, he embraced the customs of each locale, seeking to connect with audiences on a deeper level. In Japan, renowned for its rich heritage, Herrmann's displays of wonder were met with profound reverence and silent awe, contrasting with the raucous applause heard in the grand amphitheaters of Europe. The attentive and respectful nature of the Japanese audiences left an indelible mark on Herrmann, shaping his understanding of the universal appeal of magic. Across the Atlantic, in the bustling cities of America, Herrmann found an entirely different kind of reception. The exuberant, boisterous crowds greeted him with unrestrained enthusiasm, showcasing their appreciation with thundering ovations and fervent cheers. From the theaters of New York to the frontier towns of the Wild West, audiences clamored for more, embracing Herrmann as a larger-than-life figure whose artistry transcended geographical boundaries. The genuine warmth and genuine curiosity of the audience spurred Herrmann to continuously refine his craft, striving to deliver performances that resonated on a profound emotional level. It was this reciprocal exchange of admiration and inspiration that fueled his enduring commitment to enchant audiences around the globe. The resounding acclaim and heartfelt connection he established with people from every corner of the world left an enduring legacy, solidifying his status as an iconic figure in the realm of magic.

Adapting to Diverse Cultures

Adapting to diverse cultures is an essential aspect of achieving international fame as a magician. Each region has its unique customs, traditions, and sensitivities, and understanding and respecting these cultural nuances is crucial in establishing a meaningful connection with audiences around the world. When Alexander Herrmann embarked on his international tours, he recognized the significance of embracing diverse cultures, not only as a mark of respect but also as a means to enhance the impact of his performances. One of the pivotal elements in adapting to diverse cultures is language. Herrmann understood the value of effective communication. He took the initiative to become conversant in the languages prevalent in the countries he visited, allowing him to establish a deeper connection with his audience. Moreover, he made efforts to incorporate local phrases, greetings, and cultural references into his acts, demonstrating his genuine interest in and appreciation for the diverse communities he encountered. Adapting to diverse cultures also entails adjusting one's performance style to align with the preferences and sensitivities of each audience. Herrmann meticulously studied the superstitions, taboos, and beliefs of the regions he toured, ensuring that his illusions and acts were culturally sensitive and would resonate positively with spectators. This flexibility and openness to cultural adaptation allowed Herrmann to showcase his versatility as an entertainer while fostering a profound sense of inclusivity and connectedness with audiences worldwide. Embracing diverse cultures was not without its challenges for Herrmann. It required him to navigate unfamiliar territories, both geographically and culturally, often leading to moments of uncertainty or misinterpretation. However, through humility, empathy, and a genuine eagerness to learn, Herrmann triumphed over these obstacles, earning the admiration and respect of people from various backgrounds. His ability to seamlessly integrate his art with the rich tapestry of global cultures not only endeared him to audiences but also solidified his status as a truly international magician. The legacy of Alexander Herrmann's respectful and empathetic approach to cultural adaptation serves as an enduring testament to the universal language of magic, transcending borders and uniting people from all walks of life.

Challenges of Touring Abroad

Touring abroad presents a multitude of challenges for any performer, and the world of magic is no exception. The logistical aspects alone can be overwhelming: navigating foreign languages, customs, and regulations while transporting elaborate props and equipment requires meticulous planning and adaptability. Each new country brings with it a unique set of logistical hurdles, from sourcing the right materials for illusions to dealing with the technical requirements of diverse performance venues. Beyond the practical considerations, there are also cultural barriers to overcome. Magicians must carefully navigate the nuances of different traditions, beliefs, and sensitivities in order to connect with audiences without causing offense. What may be perceived as an innocuous gesture in one culture could carry unintended implications in another. Furthermore, the very nature of magic—relying on misdirection and illusion—can sometimes face skepticism or misunderstanding in certain cultural contexts. As a result, magicians must find innovative ways to bridge these cultural gaps and ensure their performances are both respectful and captivating. Moreover, the mental and emotional toll of constant travel and adaptation cannot be underestimated. Long periods away from home, coupled with the pressures of delivering high-stakes performances in unfamiliar environments, can take a significant toll on even the most seasoned performers. Maintaining peak physical and mental condition while constantly adjusting to new time zones and climates is a formidable challenge that demands unwavering dedication and resilience. Despite these challenges, the rewards of touring abroad are immeasurable. Each obstacle overcome represents a new level of growth and understanding, both artistically and personally. Through perseverance and an open heart, magicians can forge connections with people from diverse backgrounds, enrich their own craft through exposure to new ideas, and leave a lasting impact on global audiences. This chapter seeks to offer insight into the trials and triumphs of taking magic beyond familiar shores, illuminating the extraordinary efforts and sacrifices behind the glittering facade of international performances.

Collaborations with International Magicians

Alexander Herrmann's influence transcended borders, and as he embarked on his international tours, he had the opportunity to collaborate with a myriad of talented magicians from different corners of the world. These collaborations were more than just joint performances; they were exchanges of knowledge, creativity, and theatrical techniques that enriched the global magical community. Herrmann viewed these partnerships as opportunities to learn from diverse magical traditions and share his own expertise. Through these collaborations, he not only showcased his versatility but also fostered a spirit of camaraderie and collective growth within the international magic fraternity. In each country he visited, Herrmann sought out local magicians, welcomed their unique insights, and eagerly participated in the exchange of magical methods and tricks. These interactions not only broadened his repertoire but also left an indelible mark on the magicians he encountered. He believed in the transformative power of mutual collaboration and always approached these partnerships with humility and respect for the local magical customs. The cross-cultural pollination of magical ideas and techniques led to groundbreaking performances that mesmerized audiences worldwide. By blending his skills with those of his international counterparts, Herrmann created awe-inspiring spectacles that transcended language barriers and cultural differences. The synergy born from these collaborations set new standards in the art of magic, inspiring countless magicians to push the boundaries of their craft. Moreover, these collaborations played a pivotal role in fostering goodwill and understanding among different magical communities. Herrmann's respect for the traditions of his collaborators endeared him to magicians across the globe, and his willingness to share his knowledge earned him admiration and respect. This mutual exchange of artistic expression facilitated a sense of unity and shared purpose, strengthening the bonds between magicians from diverse backgrounds. The lasting impact of Herrmann's collaborations with international magicians is evident in the continued evolution of magical performances. His legacy lives on in the interwoven tapestry of global magical influences, a testament to the enduring power of collaboration and the universal language of magic.

Influence on Global Magic Communities

Alexander Herrmann's influence on global magic communities reverberates through time as a testament to his unparalleled artistry and dedication. As he ventured across continents, his performances and collaborations left an indelible mark on magicians and enthusiasts worldwide. One of Herrmann's enduring legacies is his commitment to sharing his knowledge and expertise with aspiring magicians from diverse cultural backgrounds. His willingness to engage with local magic communities during his tours fostered a spirit of camaraderie and exchange, transcending language barriers and uniting individuals through their shared passion for magic. Herrmann's genuine respect for the myriad magical traditions he encountered enriched the collective tapestry of global magic, contributing to a melting pot of ideas and innovations that continue to resonate today. His legacy lives on in the countless magicians who draw inspiration from his cross-cultural interactions and embrace a spirit of inclusivity and collaboration in their own artistic pursuits.

Memorable Performances Around the World

Alexander Herrmann's global tours showcased a mastery of illusion that transcended cultural boundaries and enchanted audiences worldwide. From the grand stages of Europe to the bustling theaters of Asia, Herrmann's performances left an indelible mark on the hearts and minds of countless spectators. Each show was meticulously crafted to resonate with the unique sensibilities of diverse societies, demonstrating Herrmann's deep respect for the art of magic and his appreciation for the varied cultures he encountered. In Paris, Herrmann mesmerized audiences with his elegant sleight of hand, effortlessly weaving a tapestry of illusions that captivated the city known for its love of artistry and sophistication. His performances in London drew acclaim for their innovation and creativity, earning him a place among the revered magicians of the Victorian era. Venturing eastward, Herrmann dazzled crowds in Shanghai, where his fusion of traditional and modern magic techniques resonated with the audience's rich heritage of mysticism and folklore. His tour of Tokyo saw him seamlessly blending the allure of Japanese storytelling with the wonder of stage magic, leaving an enduring impression on the cultural landscape of Japan. The American leg of Herrmann's world tour brought him to the bustling streets of New York, where his shows at renowned theaters astounded audiences and drew praise from critics and patrons alike. His performances in Chicago captivated audiences with their artful precision, while his appearances in San Francisco showcased his ability to infuse magic with the spirit of innovation synonymous with the city. In each locale, Herrmann's magical prowess not only entertained but also fostered a sense of unity and wonder, transcending language barriers to create shared moments of astonishment and joy. His ability to connect with audiences on a profound level, regardless of cultural background, stands as a testament to his enduring impact on the global stage. These memorable performances continue to inspire magicians and enthusiasts around the world, ensuring that Alexander Herrmann's legacy will endure for generations to come.

Legacy of International Success

Alexander Herrmann's international success left an indelible mark on the world of magic, shaping and transforming it in ways that continue to reverberate today. His ability to captivate audiences across diverse cultures and languages not only propelled him to stardom but also cemented his enduring legacy. The impact of his global influence can be seen in the countless magicians who were inspired by his performances, techniques, and showmanship. Beyond the entertainment realm, Herrmann's international triumphs helped bridge cultural divides and fostered a deeper appreciation for the art of magic. Through his unparalleled talent and unwavering dedication to his craft, he demonstrated the universal appeal of magic, transcending borders and uniting people from all walks of life. It is through his tireless efforts that magic gained a foothold in communities worldwide, enriching lives and sparking a shared sense of wonder and enchantment. Moreover, Herrmann's overseas ventures served as a catalyst for the globalization of magic, paving the way for future generations of magicians to expand their horizons and reach new audiences beyond their homelands. His contributions to the international magic community continue to inspire innovation and creativity, fostering cross-cultural exchange and mutual respect among magicians from various corners of the globe. The ripple effects of Herrmann's international success extend far beyond his own lifetime, influencing generations of magicians who have followed in his footsteps. His courage in venturing beyond familiar territories set a precedent for magicians to explore uncharted territories, share their talents on a global stage, and leave an everlasting imprint on the world of magic.

In essence, Alexander Herrmann's legacy of international success serves as a testament to the transformative power of magic, transcending linguistic and cultural barriers to unite humanity in awe and disbelief. His global impact endures as a shining beacon, illuminating the path for aspiring magicians to embrace the richness of diversity, celebrate the universality of wonder, and perpetuate the timeless allure of magic for generations to come.

Signature Illusions

A Vision of Impossibility

Crafting the Fantasy As we delve into the world of Alexander Herrmann's signature illusions, it becomes evident that his creations were not merely about baffling the audience with tricks, but rather about crafting a narrative of wonder and impossibility. Herrmann was driven by a profound desire to transport his spectators to a realm where anything seemed achievable. His relentless pursuit of perfection in his illusions stemmed from his deep-seated belief in the transformative power of magic. Motivated by a yearning to inspire awe and disbelief, Herrmann meticulously designed each illusion to create a sense of otherworldliness. He understood that magic was not just a series of tricks; it was a medium through which he could ignite the imagination and spark a sense of childlike wonder in his viewers. By envisioning the impossible and making it tangible on stage, Herrmann sought to instill a sense of magic and enchantment in the hearts of all who witnessed his performances. Every intricate detail of Herrmann's illusions was meticulously considered, from the selection of props to the orchestration of lighting and music. His dedication to his craft emanated from an earnest desire to unite artistry with astonishment. His illusions were not mere acts to deceive, but rather marvels designed to elicit emotions and provoke contemplation. With this approach, Herrmann elevated his performances beyond mere entertainment, transforming them into profound experiences that lingered in the minds of his audience long after the curtains had closed. Herrmann's commitment to crafting the fantasy extended beyond the technical aspects of his illusions. He recognized the importance of storytelling in magic, leveraging the power of narrative to weave an immersive experience for his spectators. Each illusion possessed a narrative arc, drawing the audience into a world where reality intertwined with the extraordinary. Through this masterful storytelling, Herrmann kindled a sense of curiosity and captivation, granting his audience permission to believe in the unbelievable and embrace the enchantment before them. In essence, 'A Vision of Impossibility' unravels the profound motivations driving Alexander Herrmann's creation of mesmerizing magic shows. It transcends the realm of trickery, aiming to unveil the heart and soul of his tireless dedication to crafting illusions that went beyond mere spectacle, aiming to etch a lasting impression on the souls of those fortunate enough to witness his enchanting performances.

Crafting the Fantasy

Crafting an illusion, for Alexander Herrmann, is a profound and deeply personal process. Each intricate detail is a piece of his soul woven into the fabric of magic, designed to evoke wonder and disbelief in his audience. From the initial conception to the final performance, every step is meticulously planned and executed with unwavering dedication. The genesis of a signature illusion lies in Herrmann's relentless pursuit of perfection. He draws inspiration from the world around him, finding magic in the ordinary and transforming it into the extraordinary. Whether it's the graceful flight of a bird or the delicate petals of a flower, Herrmann infuses his illusions with the beauty of everyday marvels. The crafting of each fantasy is a harmonious symphony of innovation and tradition. Herrmann reveres the timeless art of magic while fearlessly innovating and pioneering new techniques. His devotion to mastering classic sleight of hand is complemented by his bold exploration of cutting-edge illusions, resulting in a repertoire that spans the spectrum of magical feats. Every element of an illusion is carefully considered—the play of light, the sound of silence, the movement of shadows. Herrmann orchestrates these elements with an artist's precision, creating a sensory experience that transcends reality. The atmosphere he cultivates is as integral to the illusion as the illusion itself, immersing the audience in a world where the boundaries of possibility dissolve. Yet amidst the grandeur of spectacle, the heart of Herrmann's magic lies in the emotional connection he forges with his viewers. Each illusion is a narrative, a story told through enigmatic illusions that speak to the human spirit. Through his craft, Herrmann seeks to ignite that childlike sense of wonder within every spectator, inviting them to believe in the impossible with unwavering sincerity. The craftsmanship of a fantasy is not confined to the stage; rather, it extends to every interaction, every expression, and every moment that Herrmann shares with his audience. It is an intricate dance of trust and anticipation, a communion between performer and observer. Fulfilling his lifelong quest to transport audiences beyond the realm of logic and reason, Herrmann's illusions are a testament to the transformative power of magic. Ultimately, the art of crafting a fantasy is an homage to the human capacity for imagination and belief. Through his unparalleled dedication and artistry, Alexander Herrmann gifts the world with timeless wonders, etching his name into the annals of magical history.

Behind the Illusions

Crafting the fantastical illusions that captivated audiences around the world was just the beginning for Alexander Herrmann. Behind the curtains of his stage, a world of intricate planning and innovation unfolded, as he meticulously brought his visions to life. Each illusion was born from a mix of creativity, engineering, and an unwavering commitment to perfection, as Herrmann poured his heart and soul into every aspect of its creation. From the smallest details to the grandest designs, nothing was overlooked in the quest for enchantment. Herrmann's dedication to his craft extended beyond the mere mechanics of the illusions. He sought to evoke a sense of wonder and awe in his audience, striving to create an experience that transcended the boundaries of reality. Every concept held a deeper significance, reflecting his profound understanding of human emotion and the human desire for escapism. This passionate pursuit of emotional connection elevated his illusions from mere tricks to transformative experiences, leaving a lasting impression on all who beheld them. The process of bringing an illusion to the stage involved a symphony of collaboration. Herrmann worked closely with a devoted team of artisans, engineers, and creative minds to orchestrate every element of the performance. Countless hours were spent refining the minutiae of each illusion, ensuring that every movement, sound, and visual spectacle converged seamlessly to transport the audience into a realm of astonishment. The care and precision applied to the production of these illusions were a testament to Herrmann's unwavering commitment to excellence. Beyond the technical aspects, Herrmann understood the power of storytelling in weaving the fabric of his illusions. Each performance was more than a display of skill; it was a narrative carefully constructed to draw spectators into a world where the impossible became tangible. The stories behind the illusions were as important as the illusions themselves, adding depth and resonance to every moment on stage. Through this delicate balance of artistry and execution, Herrmann breathed life into his creations, allowing them to transcend the confines of the ordinary and etch themselves into the annals of magical history. As the curtain rose on each performance, the culmination of Herrmann's tireless dedication and creative fervor shone through. The alchemy of illusion, craftsmanship, and storytelling coalesced into an experience that transcended the boundaries of reality, inviting the audience to embrace the extraordinary. Behind the veil of mystery, dedicated to perfection, lay the heart of a visionary artist, whose enduring legacy continues to inspire and amaze.

Secrets of the Stage

Behind every breathtaking stage illusion is a carefully constructed tapestry of secrets and techniques, meticulously woven together to captivate audiences and leave them spellbound. Alexander Herrmann, a master of his craft, understood that the true art of magic lies not only in the performance itself, but also in the meticulous attention to detail behind the scenes. The stage is where the magic comes to life, where reality bends and imagination reigns supreme. From the hidden compartments and elaborate mechanics of grand illusions to the precise choreography of every movement, the secrets of the stage are what elevate a mere trick into an awe-inspiring spectacle. The construction of every illusion begins with a vision - a dream of the impossible made real. With unwavering passion and dedication, Herrmann would tirelessly work on perfecting each aspect, ensuring that the execution of the illusion was flawlessly seamless. Hours of practice, trial, and error were devoted to refining every movement, every gesture, until the illusion appeared effortless, masking the tireless effort and relentless pursuit of perfection behind the scenes. But the true magic lies in the art of misdirection, subtly guiding the audience's attention away from the mechanics of the illusion and towards the wonder it evokes. It is the careful orchestration of every move and every word, designed to captivate and enchant, leading the audience on a journey beyond the bounds of ordinary reality. Behind the curtain, technicians work alongside the magician, synchronizing the lighting, sound, and effects, transforming the stage into a realm of enchantment where disbelief is suspended and dreams take flight. Every illusion has a story to tell, and the stage becomes a canvas upon which these stories unfold. Whether it's making a grand illusion seem effortlessly natural or executing a smaller sleight of hand with finesse, Herrmann's dedication to excellence brought each illusion to life before the rapt eyes of the audience. The culmination of his efforts resulted in the creation of timeless classics that continue to evoke wonder and astonishment in the hearts of all who witness them. In unlocking the secrets of the stage, Alexander Herrmann illuminated the path for future generations of magicians. His commitment to pushing the boundaries of what was thought possible, his relentless pursuit of perfection, and his genuine love for the art of illusion continue to inspire and guide aspiring magicians around the globe. As we peel back the layers of illusion, we come to understand that the true magic lies not only in what we see on stage, but in the dedication, artistry, and passion that breathe life into every performance. The secrets of the stage offer a glimpse into the inner workings of magic, revealing the symphony of craftsmanship and creativity that transforms a mere trick into a timeless masterpiece.

Iconic Performances

Alexander Herrmann is renowned for his iconic performances that have captivated audiences around the world. His mastery of illusion and stagecraft has elevated magic to an art form, leaving a lasting impression on all who have witnessed his shows. One of his most famous illusions, 'The Vanishing Elephant,' stands as a testament to his unparalleled skill and showmanship. This grand spectacle saw an elephant mysteriously disappear before a mesmerized audience, leaving them in awe of Herrmann's seemingly supernatural abilities. Another breathtaking performance, 'The Levitating Lady,' showcased his ability to defy gravity as he elevated a lady from the audience, creating a sense of wonder and disbelief. Herrmann's meticulous attention to detail and flawless execution transformed these illusions into unforgettable moments of enchantment. In 'The Haunted House,' Herrmann transported spectators into a realm of mystery and allure as objects moved seemingly of their own accord within a mystically draped setting. The atmosphere he meticulously crafted heightened the suspense and left audiences spellbound. Such iconic performances were not merely displays of skill, but immersive experiences that transported viewers into a realm of wonder and imagination. Herrmann's genuine passion for magic and dedication to perfecting his art shone through each performance, enchanting audiences and solidifying his legacy as a master magician. As each act unfolded, it was evident that every movement, every gesture, and every carefully curated detail had been thoughtfully designed to create a sense of awe and fascination. Remarkably, even decades after his performances, they continue to inspire and evoke a sense of pure wonder in anyone who encounters them. Herrmann's iconic performances remain etched in the annals of magic history, forever revered for their profound impact and everlasting enchantment.

The Audience's Enchantment

Alexander Herrmann's performances have always been a source of wonder and enchantment for audiences around the world. His ability to captivate spectators and draw them into his world of illusions is a testament to his skill as a master magician. The audience's enchantment with Herrmann's performances goes beyond mere entertainment; it is an experience that lingers in the mind long after the final curtain falls. Each performance is carefully crafted to evoke a sense of awe and disbelief, leaving the audience questioning the very fabric of reality. Through his artistry, Herrmann invites his audience to suspend their disbelief and embrace the impossible, blurring the line between what is real and what is illusory. As the lights dim and the music swells, the audience becomes entranced, willingly relinquishing their grip on reality to be transported into Herrmann's world of magic and mystery. The palpable sense of anticipation and excitement that permeates the theater is a testament to the power of Herrmann's craft. His ability to engage and enthrall his audience is a testament to the depth of his artistry and the universal appeal of magic as a medium for storytelling and wonder. Each illusion draws the audience deeper into the narrative of the show, captivating hearts and minds with its spellbinding allure. As

Herrmann weaves his magic, the audience is taken on a journey that transcends the ordinary, leaving behind the constraints of everyday life and surrendering to the enchantment of the unknown. Throughout history, great magicians have been able to create experiences that transcend the limitations of the physical world, and Alexander Herrmann stands among them as a master of his craft. His performances are an ode to the human capacity for wonder and imagination, reminding us that there is more to existence than meets the eye. In the mesmerizing world of Alexander Herrmann, the audience becomes not just a passive observer, but an active participant in the unfolding drama of each illusion, united in their shared sense of wonder and enchantment. From the gasps of amazement to the thunderous applause that follows each astounding feat, the audience's enchantment with Herrmann's magic is a testament to the enduring power of his art to captivate, inspire, and transport. Every performance is a reminder that, in the hands of a master magician, the impossible becomes possible, and the world is transformed into a realm of endless fascination.

Pushing Boundaries

Alexander Herrmann was not content with merely astounding his audiences; he sought to push the boundaries of what was deemed possible in the realm of magic. With each new illusion, he strived to surpass his previous feats and captivate his spectators in ever more mesmerizing ways. This relentless pursuit of innovation and excellence drove him to explore uncharted territory, both in terms of technique and storytelling, constantly evolving his performances to leave an indelible impression on those who witnessed his magic. Herrmann's insatiable thirst for pushing the boundaries of magic led to the development of groundbreaking illusions that defied logic and transcended expectations. The introduction of daring escapes, mind-bending levitation acts, and seemingly impossible feats of telekinesis captivated audiences around the world. His meticulous attention to detail and unwavering commitment to perfection allowed him to create illusions that left even the most skeptical minds in awe of the inexplicable. Beyond the spectacle, Herrmann also endeavored to elevate the art form itself, challenging conventional perceptions of magic and pioneering new methodologies that redefined the possibilities within the craft. By fearlessly venturing into unexplored creative realms, he expanded the horizons of magic, inspiring future generations of illusionists to dream bigger and reach for the extraordinary. Moreover, Herrmann's dedication to pushing boundaries was not limited to the technical aspects of magic. He recognized the profound impact that magic could have on society, using his performances to challenge societal norms, stimulate imagination, and prompt introspection. Through his art, he aimed to break down barriers and spark a sense of wonder and possibility, instilling in his audience a belief that anything is achievable with vision, determination, and an unwavering commitment to excellence. His relentless exploration of the unknown and fearless ambition to stretch the limits of magic forever altered the landscape of the art form, leaving an enduring legacy that continues to inspire magicians and enchant audiences to this day. Thus, Alexander Herrmann's unwavering pursuit of pushing boundaries forever cemented his status as a visionary who reshaped the world of magic, leaving an indelible mark on its history.

Refining the Craft

Refining the craft of magic was not just a pursuit for Alexander Herrmann; it was an ongoing mission and a labor of love. Striving for perfection in every illusion, he dedicated himself to constant improvement, always pushing himself to innovate and elevate his performances to new heights. His relentless pursuit of excellence set him apart as a true master of his art. Herrmann understood that to refine the craft, one must delve deep into the intricacies of each illusion. He spent countless hours honing every movement, perfecting every gesture, and refining every nuance, leaving nothing to chance. His attention to detail was unparalleled, and his dedication to the art of magic was unwavering. Beyond the technical aspects, Herrmann also sought to infuse emotion and meaning into his illusions. He believed that magic should be more than just a series of tricks; it should be a transformative experience that captivated the audience's imagination and left a lasting impression. Through storytelling, music, and theatricality, he elevated his performances to something truly magical. In his relentless pursuit of refining the craft, Herrmann collaborated with artisans, technicians, and designers to create elaborate props and stage effects that were not only visually stunning but also seamlessly integrated into his illusions. Every aspect of his performance, from the lighting to the sound effects, was carefully orchestrated to enhance the overall spectacle and create an immersive world of wonder and enchantment. Moreover, Herrmann was generous in sharing his knowledge and expertise with aspiring magicians, recognizing that the future of the craft rested on continual innovation and inspired newcomers. He mentored and encouraged emerging talent, imparting invaluable wisdom and guidance to help them refine their own artistic visions. As a result of his unwavering commitment to refining the craft, Alexander Herrmann's legacy endures as a beacon of inspiration and aspiration for magicians around the world. His innovations and contributions continue to shape the magic industry, serving as a testament to the enduring power and timeless allure of the art of illusion.

The Legacy of His Work

Alexander Herrmann's impact on the world of magic extends far beyond his lifetime. His signature illusions and groundbreaking techniques continue to inspire and influence generations of magicians. From his awe-inspiring stage presence to his unparalleled showmanship, Herrmann left an indelible mark on the art of magic that still resonates today. His dedication to refining the craft set a standard that aspiring magicians strive to emulate, and his innovative approach continues to serve as a wellspring of inspiration. Herrmann's legacy is not just confined to the tricks he performed but also to the effect he had on the wider magical community. His commitment to excellence encouraged others to push the boundaries of what was believed possible in magic, sparking a creative renaissance within the field. Magicians worldwide studied and dissected his performances, seeking to understand the essence of his magic and how it captivated audiences with such spellbinding allure. Beyond the technical aspects of his illusions, Herrmann's work also embodied a profound sense of storytelling and emotional depth. His ability to weave narratives through his magic elevated the art form, creating experiences that transcended mere trickery and left a lasting impression on those who witnessed them. This narrative-driven approach has become a hallmark of many contemporary magicians, each seeking to replicate the emotional resonance that defined Herrmann's performances. In addition to his onstage brilliance, Herrmann's legacy encompasses a spirit of mentorship and generosity. Throughout his career, he eagerly shared his knowledge and expertise with emerging magicians, believing that cultivating talent was essential for the continual evolution of the craft. His impact lives on through the magicians he inspired and mentored, each carrying a piece of his magical essence forward into the future. Moreover, Herrmann's legacy has extended into popular culture, influencing depictions of magic in literature, film, and other artistic mediums. The enduring fascination with his life and work serves as a testament to the enduring power of his contributions, as they continue to capture the imagination of audiences across the globe. From the pages of history to the present day, Alexander Herrmann's legacy remains a guiding light for those who seek to explore the wondrous world of magic.

Inspiration for Future Magicians

Alexander Herrmann's remarkable career and artistry continue to inspire future generations of magicians. His pioneering illusions and dedication to his craft set a standard that aspiring magicians strive to emulate. Even in the present day, Herrmann's legacy serves as a wellspring of innovation and creativity for those captivated by the world of magic. The impact of his iconic performances and groundbreaking illusions has left an indelible mark on the history of magic, establishing him as a timeless figure in the realm of stagecraft. Alongside the allure of his mystifying acts, Herrmann's commitment to pushing boundaries and challenging conventional perceptions of what was achievable through magic serve as a beacon of inspiration for burgeoning magicians. His ability to captivate audiences and evoke a sense of wonder continues to resonate with contemporary performers, offering a roadmap for infusing their own acts with a transcendent quality. Moreover, Herrmann's enduring influence extends beyond the realm of performance, permeating the very fabric of magical innovation. By meticulously refining his craft and embracing technological advancements of his era, Herrmann not only elevated the art of magic but also established a blueprint for future illusionists to harness emerging tools in their pursuit of enchanting audiences. Aspiring magicians find solace in studying Herrmann's techniques, dissecting his legendary illusions, and gleaning invaluable insights from his unwavering dedication to the art form. Through deep introspection into the essence of Herrmann's work, budding magicians gain a profound appreciation for the nuances of performance, storytelling, and the seamless integration of theatrical elements to create a wholly immersive magical experience. Remarkably, Herrmann's ethos of innovation coupled with respect for tradition guides contemporary magicians in amalgamating classic principles with modern ingenuity, ensuring that the storytelling aspect remains at the forefront while incorporating cutting-edge methodologies and technologies. Indeed, Alexander Herrmann's illustrious career crystallizes into an invaluable wellspring of inspiration, guiding future magicians toward the realization of their artistic vision and the creation of a lasting impact within the esteemed lineage of magical performers.

Herrmann and His Rivals

The Magic Landscape: A World Full of Talent

During Alexander Herrmann's illustrious career, the world of magic was imbued with a sense of enchantment and wonder, teeming with an extraordinary array of remarkable talents. Across continents, from bustling metropolises to quaint towns, magicians adorned the stages, captivating audiences with their unique styles and mesmerizing performances. Each magician brought their own flair and theatricality, creating a vibrant and diverse tapestry within the magical community. From grand illusionists to humble street performers, the magic landscape was rich with innovation and creativity. As Herrmann navigated through this world filled with talent, he encountered fellow maestros who shaped the fabric of the magical realm. Their artistry and showmanship left an indelible mark on the audiences and inspired a spirit of friendly rivalry and mutual respect. The exchange of ideas and experiences among these luminaries fostered a culture of camaraderie and artistic growth, elevating the craft of magic to new heights. The allure of magic transcended language barriers and cultural differences, uniting performers and enthusiasts in their shared passion for mystery and astonishment. Herrmann found himself immersed in this kaleidoscope of magical expressions, learning and evolving alongside his peers. His encounters with the diverse talents across the globe enriched his own performances, infusing them with elements of international flair and ingenuity. Moreover, the vivid tapestry of magical talent provided Herrmann with opportunities to witness a myriad of performance styles and techniques, broadening his artistic horizons and fuelling his pursuit of excellence. It was within this fertile ground of creativity and proficiency that Herrmann honed his distinctive style, cultivating an act that would enthrall audiences and etch his name into the annals of magical history. In this thriving ecosystem of enchantment, competition coexisted with collaboration, as magicians sought to push the boundaries of their craft while celebrating each other's achievements. Through this communal spirit, the magic landscape blossomed into a veritable playground of innovation, offering Herrmann and his contemporaries an arena where they could showcase their unparalleled talents and leave lasting impressions on all who beheld their marvels.

Understanding Herrmann's Style

Alexander Herrmann's style of magic was a testament to his unwavering dedication and passion for the art. Every movement, every gesture, every word he uttered on stage conveyed a profound connection with his craft. His performances were not merely displays of skill; they were captivating narratives that enraptured the audience in a world of wonder and disbelief. Herrmann's unique style was a delicate balance of showmanship, technical mastery, and an innate understanding of human curiosity. He seamlessly wove together classical sleight of hand with larger-than-life illusions, leaving spectators spellbound at every turn. What truly set Herrmann apart was his ability to infuse emotion and storytelling into his acts. Each trick was not just a spectacle but a part of a larger, intricate tale that unfolded before the eyes of the spectators. His charismatic stage presence and effortless charm drew people into his world, creating an unforgettable experience for all who witnessed his performances. Beyond the technical aspects, Herrmann's style transcended mere tricks and illusions, becoming a source of inspiration for budding magicians and a benchmark for established performers. His dedication to his art and his relentless pursuit of perfection set a standard that few could match. Furthermore, Herrmann's style was deeply rooted in a genuine love for his audience. He treated every show as an opportunity to create moments of amazement and joy for those in attendance. His genuine connection with his spectators fostered a sense of awe and intimacy rarely seen in the world of magic. By understanding Herrmann's style, one can gain insights into the essence of magic itself – the ability to evoke wonder, provoke imagination, and kindle a sense of childlike fascination in all who bear witness. It is this enduring legacy of enchantment that continues to inspire magicians and captivate audiences worldwide.

Renowned Contemporary Magicians

Renowned in the world of magic, contemporary magicians of Alexander Herrmann's era have left an indelible mark on the art form. Their skillful performances and unique styles have captivated audiences worldwide, contributing to the rich tapestry of magical history. Among these esteemed contemporaries were luminaries such as Howard Thurston, Harry Houdini, and Adelaide Herrmann, each carving their own path of mesmerizing illusions and captivating stage presence. Their influence is undeniable, shaping the evolution of magic and inspiring future generations of magicians. Howard Thurston, known for his grand illusions and theatrical flair, brought a new level of showmanship and spectacle to the stage. His mastery of larger-than-life productions set a benchmark for ambitious magical performances. Through his innovative approach, Thurston solidified himself as a prominent figure in the golden age of magic, earning the admiration of audiences and fellow magicians alike. Meanwhile, Harry Houdini, renowned for his daring escapology and death-defying stunts, pushed the boundaries of what was thought possible in magic. His fearless performances and enigmatic persona captured the imaginations of people around the globe, elevating him to iconic status within the world of magic. Adelaide Herrmann, the Queen of Magic, dazzled audiences with her enchanting presence and expert command of the stage. As one of the few female magicians of her time, she broke barriers and earned widespread acclaim for her masterful performances. Her artistry and innovation redefined the role of women in magic and etched her name into the annals of magical history. The legacy of these incredible magicians continues to inspire and inform the contemporary landscape of magic, serving as a testament to the enduring power of the art. Their contributions, along with that of Alexander Herrmann, form a collective tapestry of wonder and enchantment, enriching the cultural heritage of magic and ensuring its timeless appeal.

Meeting the Iconic Harry Kellar

Harry Kellar, widely recognized as the dean of American magicians during the late 19th and early 20th centuries, left an indelible mark on the art of magic. His exceptional showmanship and unparalleled stage presence captivated audiences worldwide. Kellar was not only a magician but also a masterful storyteller. He intricately weaved narratives into his performances, enhancing the allure of his illusions. As Alexander Herrmann crossed paths with Kellar, their encounter marked a significant moment in magical history. The chemistry between the two luminaries was palpable, each respecting the other's distinct approach to magic. Amidst their rivalry, there existed a deep mutual admiration, rooted in the shared dedication to enchanting audiences and elevating the art form. Their meeting sparked a unique camaraderie, leading to unprecedented collaborations and a lasting legacy of camaraderie within the magic community. Kellar's influence extended beyond his awe-inspiring stage persona; he was known for his generosity, often providing guidance and support to emerging magicians like Herrmann. Their friendship flourished as they exchanged knowledge, techniques, and wisdom, inspiring each other to push the boundaries of magical artistry. It was in Kellar's company that Herrmann honed his stagecraft, refining his performances to deliver unforgettable experiences. Witnessing Kellar in action profoundly impacted Herrmann's understanding of showmanship and audience engagement. Their encounters were marked not only by a spirit of healthy competition but also by genuine affection and respect. In today's world, their enduring connection serves as an emblem of unity and collaboration within the magical community. As we reflect on the fabled meeting between Alexander Herrmann and Harry Kellar, it becomes clear that their relationship transcended mere rivalry. It laid the foundation for a tradition of mutual support, innovation, and reverence within the realm of magic – a legacy cherished by magicians and audiences alike.

Juvenile Competitor: Little Edison

As Alexander Herrmann's career continued to flourish, a new prodigy emerged onto the magic scene, none other than the young and promising illusionist, Little Edison. Despite his tender age, Little Edison mesmerized audiences with his uncanny ability to captivate and entertain. The charm and skill of this juvenile competitor were unparalleled, drawing parallels to Herrmann's early days. His fresh approach to magic and stage presence caught the attention of both spectators and fellow magicians, sparking a wave of excitement within the magical community. Little Edison's rise heralded a new era in the world of magic, captivating hearts and minds with his ingenuity and passion. As he honed his craft, the bond between mentor and mentee blossomed as Herrmann recognized the potential within the young prodigy. This growing camaraderie brought forth an unforeseen level of collaboration and friendly competition between the seasoned maestro and the budding star. Their encounters on and off stage sparked an intriguing dynamic that left audiences enchanted and yearning for more. Through their shared performances, Little Edison showcased an unparalleled prowess, drawing admiration from both fans and rivals alike. His youthful energy and innate talent injected a refreshing vigor into the magical landscape, setting the stage for an unforgettable chapter in the history of the art. Despite their differing styles and approaches, Herrmann and Little Edison's mutual respect and admiration for each other laid the foundation for an enduring legacy that continues to inspire aspiring magicians. Their remarkable relationship symbolizes the timeless allure and transcendent nature of magic, proving that age knows no bounds when it comes to weaving enchantment and wonder.

Rising Tensions with Rivals

The emergence of young competitors like the prodigious Little Edison sparked a wave of competitive dynamics within the community of magicians, including the renowned Alexander Herrmann. As these rising stars began to make their mark in the world of magic, Herrmann found himself facing an unprecedented challenge – one that would shape his own approach to his craft and ignite a fervent spirit of determination within him. The increasing proliferation of new talent introduced an air of healthy competition but also prompted a significant shift in the established order of the magical realm. The sense of camaraderie that once enveloped the industry now bore witness to a subtle undercurrent of tension, as the ambitious pursuit of acclaim and recognition brought forth both collaboration and rivalry among the practitioners of prestidigitation. Herrmann, an artist devoted to his craft, was not impervious to these changing tides. While he remained committed to uplifting and promoting the art of magic as a whole, the presence of formidable younger rivals compelled him to reevaluate and consolidate his unique style and techniques. The intensified competition warranted a renewed dedication to honing his skills and captivating audiences with ever more mystifying illusions. Amidst the mounting pressure, Herrmann sought to epitomize grace and integrity in navigating the realm of magical performances. His actions, while driven by an unyielding desire for excellence, were inevitably intertwined with the deep-rooted respect for his peers and the craft itself. Recognizing the importance of mutual support and encouragement within the community, Herrmann embarked on fostering relationships with both seasoned veterans and promising newcomers, albeit against a backdrop of burgeoning rivalry. As tensions simmered and flourished, Herrmann's approach foreshadowed a pivotal shift in the dynamics of magical craftsmanship, demonstrating an unwavering commitment to elevate the art form while striving to navigate the delicate balance between commendation and contention. Through this intricate interplay of aspiration, camaraderie, and competition, the legacy of Alexander Herrmann began to evolve, leaving an indelible imprint on the history of magic.

Professional Courtesy and Camaraderie

In the midst of fierce competition, one might expect animosity and rivalry to dominate the interactions between magicians of the era. Surprisingly, however, professional courtesy and camaraderie were prevalent among these masters of illusion. Despite their rivalry, there was a mutual respect that brought forth an unspoken code of conduct. This unique camaraderie stemmed from a deep understanding of the sacrifices and dedication required in the pursuit of magic. These magicians recognized the shared challenges and triumphs that came with their craft, fostering a sense of kinship that transcended their competitive endeavors. Professional courtesy was demonstrated through various acts of kindness and support within the magician community. It was not uncommon for magicians to share advice on techniques, offer guidance in showmanship, or even collaborate on projects. The exchange of ideas and mentorship allowed the art of magic to flourish and evolve, paving the way for groundbreaking performances and innovative illusions. This spirit of generosity and collaboration not only elevated the individual magicians but also enriched the entire magical landscape, captivating audiences across the globe. Moreover, amidst their performances and rivalries, these magicians exhibited a deep-seated respect for each other's unique styles and contributions to the world of magic. They understood that diversity in magic was essential for keeping the art form vibrant and intriguing. Rather than seeking to overshadow one another, they celebrated the distinct talents and approaches that each magician brought to the stage. This magnanimous appreciation for their peers' work reflected a profound understanding of the profound impact their collective efforts had on shaping the future of magic. The bond of camaraderie extends beyond the applause and accolades received during public performances. Behind the scenes, these magicians often lent a supportive ear, offered words of encouragement, and extended gestures of goodwill to one another. Their shared experiences forged enduring connections, binding them together as a close-knit community driven by passion and respect. Regardless of differing paths or personal ambitions, the communal ethos of the magical fraternity continued to inspire mutual admiration and solidarity. As we delve deeper into the intricate dynamics of these esteemed magicians, it becomes evident that their relationships embodied the noble principles of honor, integrity, and empathy, setting an exemplary standard for professional conduct. Indeed, the spirit of professional courtesy and camaraderie among Herrmann and his contemporaries serves as a poignant reminder of the profound impact that mutual respect and collaboration can have on an artistic discipline, transforming what could have been a cutthroat industry into a harmonious and thriving community where excellence thrives and enduring legacies are forged.

Competition Sparks Innovation

Competition in the world of magic has always been a driving force behind groundbreaking innovation. As Alexander Herrmann found himself amidst a landscape filled with talented contemporaries, the need for pushing boundaries and constantly seeking new ideas became imperative. The presence of rivals like Harry Kellar and Little Edison fueled Herrmann's determination to set himself apart through originality and showmanship. Rather than succumbing to complacency, he used the competitive energy to ignite innovation within his craft. This era of intense rivalry between magicians resulted in a surge of creativity and a passion for surpassing one another through ingenious illusions and mesmerizing performances. Each magician strived to outdo the other, leading to the development of never-before-seen techniques and awe-inspiring acts. The growing anticipation and excitement among audiences spurred the magicians to push their abilities to the limits, thus enhancing the overall magical experience. The competitive spirit instilled an unwavering commitment to delivering unparalleled entertainment, ultimately transforming the art of magic into a captivating spectacle that enthralled spectators worldwide. Furthermore, this era of fierce competition not only fostered individual growth but also elevated the collective standard of magic, inspiring each performer to continually evolve and redefine the boundaries of what was possible. The relentless pursuit of excellence propelled the entire magic community to explore new realms of creativity and innovation, solidifying the significance of healthy rivalry in driving the perpetual advancement of the craft. This period serves as a testament to the profound impact of competition in stimulating inventive prowess and enriching the magical landscape with enduring contributions. It is within this bubbling cauldron of competition and creativity that some of the most significant developments in the history of magic emerged, forever reshaping the art form and leaving an indelible mark on future generations of magicians.

Impact on Audiences and Fellow Magicians

Herrmann's unmatched skill and showmanship have not only captivated audiences worldwide but also significantly influenced the art of magic itself. His performances left an indelible mark on countless spectators, sparking a sense of wonder and enchantment that stayed with them long after the curtain fell. The impact on audiences was far-reaching, as Herrmann's unique blend of charisma, stage presence, and dazzling illusions continually set new standards for magical entertainment. Furthermore, Herrmann's influence on fellow magicians cannot be overstated. As a luminary in the field, he inspired a new generation of performers to hone their craft and elevate the art form. Emerging magicians were awed by his mastery of sleight of hand, innovative stage designs, and seamless choreography, learning invaluable lessons from his techniques and approach. Herrmann's dedication to his artistry served as a guiding light for those who aspired to leave their own mark on the world of magic. The ripple effect of Herrmann's influence extended beyond the realm of performance. His commitment to professionalism and unwavering pursuit of perfection served as a shining example for aspiring magicians, instilling in them a deep reverence for the art and its traditions. Moreover, his willingness to share knowledge and collaborate with fellow magicians fostered a culture of camaraderie and mutual respect, enriching the global magic community. Through his captivating performances and genuine passion for the art, Herrmann cultivated a deep-seated appreciation for magic, elevating it from mere entertainment to a profound and transformative experience. His influence continues to reverberate through generations of magicians, shaping the way audiences perceive magic and inspiring artists to push the boundaries of their own creativity.

Building a Lasting Legacy Amidst Rivalry

As Herrmann navigated the competitive landscape of magic, he remained deeply committed to building a legacy that would endure beyond the realm of rivalry. Despite the intense competition and inevitable conflicts that arose, Herrmann's focus on leaving a lasting impact on the world of magic never wavered. His dedication to his craft went far beyond mere ambition or desire for recognition; it was rooted in a genuine passion for the art of illusion and the profound belief that magic had the power to captivate, inspire, and transcend differences. Recognizing that his legacy would shape the future of magic, Herrmann actively sought to elevate the standards of magical performance and foster a sense of camaraderie among fellow magicians. In doing so, he strived to impart a spirit of professionalism and mutual respect that would enrich the entire magical community. Herrmann meticulously documented and preserved his signature illusions, ensuring that they would be handed down to future generations as invaluable treasures of the magical heritage. This meticulous approach to preserving his legacy mirrored his penchant for precision in every aspect of his performances, signaling a commitment to excellence that would solidify his enduring influence. Beyond creating awe-inspiring spectacles, Herrmann was driven by the profound desire to leave behind a legacy that would continue to spark wonder, imagination, and innovation in successive generations of magicians and audiences. Through his unwavering dedication to magic, Herrmann established an enduring legacy that transcended the confines of rivalry, drawing admiration and respect from contemporaries and leaving an indelible mark on the vibrant tapestry of magical history.

The Competition

Understanding the Magic Circle

The influential magic circle played a crucial role in shaping the competitive landscape Herrmann found himself in. As an exclusive society of magicians, the magic circle served as a hub for fostering magical talent and exchanging knowledge. Its members comprised esteemed performers, illusionists, and connoisseurs of the arcane arts, creating an environment of collaboration and healthy competition. This collective of magical minds not only upheld high standards of performance but also propelled the evolution of magic as an entertainment form. Within this revered community, aspiring conjurers learned from the masters, honed their craft, and refined their acts to stand out on the grand stage, seeking recognition and validation among their peers. The magic circle's influence extended beyond mere skill enhancement; it instilled a sense of camaraderie and professional ethics, intertwining the destinies of magicians striving to captivate audiences with their enchanting displays of wonder. For Herrmann, gaining acceptance into this selective fraternity symbolized a milestone in his career, bestowing upon him both prestige and formidable competition. This chapter delves into the pivotal role of the magic circle in cultivating talent, fostering innovation, and laying the groundwork for the competitive realm that thrived within its illustrious confines.

The Rise of Competitive Magic Acts

During the late 19th and early 20th centuries, the art of magic experienced a significant transformation with the rise of competitive magic acts. As the public's fascination with mystifying illusions grew, magicians were compelled to elevate their performances to new heights, resulting in an era of innovation and intense rivalry. This period marked the emergence of grand stage spectacles and elaborate stunts, captivating audiences and setting the stage for a fiercely competitive landscape within the world of magic. Magicians sought to outshine one another, not only through their technical prowess but also through the creativity and audacity of their illusions, sparking a wave of ingenuity and showmanship. The heightened sense of competition spurred performers to push the boundaries of what was deemed possible, propelling the art of magic into uncharted territory. The competitive atmosphere fostered an environment where magicians continually honed their skills, refining their acts to captivate and astound spectators. This fervent pursuit of perfection led to groundbreaking innovations in stagecraft, prop design, and illusion presentation, ultimately raising the bar for magical performances worldwide. Additionally, the rise of competitive magic acts brought forth a new level of showmanship and entertainment, as magicians vied for the spotlight with increasingly daring and breathtaking feats. Through intricate storytelling and immersive theatrical experiences, these performers endeavored to orchestrate enchanting narratives that enraptured audiences and left them spellbound. The evolution of competitive magic acts not only showcased the individual talents of magicians but also set the stage for the larger-than-life productions and legendary performances known to define the golden age of magic. Furthermore, this period of heightened rivalry nurtured a culture of mutual inspiration and respect among magicians, leading to a collective elevation of the art form. As performers pushed the boundaries of their craft, they drew inspiration from their peers' accomplishments, spurring a cycle of innovation and artistic growth that continues to influence the modern landscape of magic. The rise of competitive magic acts ignited an era of unprecedented creativity and showmanship, leaving an indelible mark on the history of stage performance and establishing a legacy of innovation and excellence that endures to this day.

Herrmann's First Brush with Competition

As Alexander Herrmann embarked on his magical journey, he encountered a pivotal moment when he first faced competition from other magicians. This experience would shape his understanding of the magical world and drive him to push the boundaries of his own craft. At the onset, encountering competition provided him with an opportunity to witness the diverse styles and techniques employed by fellow magicians. The subtle nuances and unique presentations of his contemporaries served as a source of valuable insight. Rather than viewing them solely as rivals, Herrmann chose to perceive them as potential sources of inspiration. In observing their performances, he gained a deeper appreciation for the art of magic, recognizing the endless possibilities of expression within it. The encounter with competition prompted Herrmann to reflect on his own repertoire and spurred him to explore fresh perspectives to further captivate and inspire audiences. As he immersed himself in the world of competitive magic acts, he recognized the need for continuous innovation and refinement in his own performances. It was a turning point that motivated Herrmann to hone his skills and refine his stage presence to stay ahead in the ever-evolving landscape of magic. Instead of succumbing to feelings of rivalry or resentment, Herrmann sought to cultivate camaraderie and mutual respect with his fellow magicians, fostering an environment where they could learn from each other's successes and challenges. This approach not only enhanced his own growth but also contributed to the overall advancement of magical arts. Herrmann's initial encounter with competition ignited a fire within him, propelling him toward greatness and cementing his dedication to shaping a legacy that transcended mere illusions.

Recognizing the Talent Around Him

Having entered the competitive world of magic, Alexander Herrmann found himself surrounded by a sea of burgeoning talent. As he attended various performances and engaged in conversations with fellow magicians, Herrmann couldn't help but acknowledge the remarkable skills and creativity displayed by his peers. Each magician had their unique style and approach, leaving an indelible impression on Herrmann's understanding of the craft. Witnessing the diverse techniques and performances, Herrmann developed a deep appreciation for the artistry and dedication of his contemporaries. It was evident that the world of magic was brimming with gifted individuals, each contributing to the rich tapestry of illusions and wonder. Recognizing the breadth and depth of talent around him, Herrmann felt both humbled and inspired to elevate his own magical prowess. He understood that acknowledging the abilities of others was not a sign of weakness, but rather a testament to the collective brilliance that enriched the magical community. Herrmann's encounters with other magicians incited within him a profound sense of admiration, igniting a desire to learn from and collaborate with these masters of illusion. The camaraderie and mutual respect among magicians fostered an environment conducive to growth and innovation. This period of recognizing and celebrating the talent surrounding him became pivotal in shaping Herrmann's perspective on the limitless possibilities within the world of magic.

Analyzing Rivals' Techniques

As Alexander Herrmann ascended to prominence in the world of magic, his keen eye and astute observation endowed him with a unique perspective on his fellow magicians and their techniques. Herrmann became deeply engrossed in the study of his competitors, minutely analyzing their performances and unraveling the intricacies of their illusions. He developed a profound respect for the artistry and dedication exhibited by his rivals, recognizing that each possessed a distinct virtuosity in their craft. Herrmann's approach to analyzing his rivals' techniques was one rooted in admiration rather than mere scrutiny. He delved into the manifold layers of their performances, deciphering the nuances and cadences that defined their unique styles. Through this process, he discovered an invaluable source of inspiration, drawing from the diversity of methods and approaches wielded by his contemporaries. Beyond the surface allure of their acts, Herrmann sought to unearth the underlying principles and innovations that fueled his rivals' success. By delving deep into the mechanics of their illusions, he gleaned insights that fostered a deeper understanding of the art form itself. This introspective examination not only enriched his own performances but also contributed to the progressive evolution of magic as a whole. Inherent to Herrmann's appraisal of his rivals' techniques was the acknowledgment of their contributions to the collective tapestry of magic. Rather than viewing them solely as adversaries, he regarded them as indispensable collaborators in the perpetual pursuit of elevating the craft to new heights. His appreciation for their ingenuity fostered a sense of camaraderie, transcending the realms of competition to cultivate an ethos of mutual enrichment and collective advancement. The process of analyzing rivals' techniques profoundly influenced Herrmann's artistic journey, instilling within him a deep-seated reverence for the multitude of talents that graced the world stage alongside him. It crystallized his belief in the transformative power of embracing diversity and learning from contemporaries, forging a legacy characterized by unwavering respect, benevolence, and a steadfast commitment to the unbounded potential of magic.

Facing the Challenge: Herrmann's Response

In the face of formidable competition, Alexander Herrmann approached the challenge with unwavering determination and a deep understanding of the art of magic. Rather than succumb to apprehension or doubt, he chose to harness the pressure and transform it into fuel for his creativity. He devoted countless hours to refining his craft, tirelessly honing his techniques, and experimenting with new illusions that would captivate and astonish audiences. Through intense practice and an unyielding dedication to his art, Herrmann endeavored to elevate his performances to unmatched levels of mastery. Moreover, he utilized the competition as an opportunity for self-reflection and growth, recognizing that pushing the boundaries of his own capabilities was integral to prevailing in the competitive arena. Drawing from his experiences, he embarked on an introspective journey, seeking inspiration from sources both within and beyond the world of magic. By immersing himself in diverse forms of artistic expression and engaging with fellow magicians, he gained fresh perspectives that invigorated his approach and expanded his creative horizons. In doing so, Herrmann cultivated a unique style that set him apart and enabled him to distinguish himself amid a crowded field of talent. Embracing the challenges presented by his rivals, Herrmann's response was not simply to surpass them, but to transcend the confines of traditional magical performance, forging a path that was distinctly his own. His unwavering commitment to innovation, coupled with a steadfast belief in the transformative power of magic, propelled him towards the pinnacle of his artistry, where he stood ready to confront any challenge that lay ahead.

Finding Inspiration Among Peers

As Alexander Herrmann navigated the competitive landscape of magic, he found himself surrounded by an array of talented peers. These fellow magicians were not just his rivals; they became a source of inspiration and learning. Each magician brought a unique perspective and a distinct set of skills to the table, creating an environment ripe for growth and discovery. Herrmann recognized the value in observing his peers' performances, studying their techniques, and engaging in meaningful conversations with them. It was through these interactions that he gained insights into the diverse approaches to the art of magic. This exploration of varying styles not only broadened Herrmann's understanding of magic but also enriched his own performances. He embraced the opportunity to learn from his peers and saw it as a testament to the collaborative nature of magic. Moreover, witnessing the creativity and innovation displayed by other magicians motivated Herrmann to continuously push the boundaries of his craft. The camaraderie among magicians served as a constant reminder that the pursuit of excellence was not a solitary venture, but a collective journey towards mastery. In turn, Herrmann sought to contribute to this culture of mutual growth and support. He openly shared his own knowledge and experiences, fostering a community where magicians could elevate each other. By embracing the wisdom and ingenuity of his peers, Herrmann honed his artistry and solidified his place within the magical realm. It is within the bond of shared passion and respect that the seeds of greatness were sown, propelling Herrmann and his contemporaries to new heights of enchantment and wonder.

The Role of Innovation in Outperforming Competitors

In the competitive world of magic, innovation plays a pivotal role in distinguishing oneself from fellow magicians. Alexander Herrmann understood this well, recognizing that constant innovation was crucial in staying ahead of his competitors. Innovating in magic involves more than just creating new illusions or tricks; it also encompasses a deep understanding of human psychology, showmanship, and the ability to captivate audiences in unique ways. Understanding the audience's evolving expectations and tailoring one's performances to meet those demands is an essential aspect of innovation in magic. Herrmann believed in constantly refining his craft and thinking outside the box. This mindset not only allowed him to maintain a competitive edge but also contributed to the evolution of magic as an art form. One aspect of innovation in magic lies in the development of new techniques and props. Magicians must continuously push the boundaries of what is possible, introducing new elements that captivate and astound spectators. Additionally, embracing cutting-edge technology and integrating it seamlessly into performances can set a magician apart from their peers. However, true innovation in magic goes beyond mere technical advancements; it requires a deep understanding of storytelling and stage presence. Alexander Herrmann was known for his innovative use of narrative and theatricality, elevating his illusions into captivating experiences that transcended simple tricks. This ability to skillfully weave narratives into his performances allowed him to connect with audiences on a profound level, setting him apart from his rivals. Moreover, a willingness to collaborate with other creative minds and explore interdisciplinary influences can lead to groundbreaking developments in magic. Herrmann was known for seeking inspiration across various art forms, incorporating elements of theater, music, and visual arts into his shows. This holistic approach to creativity allowed him to infuse his performances with a richness and depth that left a lasting impression on audiences. Ultimately, innovation in magic is a blend of technical prowess, artistic creativity, and a deep understanding of one's audience. By constantly pushing the boundaries, embracing new ideas, and honing their craft, magicians can outperform their competitors and leave an indelible mark on the world of magic.

Embracing the Spirit of Friendly Competition

In the world of magic, competition is not merely a test of skill or talent; it is a celebration of the art form and an opportunity for growth. As Alexander Herrmann navigated the realm of competitive magic, he realized that the spirit of friendly competition was a driving force behind the collective elevation of the craft. Instead of viewing his fellow magicians as adversaries, Herrmann embraced them as compatriots in a shared pursuit of excellence. The camaraderie among magicians transcended the need to constantly outdo each other. It fostered an environment where ideas were freely exchanged, techniques were honed, and creativity flourished. The interactions with his peers propelled Herrmann to continually push the boundaries of his own abilities, inspiring him to seek new approaches and innovate in ways that not only set him apart but also enriched the entire magical community. While the competitive landscape posed its challenges, it also offered invaluable lessons and insights. Herrmann recognized that observing the performances of his counterparts allowed him to gain different perspectives, learn from diverse styles, and identify areas for improvement. When faced with friendly competitors who showcased exceptional talents, Herrmann found motivation to elevate his own artistry, igniting a positive cycle of creative inspiration and personal advancement. More than just a display of individual prowess, friendly competition in magic became a catalyst for collective progress. Magicians celebrated each other's victories, supported one another through setbacks, and collectively elevated the standards of their craft. This sense of community not only enriched the experiences of both performers and audiences but also solidified a legacy of mutual respect and admiration within the magical fraternity. Embracing the spirit of friendly competition meant recognizing that the success of one magician enhanced the success of all. It led to collaborations, mentorships, and friendships that transcended the confines of rivalry, enriching the lives of those within the magical community. By embracing this ethos, Alexander Herrmann not only honed his own skills but also contributed to the growth and dissemination of magic as an enduring art form.

Reflection on Personal and Professional Growth

As I reflect on the journey of personal and professional growth, I cannot help but acknowledge the profound impact that the spirit of friendly competition has had on my development as a magician. Engaging in healthy rivalry with fellow magicians has not only pushed me to hone my craft and elevate my skill set but has also allowed me to delve deeper into self-discovery and self-improvement. Through the lens of competition, I have been able to identify my strengths and weaknesses, continually striving to refine my performances and enrich the art of magic. This process has been instrumental in shaping my character and fortifying my resilience amidst challenges. Additionally, navigating the realms of competitive magic has fostered a sense of camaraderie and mutual respect among peers, fostering an environment of shared growth and collective inspiration. Witnessing the diverse styles and techniques of other magicians has broadened my perspective and enriched my creative arsenal, propelling me towards greater innovation and artistic expression. Moreover, the interactions within the magical community have instilled in me a profound humility, reminding me that there is always more to learn and discover, regardless of one's expertise. In essence, the embrace of friendly competition has woven a tapestry of invaluable experiences, equipping me with the tools not only to flourish as a performer but also to evolve as an individual. It has ignited a relentless pursuit of excellence while nurturing a profound appreciation for the transformative power of collaboration, empathy, and continual growth. This reflection serves as a testament to the profound lessons and growth opportunities that lie at the heart of engaging in cordial competition within the world of magic.

Magic Wars

An Era of Intense Rivalry

During the formative years of Herrmann's career, the world of stage magic was characterized by an intense spirit of competition and rivalry. As a young performer, Herrmann was immersed in an environment where every illusionist strived to outdo their peers, constantly seeking to captivate audiences with more captivating and impressive performances. This atmosphere fueled Herrmann's determination to push the boundaries of traditional magic and carve out his own unique style. It was this era of intense rivalry that laid the foundation for Herrmann's relentless pursuit of excellence and innovation in the realm of magic. The pressure to stand out from his competitors motivated Herrmann to experiment with new illusions and develop his signature acts, ultimately shaping his understanding of stage magic. In the crucible of competition, Herrmann honed his craft, refining his techniques to create a mesmerizing experience for spectators. This period of rivalry was instrumental in shaping Herrmann's artistic vision and instilled in him a commitment to continually elevate the standards of stage magic. Despite the fierce competition, it also fostered a sense of camaraderie and mutual respect among fellow illusionists, as they recognized and acknowledged the dedication and artistry required to master the craft. As such, this era of intense rivalry not only pushed Herrmann to evolve as a performer but also contributed to the broader evolution of stage magic, setting the stage for an era of innovation and creativity that would redefine the art form for generations to come.

Famous Duels Between Illusionists

Throughout history, the world of magic has witnessed epic duels between rival illusionists that have captivated audiences and left an indelible mark on the art form. These confrontations were not just about showcasing magical prowess but also about asserting dominance and leaving a lasting legacy. One such legendary duel took place between the renowned Herrmann the Great and his arch-rival, the enigmatic Mystical Margery. Their clash of talents and personalities created a sensation in the magic world, drawing eager spectators from far and wide. The rivalry between Herrmann and Margery reached its peak during a spectacular performance at the prestigious Royal Opera House. Both illusionists spared no effort in outshining each other, unleashing their most awe-inspiring tricks and illusions to both mesmerize and confound the audience. As the tension mounted, the duel became as much about showmanship and theatrics as it was about magic itself. Their famed acts of one-upmanship extended beyond the stage, permeating every aspect of their public lives. They engaged in a battle of wits and innovation, constantly striving to unveil groundbreaking illusions that would upstage their adversary. This fierce competition fueled a period of extraordinary creativity, leading to an explosion of new magical effects and techniques that continue to influence magicians to this day. One of the most memorable encounters occurred during a series of performances in Paris, where both Herrmann and Margery pushed the boundaries of magical spectacle. Each sought to enthrall the audience with increasingly daring feats, causing a sensation that reverberated throughout the magical community. Their rivalry spurred them to devise never-before-seen illusions, transforming the art of magic and captivating audiences with unprecedented wonder and mystery. As the world eagerly anticipated their next showdown, the rivalry between these two maestros brought unprecedented attention to the realm of magic. Audiences were enthralled by the drama and suspense that unfolded on and off the stage, and the illustrious careers of Herrmann and Margery forever intertwined in the annals of magical history, their legacy enduring as a testament to the enduring power of competition and creativity in the world of illusion.

The Quest for New Illusions

Magicians throughout history have been driven by an insatiable thirst for innovation, constantly seeking to push the boundaries and defy expectations. The quest for new illusions is a reflection of the profound dedication and creativity that define the world of magic. It represents a relentless pursuit of captivating and awe-inspiring feats that captivate audiences and leave them spellbound. This pursuit is deeply rooted in a desire to create experiences that transcend the ordinary and transport spectators into a realm of wonder and disbelief. Magicians embark on this journey with unwavering passion, pouring their hearts and souls into crafting illusions that challenge conventional perceptions and leave an indelible mark on the collective imagination. The quest for new illusions is not merely a technical endeavor; it embodies an artistic and emotional expression that resonates with both performers and viewers alike. Each illusionist endeavors to carve out a unique niche, driven by an unyielding commitment to offering something truly extraordinary. This tireless pursuit of originality fuels a vibrant ecosystem of experimentation and ingenuity, where magicians strive to unveil never-before-seen marvels that push the boundaries of what was previously deemed possible. As innovators in their craft, they laboriously refine their techniques, leveraging cutting-edge technologies and drawing inspiration from diverse sources, from classic literature to contemporary innovations in science and technology. This relentless exploration leads to the creation of illusions that astound and entrance, leaving an enduring impact on the history and evolution of magic. However, the quest for new illusions is fraught with challenges and risks. Each groundbreaking creation carries the weight of expectation and the possibility of failure. The path to innovation is often riddled with setbacks, requiring magicians to confront disappointments and setbacks with resilience and unwavering determination. Furthermore, the relentless pursuit of novelty can strain the boundaries of ethical practice, raising questions about authenticity and the use of deceptive techniques. Despite these challenges, the search for new illusions remains a cornerstone of magical artistry, driving magicians to stretch the limits of their creativity and stage performances that defy comprehension. Ultimately, the quest for new illusions continues to shape the evolution of magic, fueling a never-ending cycle of innovation and reinvention that ensures the perpetuation of wonder and enchantment for generations to come.

Innovation: A Double-Edged Sword

In the world of magic, innovation has always been a double-edged sword. On one hand, it is the lifeblood that keeps the art form relevant and captivating for audiences. It pushes magicians to constantly strive for new heights, to challenge themselves to create illusions that are more awe-inspiring than anything seen before. Innovation opens the door to untold possibilities, allowing magicians to surprise and dazzle their spectators in ways previously unimagined. The relentless pursuit of innovation has led to some of the most iconic and unforgettable moments in magic history. From cutting-edge technology to groundbreaking techniques, every breakthrough brings with it the potential to change the landscape of magic forever. However, on the other hand, the pressure to innovate can also be daunting for magicians. The relentless quest for the next big illusion can lead to burnout and mental exhaustion. The fear of falling behind in an industry driven by novelty can create an atmosphere of intense competition, where magicians are constantly vying to outdo one another, sometimes at the expense of their own well-being. Moreover, the demand for constant innovation can overshadow the timeless elegance of classic magic, leading to an erosion of traditional techniques and performances. It becomes a delicate balancing act for magicians - how to embrace innovation while preserving the essence of what makes magic truly enchanting. The history of magic is replete with examples of magicians who found themselves caught in the whirlwind of innovation, and the impact it had on their careers and personal lives. Some embraced the challenge wholeheartedly, using it as a catalyst for reinvention and revitalization. Others struggled to keep up, feeling the weight of expectation bearing down upon them. As we delve into the stories of these magicians, we gain a deeper appreciation for the complexities of innovation in the magical arts - how it can propel success and yet also present profound challenges. In this chapter, we will explore the fascinating interplay between innovation, creativity, and the very soul of magic itself. We will uncover the triumphs and tribulations that come with striving for originality and staying ahead of the ever-changing tide of audience expectations.

The Role of Theatres and Promoters

The success of illusionists during the Magic Wars era was not solely dependent on their skills and innovations, but also on the crucial role played by theaters and promoters. Theaters served as the battlegrounds where illusionists showcased their talents and competed for public attention. It was within the walls of these venues that magical performances were elevated to unprecedented levels of grandeur, captivating audiences and leaving them in awe. The elaborate stages and state-of-the-art equipment provided by theaters allowed illusionists to bring their visions to life, creating spellbinding experiences for spectators. The support and collaboration of theater owners and managers were instrumental in fostering an environment where magical spectacles flourished. Furthermore, promoters played a pivotal role in shaping the narrative surrounding magical performances. Through strategic marketing and publicity campaigns, they generated anticipation and excitement, drawing large crowds to witness the enchanting displays of skill and artistry. Their efforts helped elevate the profiles of illusionists, transforming them into larger-than-life figures whose names became synonymous with wonder and mystery. By leveraging media channels and word-of-mouth buzz, promoters succeeded in casting a spell of fascination over the masses, propelling the world of magic into the forefront of popular entertainment. At the heart of this dynamic relationship between theaters, promoters, and illusionists lay a shared passion for preserving the allure of magic and enriching cultural experiences. Together, they coalesced to weave a tapestry of enchantment, inviting audiences into a realm where imagination reigned supreme. The harmonious synergy between these stakeholders not only propelled the careers of illusionists but also contributed to the enduring legacy of magic as a revered art form. As we delve into the intertwined histories of these influential entities, a profound appreciation emerges for the indelible mark they left on the landscape of magic, forever shaping its trajectory and securing its place in the annals of entertainment history.

Public Perceptions and Loyalties

The world of magic during the 19th century was marked by a fascinating interplay of public perceptions and loyalties. As audiences flocked to theatres to witness the extraordinary feats of illusionists, their perceptions of these performers were shaped by a complex interweaving of factors. The inherent mystique of magic created an aura of wonder and awe around these artists, leading to a sense of admiration and reverence among the public. Their ability to defy logic and manipulate reality captivated the masses, elevating magicians to almost mythical status in the eyes of their audience. Magicians became more than mere entertainers; they became purveyors of marvel and enchantment. The loyalty and devotion of their fans knew no bounds, as audiences eagerly anticipated their every performance, holding these magicians in high esteem. However, this adulation was not without its nuances. As the popularity of magic soared, so did the expectations of the audience. In such a climate, the slightest misstep or perceived failure could spark whispers of doubt and criticism. The relationship between illusionist and audience was a delicate dance, with the former constantly striving to exceed the latter's expectations.

Scandals and Sabotage On Stage

Scandals and sabotage often marred the world of magic during this fiercely competitive era. Illusionists, desperate to outshine their rivals, were not immune to resorting to underhanded tactics in order to gain an edge. The allure of success often led some performers down a treacherous path, where deceit and trickery extended beyond the boundaries of the stage. In an age where the stakes were high and reputations were everything, scandals were not uncommon. Whether it was the surreptitious theft of a rival's illusion, the spreading of malicious rumors, or the manipulation of audience perception, these devious acts tarnished the otherwise enchanting world of magic. Such actions not only sullied the names of those involved but also generated skepticism and distrust among audiences. The insidious nature of these scandals cast a shadow over the integrity of the art, threatening to undermine the genuine talents and creativity of honest performers. However, it is important to note that while some succumbed to such temptations, many others stood firm against these morally questionable practices, upholding their integrity and dedication to the craft. These individuals refused to compromise their values for fleeting success. Together, they sought to restore trust and honor to the magical community, proving that true greatness is achieved through hard work, authenticity, and respect for both fellow magicians and the audience. As the tales of scandals and sabotage unraveled, they served as cautionary reminders of the pitfalls of unchecked ambition and the importance of maintaining ethical principles in the pursuit of excellence. Despite the dark shadows cast by these unfortunate events, they ultimately paved the way for a renewed commitment to honesty, integrity, and the pure wonder of magic, guiding the art form toward a brighter and more virtuous future.

Adapting to Survive the Competition

In the cutthroat world of magic during the early 20th century, surviving the relentless competition required extraordinary resilience and adaptability. Illusionists were constantly challenged by their peers who sought to outdo them in every performance. The pressure to innovate and impress a demanding audience was immense. Magicians had to navigate through a landscape of ever-evolving techniques, and each performer had their own unique style and signature illusions. Adapting to survive the competition meant regularly honing their craft, developing new tricks, and devising fresh, unprecedented forms of entertainment that would captivate and astound audiences anew. The competitive spirit spurred magicians to look within and dig deeper into their creativity, sometimes leading them to explore uncharted territories in the realm of magical arts. Moreover, the need to stand out often sparked intense rivalries among illusionists, culminating in legendary duels and public feuds that fueled the passion for their art. It was a time of daredevilry and bold experimentation as magicians dared to push the boundaries further, reaching for the unattainable and crafting spectacles that would amaze even the most skeptical minds. As they adapted and evolved, magicians not only battled on stage but also behind the scenes, securing prime venues and negotiating complex contracts to ensure they stayed at the top of their game. Adapting to survive the competition was more than just about securing one's place in the limelight; it was about leaving an indelible mark on the history of magic and cementing a legacy that would endure the test of time.

Personal Reflections

As the magic community entered an era of intense competition, many illusionists found themselves reflecting on their personal journeys. The pressure to innovate and captivate audiences led to moments of introspection and self-doubt. Illusionists began to question their purpose and legacy, considering the impact they hoped to leave on the world of magic. It was a time of deep contemplation, as magicians grappled with the shifting tides of public perception and the relentless pursuit of excellence. Each performer sought to carve out a distinctive identity while navigating the treacherous waters of rivalry and aspiration. Amidst the fervent quest for supremacy, personal reflections often delved into the emotional toll of competing in an unforgiving industry. The unrelenting schedule of performances, the cutthroat nature of backstage politics, and the ever-present specter of failure weighed heavily on the hearts and minds of illusionists. These reflections revealed the raw, vulnerable side of artists who poured their souls into crafting magical experiences for their audiences, day after day. Moreover, personal reflections extended beyond the confines of professional challenges, encompassing the intricate tapestry of an illusionist's personal life. Family dynamics, friendships, and the pursuit of balance amidst the demands of fame and fortune were all integral facets of this introspective journey. Magicians grappled with the need to maintain authenticity while adapting to the evolving landscape of the entertainment industry. Through these personal reflections, they uncovered the profound interplay between artistry and the human experience. Despite the tumultuous nature of the 'magic wars,' these personal reflections also unearthed moments of resilience and strength. Illusionists discovered newfound depths within themselves, drawing inspiration from their struggles and triumphs. They celebrated the unwavering passion that fueled their artistic pursuits and embraced the interconnectedness of the magic community. Ultimately, these personal reflections served as a testament to the indomitable spirit of those who dared to weave enchantment into the fabric of reality. In recounting their personal reflections, illusionists forged an enduring bond with their craft, acknowledging the transformative power of magic as a force capable of transcending barriers and touching the hearts of audiences worldwide. These introspective musings laid the foundation for what would become known as the golden era of magic—a period defined by innovation, camaraderie, and a collective commitment to elevating the art form to unprecedented heights.

Setting the Stage for a Golden Era

As I reflect on the turbulent times of magic wars and intense rivalry among illusionists, it becomes clear that those challenges paved the way for what would be known as the golden era of magic. The personal reflections shared by renowned magicians during this era reveal a deep sense of camaraderie, mutual respect, and an unwavering commitment to elevating the art form. It was at this juncture that the stage was being set for a period marked by unprecedented creativity, innovation, and a renewed public fascination with magic. The intense competition from the magic wars spurred a spirit of innovation unlike anything seen before. Magicians sought to push boundaries, not only in the technical execution of illusions but also in storytelling and theatricality. This period witnessed the birth of iconic illusions that continue to captivate audiences to this day, demonstrating the enduring legacy of this golden era. Illusionists tirelessly worked to infuse their performances with a sense of wonder, pushing the limits of human imagination and defying what was previously thought impossible. Moreover, the era's emphasis on collaboration and mentorship created an environment where experienced magicians took aspiring talents under their wings, nurturing the next generation of performers. This passing down of knowledge and refinement of techniques added depth and sophistication to the art of magic, ensuring its longevity and relevance in an ever-changing world. The heightened public interest in magic during this era cannot be overstated. The allure of mystery and the unexplainable captured the collective imagination, leading to a widespread embrace of magic as a legitimate and culturally significant form of entertainment. The golden era saw magic transition from being perceived as mere trickery to a respected and revered art form that transcended language, culture, and socio-economic barriers. Furthermore, advancements in stagecraft and technology played a pivotal role in propelling magic into the mainstream. Innovations in lighting, sound, and special effects transformed magic performances into immersive spectacles, captivating audiences on a grand scale. The convergence of artistry and technical wizardry defined this transformative period, establishing magic as a truly multi-sensory experience that left a lasting impact. In closing, the chapter of 'Magic Wars' ultimately sowed the seeds for a golden era that reshaped the landscape of magic. It was a time characterized by collaboration, ingenuity, and an unwavering dedication to the craft. As we delve deeper into this wondrous period, we begin to understand how the collective passion and perseverance of magicians laid the foundation for a renaissance in the art of magic—the echoes of which continue to resonate through the corridors of history.

The Golden Age of Magic

Introduction to the Golden Era

The Golden Era of magic represents a pivotal period in history when the art form transcended its previous boundaries and became an integral part of popular culture. This era, which spanned from the late 19th century into the early 20th century, saw a remarkable surge in the public's interest and fascination with magic. It signified not only a shift in how magic was perceived but also a transformation in the way magicians embraced their craft and interacted with their audiences. The period marked a departure from the more exclusive and secretive nature of magic, opening its doors to a wider audience and garnering widespread appreciation. The Golden Era was characterized by a merging of innovation, showmanship, and a heightened sense of wonder that captivated audiences across the globe. Magicians of this time were instrumental in redefining the art form, pushing boundaries, and pioneering new techniques that set the stage for modern magic as we know it today. Furthermore, the Golden Era witnessed a significant cultural shift that elevated magic to a status enjoyed by few other forms of entertainment, positioning it as a source of awe, inspiration, and sheer delight for people from all walks of life. This section will delve into the societal factors and emergent trends that contributed to the meteoric rise of magic, shedding light on its ascent from niche amusement to mainstream fascination. By examining the historical context and key influencers of this era, we can gain a more profound understanding of how magic transitioned from an esoteric pursuit to a global phenomenon with enduring appeal.

Cultural Shifts and Magic's Ascendancy

During the Golden Age of Magic, cultural shifts had a profound impact on the ascendancy of magic as an art form and entertainment. As society evolved, so did the preferences of the audience, sparking a heightened interest in the enigmatic allure of magic. The late 19th and early 20th centuries were marked by significant advancements in technology, rapid urbanization, and a growing fascination with the unknown. Amidst this backdrop, magic captured the imaginations of people from all walks of life, offering an escape from the rigors of industrialized living. As the world transformed, so did the role of magicians, who became cultural icons and purveyors of wonder. This era saw a convergence of diverse cultures, ideas, and beliefs, fostering a fertile environment for the propagation of magic. Magicians leveraged these cultural shifts to craft performances that resonated with audiences on a deep, visceral level. They tapped into the collective yearning for magic and mystery, embedding their acts within the prevailing zeitgeist. The ascendancy of magic during this period was not merely a novelty, but a reflection of societal values and aspirations. Magicians rose to prominence as arbiters of imagination, enchanting audiences with their ability to defy the laws of nature and transport them to realms beyond the mundane. The golden era of magic witnessed an unprecedented surge in the popularity of live performances, captivating theaters and venues worldwide. Audiences flocked to witness spectacles that defied conventional reasoning, seeking respite from the tumultuous realities of an ever-changing world. The cultural significance of magic's ascendancy cannot be overstated, as it mirrored the collective desire for escapism, wonder, and a renewed sense of awe in an increasingly mechanized society. In essence, this era marks a pivotal point in history where magic transcended mere entertainment, becoming a symbolic representation of humanity's enduring thirst for the extraordinary.

Notable Magicians of the Time

During the Golden Age of Magic, numerous remarkable magicians emerged, leaving an indelible mark on the global landscape of conjuring arts. Their contributions not only entertained audiences but also shaped the future of magic as an art form. One such luminary of the era was Jean Eugène Robert-Houdin, often hailed as the 'Father of Modern Magic'. His innovative approach to magic and his rejection of traditional wizard garb in favor of formal attire set the stage for modern magicians. Robert-Houdin's influence extended beyond his captivating illusions; he also authored books and treatises that enriched the theoretical underpinnings of magic. Another iconic figure was Harry Houdini, renowned for his daring escape acts and ability to mesmerize audiences with his stunts. Beyond his performances, Houdini championed the rights and recognition of magicians, advocating for ethical standards and helping elevate magic to a respected profession. In England, John Nevil Maskelyne and George Alfred Cooke established the Egyptian Hall as a prominent venue for magic, where they dazzled audiences with their groundbreaking acts and inventions. Across the Atlantic, Howard Thurston gained fame for his grand-scale illusions and theatrics, captivating crowds with his eloquence and showmanship. Furthermore, Adelaide Herrmann, known as the 'Queen of Magic', broke gender barriers in the male-dominated world of magic, carving her own place through her mastery of classic illusions and captivating stage presence. The roster of exceptional magicians during this period is extensive, from Harry Kellar to Chung Ling Soo, each contributing unique styles and innovations to the rich tapestry of magic. Their enduring legacies continue to inspire and inform modern magicians, ensuring that the golden era's enchanting spirit lives on in the contemporary world of magic.

Innovation and Creativity in Magic

Innovation and creativity have always been at the heart of magical performances. During the Golden Age of Magic, magicians pushed the boundaries of what was possible, constantly seeking to amaze and enthrall their audiences. One significant aspect of this innovation was the development of new illusions and tricks that had never been seen before. Magicians like Harry Houdini, Howard Thurston, and Harry Kellar pioneered a wave of novel effects that captivated spectators and left them in awe. These performers were relentless in their pursuit of originality, dedicating countless hours to perfecting their craft and introducing never-before-seen feats. Furthermore, technical advancements in stagecraft and theatrical effects allowed magicians to create increasingly grand and spectacular spectacles, elevating magic to a level previously unattainable. Moreover, the era saw a surge in interdisciplinary collaboration, as magicians drew inspiration from fields such as engineering, psychology, and art. This interdisciplinary approach facilitated the creation of groundbreaking illusions that seemed to defy logic and reason. For instance, the inventive use of lighting, mirrors, and mechanical contraptions brought to life illusions that astonished audiences and sparked a sense of wonder. Magicians also delved into the realms of psychology and perception, leveraging their understanding of human cognition to devise illusions that played with the audience's senses and challenged their notions of reality. It was a period of exploration and experimentation, where magicians fearlessly ventured into uncharted territory, driven by an unyielding desire to push the boundaries of what magic could achieve. Additionally, the Golden Age of Magic witnessed a surge in the integration of storytelling and narrative into magical performances. Magicians realized that the power of narrative could profoundly enhance the emotional and psychological impact of their acts. By weaving compelling stories into their illusions, they were able to transport audiences to fantastical realms and create a sense of enchantment. This innovative marriage of storytelling and magic elevated the art form, transforming it into a multifaceted experience that engaged both the intellect and the emotions of the viewers. The spirit of innovation and creativity during this era not only revolutionized magical performances but also laid the foundation for the modern conception of magic as an art form. The enduring influence of the innovations introduced during the Golden Age continues to resonate in contemporary magic, serving as a testament to the boundless ingenuity and imagination of the magicians who shaped this remarkable period.

Magic as Entertainment: Theaters and Venues

During the Golden Age of Magic, theaters and performance venues played a significant role in shaping the landscape of magic entertainment. Magicians were not only masters of illusion; they were also captivating performers who knew how to command an audience's attention within these spaces. Theaters became enchanted realms where the impossible seemed possible, and audiences eagerly anticipated the thrill of witnessing extraordinary feats on stage. With the emergence of grand theaters, magicians had a platform to showcase their artistry on a scale never seen before. These majestic settings provided the perfect backdrop for creating an immersive and unforgettable magical experience. In cities around the world, theaters dedicated specifically to magic performances began to emerge. These venues became hubs for both established magicians and rising stars to showcase their skills. Audiences flocked to these theaters, eager to witness mesmerizing illusions and breathtaking acts of prestidigitation. Each theater carried its own unique atmosphere, often enhancing the sense of wonder and mystery that surrounded the art of magic. Additionally, these venues allowed magicians to experiment with new effects, push the boundaries of their craft, and continually innovate to captivate their audiences. One of the most remarkable aspects of magic in theaters was the interaction between performer and spectator. Unlike other forms of entertainment, magic thrived on the ability to directly engage and involve the audience. Whether it was a magician performing intimate close-up magic or executing awe-inspiring illusions on a larger scale, the theatrical setting provided the perfect space for fostering a sense of wonder and enchantment among the spectators. The shared experience of witnessing magic live in a theater setting created an indelible connection between the performer and the audience, fostering a profound appreciation for the art form. Moreover, the theaters themselves underwent transformations to accommodate the intricate technical requirements of magic performances. Elaborate stage designs, concealed trapdoors, and state-of-the-art lighting and sound systems became essential elements in bringing the illusions to life on stage. These innovations not only elevated the quality of the performances but also contributed to the overall spectacle and allure of the magic shows. As the popularity of magic continued to soar during this era, theaters and venues became focal points for the convergence of diverse magical traditions from around the world. This international exchange of ideas and techniques enriched the art of magic, leading to the evolution of new styles and approaches to captivating an audience. Magicians from different cultures and backgrounds brought their distinctive influences to these theaters, resulting in a vibrant tapestry of magical performances that transcended geographical boundaries.

The International Exchange of Ideas

During the Golden Age of Magic, there was a remarkable exchange of ideas and techniques that transcended geographical boundaries. Magicians traveled extensively, learning from their peers and adapting their acts to incorporate new illusions and sleight of hand methods. This international exchange enriched the art of magic, infusing it with diverse cultural influences and captivating performances. One of the key drivers of this exchange was the rise of vaudeville circuits and variety shows across Europe and North America. These platforms provided magicians with opportunities to showcase their talents to diverse audiences and connect with other performers from around the world. As they traversed continents, magicians encountered different styles of magic, presentation techniques, and stagecraft, leading to a melting pot of magical innovation. The emergence of international magic conventions further fostered collaboration and the sharing of knowledge among magicians. These gatherings became pivotal events where magicians from various countries could come together to demonstrate their latest feats, discuss new trends, and learn from one another. The camaraderie and mutual respect within the magical community spurred the cross-pollination of ideas that propelled the art form to unprecedented heights. Additionally, the advent of mass communication, such as the dissemination of magic magazines and journals, played a crucial role in disseminating magical innovations. Magicians could now keep abreast of developments in the field, no matter where they were based, and draw inspiration from the work of their counterparts across oceans and continents. Furthermore, international tours by renowned magicians contributed to the global spread of magical practices. These tours not only exposed audiences to diverse styles of magic but also facilitated cultural exchanges, as magicians incorporated elements from different traditions into their acts, thus broadening the appeal and impact of their performances. The spirit of collaboration and cross-cultural exchange during the Golden Age of Magic left an indelible mark on the art form, influencing the evolution of magic for generations to come. The diverse influences and innovative techniques that emerged from this era continue to shape the modern landscape of magic, exemplifying the enduring impact of the international exchange of ideas.

Audience Reactions and Public Perception

In the Golden Age of Magic, audience reactions played a pivotal role in shaping the public perception of magicians and their craft. Spectators were captivated by the extraordinary feats performed by magicians, fostering a sense of awe and wonder that transcended societal divides. The palpable anticipation and gasps of amazement that filled the air in theaters and venues were indicative of the profound impact magic had on audiences of all ages and backgrounds. Magicians became cultural icons, captivating the hearts and minds of the public with their astonishing acts. Audience reactions varied from sheer disbelief to unbridled joy. Witnessing seemingly impossible illusions and mind-boggling escapades, spectators were left spellbound, pondering the mysteries that unfolded before their eyes. The art of magic not only evoked wonderment but also sparked conversations, debates, and fervent curiosity. The public perception of magic evolved from mere entertainment to a form of enchantment that enraptured the collective imagination. Moreover, the emotional resonance of magic performances cannot be understated. The gasps, applause, and exclamations from the audience mirrored the deep connection between magician and spectator. Through innovative storytelling and captivating showmanship, magicians wove an intricate tapestry of emotions, eliciting laughter, astonishment, and sometimes even contemplation. These intimate connections forged an indelible bond between performers and their audience, elevating magic beyond mere tricks to an immersive, emotionally charged experience. Yet, alongside adoration, there existed skepticism and scrutiny. Some skeptics sought to demystify magic, dissecting illusions in an attempt to unravel the secrets behind the spectacle. Nonetheless, such skepticism only served to elevate the artistry of magicians, pushing them to further innovate and create illusions that defied explanation. The interplay between skepticism and belief underscored the complex fabric of public perception surrounding magic. In the realm of public perception, the Golden Age of Magic marked a turning point. Magicians transitioned from mere entertainers to revered figures capable of enchanting and inspiring generations. The lasting impact of audience reactions and public perception during this era continues to shape the legacy of magic, cementing its status as a timeless art form that transcends boundaries and captivates the human spirit.

Magic in Print Media and Publications

During the Golden Age of Magic, the evolution of magic in print media and publications played a pivotal role in shaping the perception and dissemination of magical knowledge. Magicians, eager to share their craft, penned countless books, journals, and periodicals dedicated to the art of illusion. These publications became invaluable resources for aspiring magicians, providing detailed instructions, historical insights, and theoretical discourses on the intricacies of magic. By documenting and sharing their expertise, these luminaries made significant contributions to the preservation and advancement of magical arts. One of the most influential publications of the era was 'The Conjuror's Magazine,' a groundbreaking periodical that provided a platform for magicians to exchange ideas and showcase their latest creations. This periodical not only fostered a sense of community among magicians but also facilitated the widespread dissemination of new techniques and illusions. As magicians eagerly awaited each issue, they were inspired by the innovative content, fueling a resurgence of creativity and experimentation within the magical community. In addition to periodicals, the publication of comprehensive magic books became increasingly popular. Renowned magicians authored instructional works that chronicled their most renowned acts and divulged closely guarded secrets of their trade. These volumes, meticulously detailed and illustrated, served as indispensable learning tools for budding magicians, offering step-by-step guides to mastering the art of prestidigitation and illusion. Moreover, these books provided insight into the ethos and philosophy of magic, enlightening readers about the dedication and discipline required to excel in the magical arts. Furthermore, the proliferation of print media enabled magicians to transcend geographical boundaries, allowing their magical expertise to reach audiences far and wide. As transatlantic voyages and global communication networks expanded, magic publications became instrumental in fostering an international exchange of magical knowledge. Magicians from diverse cultural backgrounds shared their unique perspectives, enriching the global magical landscape with a tapestry of traditions, techniques, and performance styles. The impact of magic in print media also reverberated beyond the confines of the magical community, captivating the public imagination and elevating magic to a revered form of entertainment. The publication of exposés and articles detailing the wonders of magic captivated readers, sparking widespread fascination with the enigmatic world of illusion. Thus, the convergence of magic and print media not only elevated the status of magicians but also generated enthusiasm for magic as a source of wonder and enchantment among the general populace. In retrospect, the proliferation of magic in print media during the Golden Age of Magic stands as a testament to the enduring allure and cultural significance of the magical arts. Through their publications, magicians indelibly shaped the history of magic, fostering a legacy that continues to inspire and captivate audiences worldwide.

Challenges Faced and Overcome

The Golden Age of Magic was not without its fair share of challenges. As magic gained popularity, it also faced scrutiny and skepticism from various quarters. Magicians encountered resistance from traditionalists who viewed magic as mere trickery and deception. Additionally, there were challenges in maintaining the secrecy and exclusivity of magical techniques, especially with the proliferation of exposés and unauthorized disclosures. Furthermore, the competition among magicians during this era was fierce. Each performer endeavored to outdo their peers, leading to an arms race of innovation and showmanship. This intense rivalry drove magicians to continuously push the boundaries of what was deemed possible, resulting in groundbreaking illusions and performances. However, this competitive environment also heightened the pressure on magicians, requiring them to consistently deliver awe-inspiring feats to captivate audiences. Beyond internal competition, magicians also grappled with external factors such as technological advancements and changing audience tastes. The emergence of new technologies posed a threat to traditional magic acts, compelling magicians to adapt and integrate modern elements into their performances. Moreover, evolving audience preferences demanded that magicians evolve their storytelling and presentation styles to remain relevant and engaging. Amidst these challenges, the resilience and determination of magicians shone through. They harnessed adversity as a catalyst for innovation, leading to the development of new magical techniques and the revitalization of classic illusions. Magicians also formed tight-knit communities to support and learn from one another, fostering a spirit of collaboration amidst the competitive backdrop. Through collective efforts, they endeavored to preserve the artistry and wonder of magic in the face of mounting obstacles. Ultimately, the challenges encountered during the Golden Age of Magic became transformative opportunities for growth and evolution within the magical community. Magicians overcame these hurdles by embracing change, upholding the allure of mystique, and reaffirming the timeless appeal of enchantment. Their resilience and creativity laid the foundation for the enduring legacy that continues to inspire and captivate audiences to this day.

Legacy of the Golden Age

The legacy of the Golden Age of Magic continues to cast a profound influence on modern magic and entertainment as a whole. The innovations, creativity, and cultural impact of this era have reverberated through time, shaping the very essence of what magic represents today. At its core, the legacy of the Golden Age lies in the transformation of magic from mere trickery to a sophisticated art form that captivated audiences and elevated performers to legendary status. One of the most enduring legacies of this era is the elevation of magicians to the realm of respected artists. Magicians during the Golden Age were no longer perceived simply as purveyors of illusions, but as creators of awe-inspiring experiences that transcended the boundaries of reality. This shift in perception laid the foundation for the modern appreciation of magic as a legitimate and respected form of entertainment and artistic expression. Furthermore, the Golden Age engendered a spirit of innovation and creativity that continues to drive the evolution of magic. Pioneering magicians of the time broke new ground in developing elaborate illusions, pioneering techniques, and pushing the boundaries of what was thought possible. Their willingness to experiment and take risks set a precedent for future generations of magicians, inspiring them to constantly push the limits of magical performance. The Golden Age also left an indelible mark on the public's perception of magic. The mystique and allure surrounding the great magicians of this era captured the imagination of society at large, embedding magic into the cultural fabric. The enduring fascination with magic as a form of entertainment can be traced back to the profound impact of the Golden Age, where it became an integral part of mainstream culture. Moreover, the international exchange of ideas during the Golden Age facilitated the global dissemination of magical techniques and performances. This cross-pollination of styles and influences enriched the diversity of magical acts, leading to a rich tapestry of traditions and practices that continues to shape magic around the world. In conclusion, the legacy of the Golden Age of Magic is nothing short of enduring. Its influence permeates every facet of contemporary magic, from the public's perception to the art form's innovative spirit. By recognizing and understanding the profound impact of this era, we gain a deeper appreciation for the magic we experience today, paying homage to the individuals and cultural shifts that have shaped magic into the awe-inspiring spectacle it is.

Magic's Popularity Boom

Laying the Groundwork for Magic's Surge

The rise of magic in popular culture was not an accident, but a carefully cultivated phenomenon. It sprung from a complex tapestry woven with threads of societal fascination, technological innovation, and evolving artistic expression. At its core, the surge of interest in magic was a reflection of the human desire to transcend the ordinary—to experience wonder and awe in a world that was rapidly changing. During this transformative era, the world was experiencing profound shifts. Industrialization had ushered in an age of rapid progress and innovation, leading many to seek moments of enchantment and escape from the mundane. The allure of magic offered a chance to suspend disbelief and be transported to realms where the impossible became possible. As cities grew and societies evolved, the hunger for entertainment and diversion intensified, creating fertile ground for the growth of magic as a form of popular amusement and cultural spectacle. Central to this surge was the deep-seated human yearning for the mystical and the mysterious—elements that magic encapsulated and presented in captivating ways. Magicians, with their ability to astound and confound, tapped into this primal fascination, leveraging it as a potent force in shaping the public's appetite for extraordinary experiences. Furthermore, the rise of magic was intertwined with the expansion of mass media and communication channels. Through newspapers, posters, and word of mouth, stories of magical feats captured the imagination of audiences on a global scale. These tales served to fuel the growing appetite for wonder and spectacle, propelling magic into the spotlight of public consciousness. Additionally, the burgeoning middle class sought out new forms of entertainment, driving demand for more accessible and diverse performance art. Through innovative marketing and strategic alliances with emerging entertainment venues, magicians found themselves poised to capture the hearts and minds of a burgeoning audience eager for enchantment and diversion. As magic continued to enthrall and captivate, it also symbolized a departure from the rigidity of societal norms and orthodoxies—a rebellion against the confines of everyday life. It represented a powerful assertion of the human spirit's capacity to dream, imagine, and believe in the extraordinary. In essence, the groundwork for magic's surge was laid upon the rich soil of human curiosity, aspiration, and a collective thirst for wonder.

Cultural Context: Why the World Embraced Illusion

The embrace of illusion and magic by cultures across the world has deep roots in human history. From ancient civilizations to modern societies, the allure of magic has been a consistent thread woven into the fabric of human experience. At its core, the fascination with magic reflects the universal desire to transcend the limits of the ordinary, to momentarily escape the constraints of reality and immerse oneself in a world where the impossible becomes possible. One pivotal cultural aspect that contributed to the widespread embrace of magic is the intrinsic human yearning for wonder and enchantment. Throughout history, individuals have sought refuge from the mundane and the predictable, gravitating towards experiences that ignite their imaginations and awaken a sense of childlike awe. Magic, with its capacity to defy logic and challenge perceptions, taps into this innate craving for amazement, offering an immersive escape into realms of mystery and fascination. Furthermore, the evolution and dissemination of cultural folklore and mythology have played a significant role in shaping the receptivity to magic. Across diverse societies, tales of mythical beings and extraordinary feats have been woven into the collective consciousness, fostering an environment conducive to accepting the unexplainable and the wondrous. This rich tapestry of storytelling has primed audiences to suspend disbelief and entertain the possibility that there are forces beyond comprehension at play in the world. Every culture has its own unique traditions, rituals, and ceremonies, many of which integrate elements of illusion and magic. These practices serve as conduits for communities to connect with the mystical and the supernatural, fostering a sense of unity and collective wonder. Whether through shamanic performances, religious rites, or celebratory festivities, the rhythmic pulse of magical expression beats within the heart of human culture, resonating with people on a profound level. In addition to a steadfast connection to tradition, the embrace of illusion is also a testament to society's enduring quest for entertainment and diversion. Amidst the trials and tribulations of life, individuals seek avenues for respite, seeking out spectacles and diversions that offer reprieve from the rigors of existence. Magic, with its spellbinding allure and spectacle-driven nature, has emerged as a timeless source of joy and distraction, captivating audiences with displays of skill, wit, and mystery. Over time, the propagation of magic has transcended geographical boundaries, weaving itself into the global tapestry of human experience. The universal appeal of magic speaks to its status as a cultural unifier, transcending language barriers and ideological divides to unite people in shared moments of wonder and astonishment. Thus, the widespread embrace of illusion can be understood as a testament to the enduring allure of magic, serving as a testament to the profound impact that the art form exerts on the human spirit.

The Role of Technological Advancements

During the period when magic experienced a surge in popularity, technological advancements played a pivotal role in shaping the landscape of performance art. The advent of new technologies not only expanded the possibilities for magicians but also captivated audiences with previously unimaginable spectacles. Innovations in lighting, sound amplification, and special effects revolutionized the presentation of magic, elevating it from humble street performances to grand theatrical productions. Magicians increasingly incorporated these technological marvels into their acts, dazzling spectators with the seamless integration of traditional sleight of hand and cutting-edge innovation. Furthermore, the emergence of photography and cinematography provided magicians with new mediums through which they could reach and mystify larger audiences. Whether through posters advertising their upcoming shows or mesmerizing short films showcasing their illusions, magicians leveraged these visual mediums to spark intrigue and draw crowds. Additionally, the rise of mass communication, including newspapers and telegraph systems, enabled magicians to publicize their performances on a scale never before seen. This newfound ability to swiftly disseminate news of their extraordinary feats meant that magicians could capture the imaginations of people across vast distances, ultimately contributing to the global diffusion of magical experiences. Beyond the realm of performance, technological advancements also impacted the development of magical apparatus. Innovations in engineering and materials led to the creation of intricate devices that transformed the execution of illusions. From elaborate stage contraptions to ingeniously designed props, these advancements afforded magicians the means to weave even more enchanting narratives and leave audiences spellbound. Moreover, the increasing accessibility of travel due to advancements in transportation facilitated the cross-pollination of magical techniques and styles across different regions. Magicians had the opportunity to learn from diverse sources and merge various cultural influences into their performances, further enriching the tapestry of magical expression. In essence, technological advancements during this era not only propelled the art of magic to new heights of wonder and precision but also deeply intertwined it with the broader currents of societal progress and innovation.

Influence of Urbanization and Global Travel

Urbanization and global travel played pivotal roles in the unprecedented surge of magic's popularity during this era. As cities expanded and transformed into bustling metropolises, the demand for entertainment grew exponentially. The rapid influx of diverse cultures and traditions due to global travel brought about a fascination with exotic performances and mysticism, fueling the public's insatiable thirst for wonder and enchantment. Magicians seized this opportunity to captivate audiences with their mesmerizing acts, leveraging the allure of unfamiliar and enigmatic concepts from distant lands. The intertwining of various cultural influences within urban landscapes provided a fertile ground for magic to flourish, as it became a form of escapism, transporting city-dwellers from the mundane reality of daily life into realms of awe and disbelief. The captivating allure of illusions and sleight of hand offered a temporary respite from the rapid industrialization and urban chaos, providing a source of amazement and relief to those yearning for moments of transcendence. Furthermore, the expansion of transportation networks and means of travel facilitated the proliferation of magic across borders and continents. As magicians traveled far and wide, their performances transcended geographical boundaries, enchanting audiences with their artistry and adding an air of mystique to the experience of global exploration. Their acts became intricately intertwined with the narratives of cosmopolitan adventure, enriching the cultural tapestry of each destination they graced with their presence. The influence of urbanization and global travel on the rise of magic cannot be overstated, as they not only provided platforms for performances but also nurtured a deep-seated curiosity and appreciation for the extraordinary. These developments set the stage for an era where magic captured the collective imagination of urban societies and traversed the globe, leaving an indelible mark on the cultural landscape of the time.

Iconic Venues and Performances

During the period of magic's unprecedented popularity boom, several iconic venues emerged as the heart of mesmerizing performances. These hallowed stages, adorned with opulence and mystique, played host to some of the most captivating acts the world had ever seen. From the grandeur of opera houses to the intimacy of vaudeville theaters, magic found a home in a myriad of settings, each adding its own unique charm to the art form. One such venue that became synonymous with magical spectacle was the renowned Grand Théâtre de Bordeaux in France. The ornate architecture of this historic theater provided a breathtaking backdrop for the illusions crafted by pioneering magicians. Audiences were enthralled as they witnessed the convergence of artistry and mystery within its hallowed walls. Across the Atlantic, the esteemed Orpheum Theatre in New York City stood as a beacon of wonder and enchantment. Magicians from far and wide aspired to grace its stage, knowing that their performances would be elevated by the theater's illustrious reputation. From vanishing acts to daring escapology, the Orpheum Theatre bore witness to an array of spellbinding feats that left spectators spellbound. Beyond the brick-and-mortar venues, outdoor settings also witnessed the allure of magic. The exotic gardens of European palaces and the bustling squares of emerging metropolises served as enchanting backdrops for open-air performances. The juxtaposition of natural beauty and otherworldly illusions added an extra layer of enchantment to these shows, imprinting indelible memories upon audiences. Moreover, the advent of the traveling magic show brought enchantment to towns and cities that had never before experienced such wonder. Across continents, street corners transformed into impromptu stages where magicians wove their spells, capturing the imaginations of onlookers and sparking a newfound fascination with the art of illusion. These iconic venues and performances not only showcased the artistic prowess of magicians but also fostered a sense of community and shared wonder among attendees. As the curtains rose and the spotlights danced across the stage, the amalgamation of talent, ambiance, and sheer magic created an atmosphere that transcended the ordinary, transporting all who bore witness to a realm where the impossible became possible.

Captivating the Upper Class

The allure of magic extended its captivating embrace to the refined circles of the upper class during this era. As society's elite indulged in opulent gatherings and illustrious events, the presence of renowned magicians added an extra layer of prestige and fascination. Magicians were not merely entertainers; they were revered as purveyors of wonder and mystery, enhancing the sophistication and allure of high-society affairs. The participation of the upper class in magic performances was more than a simple spectacle. It became a culture—a mark of discernment and distinction. Hosting a celebrated magician at a lavish party or soirée was a statement of elevated taste and sophistication. The enigmatic allure of magic intertwined seamlessly with the refined tastes of the aristocracy, creating an atmosphere steeped in elegance and exclusivity. With their impeccable artistry and mesmerizing performances, magicians held court in the opulent salons and grand ballrooms of nobility. Their demonstrations of illusion and sleight of hand commingled seamlessly with the ambiance of luxury and refinement. The presence of these esteemed conjurors elevated the status of any gathering, leaving a lasting impression on those fortunate enough to witness their incredible displays of skill and dexterity. The upper class eagerly embraced the enigmatic world of magic, finding respite from the rigid protocol and societal constraints that often defined their lives. Through the artistry of magicians, nobles and aristocrats encountered a realm where disbelief was suspended, allowing them to immerse themselves in an otherworldly experience that transcended the confines of everyday life. This mutual enchantment between the upper echelons of society and the world of magic contributed to the perpetuation of the magician's prestigious standing. The impact of magic on the upper class was profound, influencing not only their leisure activities but also their cultural perspectives. These experiences with magic instilled a sense of awe and wonder, fostering a deeper appreciation for the intricacies of illusion and prestidigitation. The upper class became fervent patrons of the magical arts, supporting the advancement and evolution of magic while elevating its cultural significance to unprecedented heights.

Magic's Appeal to the Masses

Magic has an unmistakable allure that transcends societal boundaries, captivating audiences from all walks of life. The unspoken promise of wonder and impossibility draws the masses into the mesmerizing world of illusion. Unlike many other forms of entertainment, magic possesses the unique ability to unite people through a collective sense of awe and bewilderment. It bridges gaps between different social strata, bringing joy and amazement to diverse audiences. Whether performed on bustling city streets or grand stages, magic's universal appeal lies in its ability to evoke emotions that resonate with individuals and communities alike. The art of magic's appeal to the masses is ingrained in its intrinsic nature as an escape from the rigors of everyday life. For centuries, people have sought refuge in the enchanting realms created by talented magicians. Watching a magic performance is akin to experiencing a shared dream that ignites fascination and sparks conversations among strangers. Regardless of age, gender, or background, spectators find solace and elation in witnessing the impossible come to life before their eyes. This sense of shared wonder fosters a sense of unity and kinship, allowing magic to transcend social barriers and foster a spirit of inclusivity. Amidst the clamor of modern life, magic's ability to captivate the masses serves as a testament to its enduring significance in society. Moreover, the appeal of magic to the masses stems from its capacity to inspire belief in the extraordinary. In an increasingly tumultuous world, the sight of a skilled magician defying the laws of nature offers a respite from the mundane and instills a renewed sense of hope and wonder. By stirring the imagination and challenging perceptions of reality, magic imparts a sense of childlike wonder to audiences young and old. This infusion of optimism and astonishment reignites the innate curiosity and sense of magic that lies dormant within each individual, fostering an environment of collective marvel and delight. As such, magic's appeal to the masses speaks to the timeless human desire for a touch of enchantment in their lives. For centuries, magic has flourished as an art form that transcends cultural and geographic barriers, drawing people together in shared moments of awe and amazement. The enduring appeal of magic to the masses stands as a testament to its profound impact on society, forging connections and sparking joy across diverse communities. From bustling city squares to intimate theaters, the enchanting allure of magic continues to capture the hearts and minds of the masses, weaving a tapestry of wonder that binds humanity in a shared celebration of the inexplicable.

The Power of Publicizing Prestigious Performers

Publicity plays an instrumental role in elevating the status and allure of esteemed magicians. The media, including newspapers, magazines, and burgeoning forms of entertainment dissemination, have been crucial channels for showcasing the dazzling talents of renowned illusionists. Through gripping narratives and captivating imagery, these platforms capture the essence of magic, drawing in audiences and leaving them spellbound. Publicity not only serves as a means of disseminating the wonders of magic to a wider audience, but also immortalizes the mystique of extraordinary performances. The exposure garnered through publicity cements a magician's reputation and can catapult them to stardom. Coverage of their extraordinary feats and charismatic stage presence cultivates an aura of intrigue and fascination, capturing the imagination of the public. As their names become synonymous with mystique and wonder, the public eagerly anticipates their every appearance, fostering a sense of anticipation and excitement that is unparalleled. The power of publicity extends beyond mere promotion; it crafts a narrative around the magician, transforming them into larger-than-life figures whose mystique transcends the boundaries of the stage. Moreover, publicity generates immense interest in the art of magic itself. By spotlighting the exceptional talents and unyielding dedication of these prestigious performers, it inspires a new generation of aspiring magicians. Through compelling stories and awe-inspiring images, budding illusionists are drawn into the enchanting world of magic, fueling their ambition to follow in the footsteps of their revered counterparts. The widespread coverage of celebrated magicians piques curiosity and kindles a fervent passion for the craft, igniting a profound cultural appreciation for the art of magic. Furthermore, the publicizing of prestigious performers has a ripple effect on the entire magical community. It fosters a climate of innovation and excellence, driving magicians to continually push the boundaries of their craft. As their exploits and breakthroughs are broadcast far and wide, the bar for magical prowess is raised, spurring healthy competition and propelling the art to new heights. This wave of creativity and ingenuity fuels the evolution of magic, infusing it with fresh energy and captivating the imaginations of audiences worldwide. In essence, the power of publicizing prestigious performers transcends the confines of traditional promotion; it weaves a tapestry of wonder, inspiration, and aspiration. Through the captivating narratives and breathtaking visuals that grace the public eye, these esteemed magicians become icons of mystery and enchantment, leaving an indelible mark on the cultural fabric. Their influence reverberates through generations, ensuring that the timeless allure of magic continues to captivate and exhilarate.

Celebrated Magicians: Inspiring a New Generation

The era of magic's popularity boom witnessed the emergence of celebrated magicians who left an indelible mark on the art form and captivated audiences worldwide. These influential figures not only entertained with their mesmerizing performances but also inspired a new generation of aspiring illusionists. Their impact resonated far beyond the confines of the stage, shaping the cultural landscape and fueling a renaissance in the world of magic. At the forefront of this movement were magicians whose innovative techniques and charismatic stage presence set them apart. From daring escapologists to masterful mentalists, each performer brought a unique flair to their craft, pushing the boundaries of what was deemed possible and redefining the art of illusion. Their ability to connect with audiences on a profound level created a sense of wonder and fascination, igniting a passion for magic in the hearts of spectators young and old. These celebrated magicians became role models and mentors, offering guidance and inspiration to budding illusionists eager to carve their own path in the enchanting realm of magic. Through their mentorship and instructional materials, they shared their wealth of knowledge and expertise, nurturing the next generation of performers and fostering a sense of community within the magical fraternity. Their dedication to passing on the secrets of their trade ensured that the legacy of magic would continue to thrive and evolve, safeguarding its traditions while embracing innovation. Moreover, the impact of celebrated magicians extended beyond the confines of the theatrical stage, permeating popular culture and influencing artistic expression across various mediums. Their influence could be seen in literature, cinema, and even contemporary music, as the allure of magic captured the imagination of creators and audiences alike. By embodying the essence of wonder and astonishment, these iconic figures transcended the boundaries of entertainment, leaving an enduring legacy that continues to shape the modern landscape of magic. The enduring legacy of celebrated magicians continues to inspire a new generation of enchanters, ensuring that the timeless art of magic will endure for generations to come. Aspiring magicians look to these influential figures as beacons of creativity and distinction, drawing upon their expertise and innovation to push the boundaries of what is possible within the realm of illusion. Through their enduring influence, celebrated magicians have sparked a renaissance in magic, ushering in an era of unprecedented creativity and captivating performances that continue to enrapture audiences around the globe.

Reflections on a Captivated Era

As we reflect on the captivated era of magic's explosive popularity, it becomes evident that the impact of celebrated magicians transcended mere entertainment. Their mesmerizing performances left an indelible mark on society, sparking a collective fascination with illusion and wonder. During this enchanted period, audiences reveled in the thrill of witnessing grand illusions unfold before their very eyes, cultivating a sense of amazement and enchantment that was unparalleled. The influence of these renowned conjurers extended far beyond the confines of the stage, permeating various facets of culture and shaping the zeitgeist of the time. Moreover, the emergence of celebrated magicians instigated a renaissance of creativity within the realm of magic, inspiring a new generation of aspiring illusionists to push the boundaries and redefine what was previously deemed impossible. Through their artistry and innovation, these luminaries instilled an enduring legacy, bestowing upon the world a priceless gift—a timeless tradition of enchantment. The captivated era not only bore witness to the rise of legendary performers but also heralded a new dawn of appreciation for the art form itself. As magicians enthralled audiences from all walks of life, they bridged divides and ignited a shared sense of wonder and excitement, uniting people through the universal language of magic. This captivating epoch etched its mark on history, leaving an unforgettable tapestry of mystique, spectacle, and transcendence. Even today, the echoes of this mesmerizing era continue to reverberate through the annals of time, reminding us of the enduring allure of magic and its profound impact on the human experience.

Innovating the Art

Envisioning a New Era of Magic

Throughout his illustrious career, Alexander Herrmann was driven not only by the desire to perform extraordinary feats of magic, but also by an unwavering commitment to reshape and redefine the art form itself. With an unyielding vision that transcended the boundaries of convention, Herrmann consistently sought to pioneer pioneering techniques and transformations that would captivate and astonish audiences in ways never before seen. His dreams were grand and far-reaching, fueled by an insatiable curiosity and an unrelenting passion for pushing the boundaries of what was perceived as possible within the realm of magic. As he forged ahead, Herrmann emphatically believed in the potential to revolutionize the very essence of magical performance, captivating the hearts and minds of all who experienced his astounding creations. From the intricacies of masterful sleight of hand to the breathtaking illusions that defied logic, Herrmann's relentless pursuit of excellence propelled him to imagine a new era of magic that would leave an indelible mark on the world stage. Each day brought with it a renewed fervor to explore and innovate, and his determination to unlock the secrets of wonderment spurred him to reach unparalleled heights in his artistic endeavors. His visionary leadership in envisioning a new era of magic set a standard that continues to inspire magicians and illusionists to this day, reminding them that the realm of the impossible is merely a canvas waiting to be transformed into breathtaking reality. Herrmann's commitment to reshaping the magical arts transcended mere showmanship; it embodied a deeply-rooted belief that the evolution of magic held the power to uplift and astound audiences across the globe. Through his unwavering dedication to realizing his dreams, Herrmann set in motion a paradigm shift that forever altered the landscape of modern magic, leaving an enduring legacy that continues to ignite the imaginations of countless illusionists who dare to dream as boldly as he did.

Pioneering Techniques and Transformations

In the quest to pave new avenues of wonder and amazement, Alexander Herrmann delved deeply into pioneering techniques and transformations that would redefine the art of magic. His relentless pursuit of pushing boundaries and creating unforgettable experiences led him to explore a myriad of ingenious methods. By immersing himself in the realms of illusion, sleight of hand, and showmanship, Herrmann sought to revolutionize the very essence of magic. Through tireless experimentation, he harnessed the power of innovation to breathe life into illusions that captivated audiences around the world. At the heart of his craft lay the seamless integration of traditional magic with groundbreaking innovations. Herrmann was adamant about preserving the core principles of classic magic while infusing it with a modern twist. This delicate balance not only paid homage to the revered traditions of the art but also propelled magic into an era of unprecedented fascination. His innovative spirit gave rise to a new wave of transformative performances that left spectators spellbound and craving more. Herrmann's journey was marked by the relentless pursuit of perfecting techniques that had never been seen before. He meticulously refined the art of vanishing acts, levitation, and mind-reading, ushering in a revolution of magic that transcended conventional perceptions. By ingeniously crafting and adapting his methods, he cultivated a repertoire of illusions that defied the boundaries of what was deemed possible. The mastery and precision with which Herrmann executed each transformation elevated his performances to unparalleled heights, leaving an indelible mark on the history of magic. In his unyielding dedication to pioneering techniques, Herrman collaborated with fellow innovators and craftsmen who shared his vision. Their collective efforts birthed groundbreaking inventions, from intricately designed props and mechanical marvels to the seamless fusion of technology with age-old wizardry. Each breakthrough introduced an element of novelty and wonder, enhancing the enchantment woven into his performances. The lasting impact of these pioneerings reverberated across the magical community, inspiring future generations to persist in redefining the landscape of illusion and awe. As Herrmann's pioneering techniques and transformations unfolded, they encapsulated the very essence of magic's evolution, heralding an era where the impossible became a tangible reality. His legacy stands as a testament to the enduring influence of a visionary who dared to push the boundaries of wonder, championing the art of magic into unprecedented realms of ingenuity and enchantment.

Blending Tradition with Innovation

Magic has always been rooted in tradition, with centuries of secrets and techniques passed down from one magician to the next. However, the allure of innovation has always beckoned, challenging magicians to push the boundaries of what was once thought impossible. Blending tradition with innovation is a delicate dance, requiring a deep understanding and appreciation of the foundations while daring to explore uncharted territories. In this pursuit, magicians have sought to honor their predecessors while simultaneously introducing groundbreaking methods and effects that captivate modern audiences. This delicate balance between old and new has resulted in some of the most awe-inspiring performances and magical feats ever witnessed. Magicians, throughout history, have revered the classic acts and illusions that have withstood the test of time, infusing them with fresh perspectives and contemporary twists. By marrying traditional elements with innovative approaches, they breathe new life into age-old tricks, ensuring that the essence of magic endures and evolves with each passing generation. Through the artful blending of tradition with innovation, magicians pay homage to the legacy of their craft while paving the way for its continued relevance in today's fast-paced world. Every new innovation stands as a testament to both the ingenuity of the magician and the enduring appeal of magic as an art form. It is through this delicate fusion that the beauty of magic shines brightest, captivating audiences and leaving them spellbound by the seamless convergence of the old and the new.

Crafting the Unseen Wonders

In the world of magic, crafting the unseen wonders is an art that requires a delicate balance of skill, creativity, and a touch of the extraordinary. Magicians take pride in their ability to conceive and bring to life illusions that transcend the boundaries of what is perceivable by the human eye. These unseen wonders hold the power to captivate and mystify audiences with the sheer brilliance of their conception and execution. Crafted with meticulous attention to detail, these illusions blur the line between reality and imagination, leaving spectators spellbound. It is within these unseen wonders that the true essence of magic is unveiled, awakening a sense of wonder and awe in those who bear witness. The process of crafting the unseen wonders involves an intricate fusion of traditional magical techniques with innovative approaches. Magicians draw upon age-old principles of misdirection, sleight of hand, and illusion, infusing them with contemporary allure and sophistication. Each movement, gesture, and prop is meticulously choreographed to create an enchanting spectacle that defies logic and leaves an indelible mark on the mind of the viewer. At the heart of crafting the unseen wonders lies an unwavering dedication to pushing the boundaries of what is achievable within the realm of magic. Magicians pour countless hours into perfecting each aspect of their illusions, from the seamless execution of complex maneuvers to the seamless integration of cutting-edge technology. With an unrelenting quest for perfection, they strive to create experiences that transcend mere entertainment, delving into the realm of profound artistic expression. These unseen wonders also serve as a testament to the resilience and adaptability of the art of magic. As technology advances and societal norms evolve, magicians continue to innovate and redefine what is possible within their craft. The allure of the unseen wonders lies in their timelessness, as they seamlessly integrate traditional charm with modern ingenuity, ensuring that the spirit of magic remains perpetual and relevant in an ever-changing world. Beyond their technical intricacy, the unseen wonders hold a profound emotional resonance, forging an unspoken connection between the magician and the audience. In unveiling these awe-inspiring spectacles, magicians invite viewers to suspend disbelief and embrace the inexplicable, fostering a sense of childlike wonder and enchantment. Throughout history, these unseen wonders have served as conduits for transporting audiences to realms where the impossible becomes tangible, igniting a sense of joy and curiosity that transcends cultural and linguistic barriers. Ultimately, in the realm of magic, crafting the unseen wonders represents an act of pure artistry and storytelling. Magicians harness their boundless imagination to weave narratives that unfold before the eyes of the beholder, leaving an enduring imprint on the collective consciousness. These unseen wonders stand as testaments to the transformative power of magic, illuminating the boundless potential of the human mind and spirit.

The Influence of Emerging Technology

In the ever-evolving world of magic, emerging technology has played a pivotal role in reshaping the art form and pushing the boundaries of what was once considered impossible. With advancements in engineering, digital effects, and specialized materials, magicians have been able to create awe-inspiring spectacles that captivate audiences around the globe. One of the most profound impacts of emerging technology on magic has been the integration of high-tech illusions into live performances. From holographic projections to augmented reality experiences, magicians are using cutting-edge technology to blur the lines between reality and illusion, transporting audiences to otherworldly realms where the laws of physics seem to bend at will. These innovations have not only elevated the visual appeal of magic shows but have also redefined what audiences perceive as magical. Moreover, the rise of social media and online platforms has revolutionized how magicians connect with their fans and share their craft with the world. Through captivating videos and interactive virtual performances, magicians harness the power of technology to engage global audiences, bringing the wonder of magic into the digital age. This accessibility has allowed for a wider appreciation of the art form and has sparked renewed interest in traditional and contemporary magic alike. Additionally, the use of specialized equipment and state-of-the-art tools has empowered magicians to execute feats that were previously deemed unimaginable. From levitating objects with electromagnetic principles to utilizing drones for grand-scale illusions, these technological advancements have broadened the scope of what magicians can achieve, leading to groundbreaking displays of skill and creativity. The synergy between magic and emerging technology has also fostered cross-disciplinary collaborations, as magicians partner with tech innovators to push the boundaries of what is possible. Such partnerships have not only fueled the development of revolutionary illusions but have also inspired a new generation of magicians to blend traditional techniques with cutting-edge inventions, ensuring that the art of magic continues to evolve and enthrall for years to come. Ultimately, the influence of emerging technology on magic has transcended mere spectacle, serving as a catalyst for innovation and redefining the very essence of what it means to experience wonder. As we continue to embrace the ever-changing landscape of technology, one thing remains certain:

the union of magic and innovation will continue to shape the future of this timeless art, captivating and inspiring audiences for generations to come.

Creating the Impossible

In the realm of magic, the concept of creating the impossible forms the cornerstone of a magician's repertoire. It transcends mere illusions and delves into the art of crafting experiences that defy the boundaries of reality. Magicians are artisans of wonder, weaving narratives that challenge the very notion of what is possible. When a magician sets out to create the impossible, they embark on a profound journey of creativity and innovation. This endeavor goes beyond traditional tricks and illusions; it requires a deep understanding of psychology, physics, and the intricacies of human perception. Each element meticulously orchestrated to elevate the audience's experience to new heights of astonishment. The process of crafting the impossible involves meticulous attention to detail. Every movement, every gesture, and every word uttered by the magician is purposefully designed to maintain an air of mystery and captivation. Whether it's making objects vanish into thin air or redefining the laws of physics, these remarkable feats demand dedication, skill, and an unwavering commitment to perfection. Moreover, at the heart of 'creating the impossible' lies the desire to evoke a sense of childlike wonder and enchantment in the audience. It's about igniting the spark of imagination and fostering a belief in the extraordinary. The magician becomes an orchestrator of dreams, intertwining reality with fantasy to transport spectators to a realm where the impossible unfolds before their eyes. Furthermore, the magicians who venture into this terrain often find themselves pushing the boundaries of conventional magic. Innovation becomes their ally as they seek to introduce groundbreaking techniques and effects that redefine the very essence of magic. With a relentless pursuit of the uncharted, they unravel new dimensions of marvel, propelling the art form into uncharted territories. However, creating the impossible isn't solely about the prowess of the magician; it's also a testament to the unwavering fascination and belief of the audience. Their suspension of disbelief, their willingness to be enraptured by the inexplicable, fuels the magic, elevating it to an ethereal realm that transcends conventional comprehension. Ultimately, to create the impossible is to invite the audience into a world where skepticism and cynicism yield to awe and delight. It's an invitation to embrace the unknown, to revel in the enigma, and to celebrate the boundless potential of the human imagination. In doing so, magicians etch their legacy in the annals of time, leaving behind moments of wonder that endure in the hearts and minds of all who bear witness.

Innovations that Changed the Magic Landscape

In the world of magic, innovation has been a driving force behind some of the most remarkable transformations in the art form. Throughout history, numerous innovations have fundamentally altered the landscape of magic, captivating audiences with new wonders and pushing the boundaries of what was once deemed impossible. From the groundbreaking illusions of Jean Eugène Robert-Houdin to the modern marvels of David Copperfield, the evolution of magic has been marked by key innovations that continue to shape the art today. One such pivotal innovation is the development of the levitation illusion. Originally performed using simple mechanisms and hidden supports, the challenge of creating convincing and breathtaking levitation acts spurred magicians to explore new techniques and materials. The quest for the perfect levitation led to the use of advanced engineering, innovative materials, and creative stagecraft, revolutionizing not only the performance of levitation but also inspiring other magicians to push the boundaries of their own illusions. In addition to stage illusions, the introduction of close-up magic as a distinct and compelling form of entertainment was a game-changer for the art of magic. Close-up magicians, such as Dai Vernon and Slydini, brought magic directly to the audience, engaging them with intimate and bewildering displays of skill and dexterity. This shift from grand stage performances to up-close encounters ushered in a new era of interactive and personal magic, captivating audiences in unprecedented ways. Moreover, the advent of multimedia technology brought about a revolution in the presentation of magic. Magicians embraced the possibilities of video projections, LED screens, and digital effects to enhance their performances, creating immersive and visually stunning experiences for their audiences. By seamlessly integrating technology with traditional magic acts, these innovators transformed the way magic was presented, blurring the lines between reality and illusion. Another significant innovation that reshaped the magic landscape was the incorporation of storytelling into magical performances. Magicians such as Juan Tamariz and Derren Brown elevated the art form by weaving intricate narratives into their acts, captivating audiences on a deeper emotional level. Through the power of storytelling, these visionaries transported spectators into a world where wonder and imagination converged, leaving a lasting impact long after the curtains closed. Each of these innovations has left an indelible mark on the rich tapestry of magic, propelling the art form into new realms of creativity and enchantment. As we continue to embrace the spirit of innovation, we honor the trailblazers and visionaries who have forever changed the magic landscape, inspiring future generations to push the boundaries of what is possible and keep the wonder alive.

Collaboration with Visionaries

Collaboration with visionaries has been a defining aspect of Alexander Herrmann's journey in revolutionizing the art of magic. Throughout his illustrious career, Herrmann sought out collaborations with forward-thinking inventors, artists, and engineers who shared his passion for pushing the boundaries of what was thought possible within the realm of illusion and wonder. One of Herrmann's most notable collaborations was with the esteemed inventor and stagecraft innovator, Jean Eugène Robert-Houdin. Their partnership not only paved the way for groundbreaking illusions but also elevated the production value of magic performances. This alliance bore witness to the creation of astonishing effects that had never before graced the stages of Europe. Furthermore, Herrmann's dedication to collaborating with visionaries extended beyond the world of magic. He eagerly engaged with experts in fields such as optics, mechanics, and even psychology, recognizing the multidisciplinary nature of creating truly spellbinding experiences for his audiences. The symbiotic relationship between Herrmann and these visionaries resulted in the development of sophisticated contraptions, intricate stage designs, and awe-inspiring storytelling techniques. Collaborative brainstorming sessions often led to ingenious solutions for overcoming technical limitations and enhancing the emotional impact of the illusions. In reflecting on these collaborations, it becomes evident that Herrmann's openness to innovation and willingness to embrace unconventional ideas allowed him to establish himself as a transformative figure in the history of magic. His ability to harness the collective creativity of diverse talents produced enduring works of art that continue to inspire contemporary magicians and illusionists. Ultimately, collaboration with visionaries was more than a means to an end for Alexander Herrmann; it represented a profound philosophy that celebrated the fusion of artistry, innovation, and human ingenuity. The legacy of these collaborations serves as a testament to the power of unity in crafting experiences that transcend the ordinary and transport audiences into realms of amazement and enchantment.

Audience Reactions to New Marvels

Magic has always had the unique power of evoking awe and wonder in its spectators. As the art of magic continued to evolve, so did the reactions from audiences to the introduction of new marvels. The unveiling of groundbreaking illusions and innovations often left audiences spellbound, their disbelief suspended as they bore witness to feats that seemed to defy the laws of nature. This chapter explores the fascinating and diverse spectrum of emotional and psychological responses elicited by these new marvels. When audiences encounter a revolutionary illusion for the first time, their reactions are a symphony of astonishment, curiosity, and sheer amazement. It is the exhilarating moment when the seemingly impossible becomes a tangible reality before their eyes. Such experiences create lasting memories that continue to astound and inspire. For some spectators, the initial response to witnessing a new marvel may be one of skepticism or disbelief. As the mind grapples with the perceived impossibility of what it has just seen, a sense of wonder unfolds, giving rise to an insatiable desire to unravel the mystery behind the spectacle. This transformative process reflects the unique ability of magic to captivate not only the senses but also the intellect, sparking a quest for understanding and exploration of the unknown. Moreover, audience reactions to new marvels often extend beyond mere fascination. The profound impact of witnessing these extraordinary displays can spark creative inspiration, fueling a desire for personal innovation and artistic expression. Through the lens of these innovative spectacles, observers gain a newfound appreciation for the boundless potential of human creativity and ingenuity. This revelation moves beyond mere entertainment, serving as a source of motivation and empowerment, igniting a thirst for discovery and advancement. Beyond the individual experience, the collective reactions of audiences to new marvels serve as a testament to the universal appeal of magic. Shared moments of astonishment can forge powerful connections among diverse individuals, transcending cultural and societal boundaries. This shared sense of wonder has the power to unite communities and foster a collective appreciation for the art of magic, creating bonds that endure long after the curtains have closed. The enduring legacy of audience reactions to new marvels underscores the timeless allure and significance of magic as a medium that continues to enthrall, inspire, and unite people from all walks of life.

A Legacy of Inspiration and Transformation

The legacy of inspiration and transformation left by Alexander Herrmann's innovative contributions to the art of magic continues to reverberate throughout the centuries. His unyielding dedication to pushing the boundaries of magical performance has indelibly shaped the way modern magicians conceive and execute their craft. As his visionary creations continue to captivate and amaze audiences, they serve as a testament to his enduring influence and creative prowess. Herrmann's inventive techniques and pioneering stagecraft have inspired countless magicians to expand their artistic horizons and challenge conventional norms. By fearlessly exploring new realms of illusion and enchantment, he set a precedent for future generations to embrace innovation as a means of revitalizing the timeless allure of magic. His unwavering commitment to perfection and finesse has not only transformed the very fabric of magical entertainment but also brought about a renaissance in the way magic is perceived and appreciated. The transformative impact of Herrmann's artistic ingenuity extends beyond the realm of traditional magic, transcending cultural and geographical boundaries. His enduring legacy has manifested in the evolution of contemporary magic shows, where his influence can be seen in the seamless fusion of technology, storytelling, and unparalleled showmanship. Magicians today draw inspiration from his legacy, using it as a foundation upon which they build new feats of wonder and mystique. Furthermore, the ethos of collaboration and sharing that underpinned Herrmann's innovative spirit has sparked a collective pursuit of elevating magical performances worldwide. Through partnerships with like-minded visionaries and fostering a supportive community, Herrmann's legacy endures as an emblem of unity and cooperation within the global magic fraternity. As we reflect on Herrmann's enduring legacy, it becomes apparent that his revolutionary approach to magic transcended mere entertainment; it became a source of profound inspiration for generations of aspiring magicians. The transformative impact of his legacy extends to every facet of the art form, serving as a constant reminder that innovation and creativity are the hallmarks of a truly remarkable magician. Alexander Herrmann's legacy will continue to inspire and shape the future landscape of magic, ensuring that his contributions remain integral to the enduring allure of this captivating performing art.

Behind the Curtain: Life Beyond the Stage

A Glimpse of the Man Behind the Mystique

Alexander Herrmann, known to the world as the master magician, demonstrated a duality that was both mesmerizing and captivating. While on stage, he dazzled audiences with his unparalleled showmanship and magical prowess, but beyond the spotlight, there lay a man whose depth and complexity added another layer to his enigmatic allure. Amidst the grandeur of his performances, Alexander displayed an unassuming humility, often choosing solitude over the clamor of adulation. His private persona was marked by introspection, a thoughtful contemplation of life's intricate tapestry that served as a stark contrast to the flamboyant spectacle of his public image.

Family Ties and Relationships

Family relationships are the foundation upon which we build our lives, and for Alexander Herrmann, they were the bedrock of his existence. At the core of his being lay an unwavering devotion to his loved ones, a trait that would become evident through his actions both on and off the stage. His familial ties were not merely relegated to blood relations; instead, they extended to include a close-knit circle of friends and colleagues who became his chosen family. Central to Herrmann's world was his deep bond with his brother, Compars Herrmann, who was not only his mentor but also his lifelong companion. Beyond the confines of their professional partnership, they shared a profound emotional connection that sustained them through triumphs and tribulations alike. It was this unbreakable fraternal bond that fueled their shared pursuit of excellence in the realm of magic, driving them to conquer new heights in their craft. In addition to his brother, Alexander

Herrmann's family extended to his beloved wife, Caroline. Their union was characterized by a rare depth of understanding and companionship, transcending the conventional roles of husband and wife. Caroline's unwavering support and encouragement provided a source of strength for Herrmann, allowing him to flourish in his artistic endeavors. Together, they formed a formidable team, weathering the storms of life with grace and resilience. The familial warmth that emanated from Herrmann extended to his interactions with his fellow magicians and performers. Within the community, he fostered genuine connections and nurtured friendships built on mutual respect and admiration. These relationships, forged amidst the backdrop of shared passion and creativity, served as a source of inspiration and camaraderie for Herrmann, enriching his personal and professional pursuits. Beyond the realms of fame and illusion, it was these familial ties and relationships that shaped Alexander Herrmann's essence, infusing his life with profound meaning and purpose.

The Quiet Moments of Solitude

In the midst of the dazzling lights and thunderous applause, Alexander Herrmann cherished the quiet moments of solitude. Away from the uproar of the stage, he found solace in the tranquility of his own thoughts. Whether it was a peaceful morning stroll or a moment of contemplation before bed, these serene interludes were essential for rejuvenating his spirit. During these tranquil times, Herrmann often sought refuge in nature, finding inspiration in the beauty of the world around him. The gentle sway of the trees, the serenade of birdsong, and the calming rhythm of flowing streams provided him with a sense of peace that transcended the excitement of his performances. These moments allowed him to reflect on his journey, pondering the intricacies of life, love, and the pursuit of happiness. His introspective nature led him to explore the depths of his soul, contemplating his purpose and the impact he wished to leave on the world. While many saw him as a master of illusion, in these solitary moments, he grappled with the very real questions that defined his existence. Despite the demands of his career, Herrmann's commitment to self-reflection and meditation remained unwavering. These quiet moments served as a sanctuary from the relentless pace of fame, offering him a respite from the constant scrutiny and adulation. Here, he found the freedom to simply be, away from the spotlight that so often defined him. In these timeless moments, he rediscovered a sense of balance and harmony, grounding himself in the simple pleasures that nurtured his soul. The quiet moments of solitude were where he found clarity amidst the whirlwind of his extraordinary life. As the world clamored for his attention, these secluded respites became his anchor, providing the strength and wisdom necessary to navigate the complexities of his public persona and his private self. It was within these silent reveries that Alexander Herrmann unearthed the profound truths that shaped his artistry, his relationships, and his legacy.

Passions Beyond Magic

Alexander Herrmann's life was not solely defined by his illustrious career in magic. Behind the curtain, away from the stage's spotlight, Herrmann was a man of multifaceted passions that enriched his existence and inspired those around him. An avid lover of nature, he found solace and rejuvenation amidst the tranquility of the outdoors. Whether it was wandering through lush forests, gazing at the starry expanse of the night sky, or tending to his garden, Herrmann reveled in the beauty and wonder of the natural world. Through his writings and personal accounts, it becomes evident that these encounters with nature provided him with profound inspiration, nurturing his creativity and grounding his spirit. Beyond his magical performances, Herrmann dedicated himself to fostering an appreciation for the arts, supporting aspiring artists, and nurturing their talents. His unwavering belief in the transformative power of art manifested in his fervent advocacy for artistic endeavors, leaving an indelible impact on the cultural landscape. Additionally, Herrmann possessed an insatiable curiosity and a hunger for knowledge. He delved into a diverse array of subjects, from literature and philosophy to science and history, amassing a wealth of wisdom that permeated his conversations and performances. His voracious appetite for learning manifested in his library, a treasure trove of rare manuscripts and volumes that reflected his eclectic interests and intellectual pursuits. Ultimately, Alexander Herrmann's passions transcended the realm of magic, painting a portrait of a man whose ardor for life extended far beyond the confines of his profession, enriching the world around him and echoing through the annals of time.

The Balance Between Fame and Privacy

In the world of magic, Alexander Herrmann captivated audiences with his extraordinary talents, drawing the spotlight onto himself time and again. However, behind the mesmerizing performances and the glittering stage, there existed a delicate equilibrium between his fame and personal privacy. Striking this balance was no small feat for a man whose every move was scrutinized by fans and critics alike. The constant presence of public attention posed a significant challenge as he navigated through his daily life. Nevertheless, Herrmann cherished the moments where he could retreat into a realm of solitude, away from the watchful eyes of the world. It was during these tranquil interludes that he recharged his spirit, finding solace in the simple pleasures of life. Whether it was a quiet walk through nature or engrossing himself in a cherished book, these moments offered respite from the demands of his larger-than-life persona. Despite the allure of fame, he held dear the value of maintaining boundaries around his private affairs. This unwavering dedication to safeguarding his personal life served as a shield against the overwhelming effects of stardom. His deliberate efforts to shield his innermost thoughts from the public gaze underscored the importance of nurturing a sense of self away from the limelight. Moreover, Herrmann understood the significance of finding stillness amidst the clamor of admiration and expectation. Privately, he sought introspection and contemplation, grasping at elusive moments of tranquility that eluded him in the throes of his illustrious career. By meticulously preserving the sanctity of his privacy, he not only forgave himself the space to breathe but also set an example for others grappling with similar challenges in the pursuit of their dreams. As readers immerse themselves in the complexities of Herrmann's quest for equilibrium, they gain insight into the price of fame and the profound impact of safeguarding one's privacy amidst the sea of adoration. With sincerity and vulnerability, this chapter serves as a poignant reminder that even the most celebrated individuals tread the tightrope of balancing fame and privacy, ultimately emerging as symbols of resilience and authenticity.

Cherished Friendships and Bonds

Friendship is an essential thread that weaves through the tapestry of Alexander Herrmann's life. Beyond the stage, beyond the illusions and enigma, lay a man who valued the beauty of human connection. His genuine warmth and kindness endeared him to many, creating a network of cherished friendships and indelible bonds that lasted a lifetime. As he traveled the world, captivating audiences with his magic, Herrmann also cultivated deep relationships with fellow magicians, patrons, and admirers alike. These bonds were not merely transactional or professional; they transcended the realms of magic and touched the core of his being. One cannot reflect on Herrmann's life without unraveling the stories of these treasured friendships. One such friendship that defined Herrmann's life was his enduring camaraderie with the esteemed magician Harry Houdini. Their bond went beyond the shared love for magic; it was a testament to mutual respect and unwavering support. Through their correspondence and collaborations, they found solace in each other's company and fueled each other's creative spirits. Furthermore, throughout his extensive tours, Alexander Herrmann formed lasting connections with individuals from all walks of life. His humility and genuine interest in people endeared him to countless hearts, transcending cultural barriers to create profound friendships. These bonds extended beyond the confines of his profession, blossoming into lifelong associations filled with camaraderie and mutual admiration. Even offstage, Herrmann's gracious nature and infectious enthusiasm forged unbreakable ties with companions who stood by him through triumphs and tribulations. Their unwavering belief in him fuelled his artistry and offered solace in times of struggle. The anecdotes and heartfelt recollections of those whose lives intersected with his are testaments to the impact of Herrmann's friendships on those around him. Their narratives paint a vivid picture of a man whose charisma and compassion left an indelible mark on the lives of many. These friendships were not merely footnotes in his legacy; they were an integral part of the man who continues to enchant and inspire generations of performers and enthusiasts. In commemorating Alexander Herrmann, it is essential to honor the companions who colored the canvas of his existence and enriched his journey with their unwavering support and enduring friendship.

Philosophies and Beliefs

Alexander Herrmann, though known for his captivating mastery of magic on stage, was also a man of profound philosophies and deeply held beliefs. Beyond the allure of illusion, he often contemplated the nature of reality and the human experience. At the core of his beliefs was a profound reverence for wonder and the unseen forces that shape our world. He saw the art of magic not merely as a performance, but as a medium through which to unveil the mysteries that dwell within and around us. In his personal reflections, Herrmann often delved into the interconnectedness of all things, embracing the intricate web of life and the beauty of its complexities. He spoke of the importance of humility in the face of the unknown, emphasizing that the more one learns, the greater the recognition of how much remains beyond our grasp. His musings on the enigma of existence were peppered with an unwavering sense of awe, showcasing a man who sought to inspire awe in others while being overtaken by it himself. His philosophical ruminations extended beyond the ephemeral nature of life and the allure of mystery. With empathy at the forefront, Herrmann explored the significance of compassion, kindness, and understanding in forging meaningful connections with others. He firmly believed that the truest magic lies in the ability to touch the hearts and souls of people, transcending the boundaries of language, culture, and time. Through his writings, it is evident that he viewed every encounter as a chance to invoke joy, provoke contemplation, and leave a lasting imprint on the human spirit. Additionally, Herrmann's spiritual inclinations shaped his worldview, instilling in him a deep respect for the intangible forces that govern the universe. His thoughts on spirituality were not confined to traditional dogmas but rather revolved around the universal essence that unites all living beings. He sought to uncover the ethereal threads that bind humanity, nurturing a spirit of inclusivity and acceptance. This foundation in spiritual interconnectedness permeated every facet of his life, infusing his performances with a sense of reverence for the collective human experience. Ultimately, Alexander Herrmann's personal philosophy encapsulates a profound celebration of the infinite intricacies that define existence. Through his intimate reflections and boundless curiosity, he invites readers to embark on a journey of introspection, urging them to embrace the wondrous spectacle of life with open hearts and unyielding wonder.

Letters and Personal Reflections

Throughout his illustrious career, Alexander Herrmann diligently documented his innermost thoughts and reflections in a series of personal letters and notes. These heartfelt missives offer a poignant insight into the man behind the magician, revealing a profound depth of emotion and introspection that often remained hidden from the adoring public eye. As we delve into these private correspondences, we are granted a rare glimpse into Herrmann's soul, discovering the hopes, dreams, and vulnerabilities that shaped his extraordinary journey. In these letters, penned in moments of quiet contemplation or fervent inspiration, Herrmann bares his raw emotions with an unguarded sincerity, providing an authentic portrayal of his inner world. There is an undeniable sense of intimacy as he shares glimpses of his triumphs, struggles, and personal philosophies, inviting readers to empathize with his joys and sorrows. Moreover, through his candid self-examinations, we witness the evolution of his beliefs and values, laid bare with unwavering honesty. The contents of these treasured letters also illuminate the profound impact of meaningful relationships on Herrmann's life. Within their pages, we encounter stirring accounts of camaraderie, love, and loss, each penned with emotional eloquence that resonates across the ages. Whether celebrating joyful milestones or seeking solace during times of adversity, Herrmann's words convey a deep sense of appreciation for the enduring bonds that enriched his existence. Moreover, embedded within these personal reflections are nuggets of wisdom and insight that transcend time, offering valuable lessons that continue to inspire and uplift. Each anecdote and observation serves as a testament to Herrmann's unwavering spirit and unwritten legacy, leaving an indelible imprint on the hearts and minds of those who encounter his written musings. It is through this intimate literary journey that we come to understand not only the celebrated showman, but also the profound humanity that resided within him. In revealing his vulnerabilities and triumphs alike, Herrmann imparts a timeless wisdom that encourages us to embrace our own complexities and cherish the beauty of shared experiences.

Endearing Anecdotes from Close Friends

As we delve into the personal sphere of Alexander Herrmann, we are privy to an array of heartwarming anecdotes shared by those closest to him. These endearing stories offer a glimpse into the man behind the magician—the compassionate, humorous, and deeply cherished individual that his friends knew and loved. One such story recounts a moment when Herrmann selflessly aided a struggling colleague, offering not only advice but also unwavering support during trying times. His generosity and kindness consistently surfaced in interactions with fellow magicians, as well as in his social circles. Another poignant anecdote recalls how Herrmann's wit and charm lit up every room he entered, bringing joy and laughter to those around him. His quick sense of humor and infectious energy created an atmosphere of warmth and camaraderie, leaving a lasting impression on all fortunate enough to bask in his presence. Close friends also reminisce about Herrmann's unwavering dedication to both his art and the people in his life. They speak of his tireless efforts to inspire and mentor aspiring magicians, never failing to impart invaluable wisdom and encouragement to those following in his footsteps. In more intimate moments, Herrmann's friends affectionately share tales of his love for simple pleasures—be it a fondness for a particular type of tea or his quiet enjoyment of stargazing. These glimpses into his private world humanize the larger-than-life figure known to the public, emphasizing the depth and richness of his character beyond the glitz and glamour of the stage. Furthermore, these anecdotes paint a touching portrayal of the friendships Herrmann held dear. Whether through impromptu gatherings or heartfelt conversations, his genuine connections with others reflected the authenticity and depth of his relationships. The enduring impact of Alexander Herrmann's kindness, humor, and generosity weaves a tapestry of beautiful memories, treasured by those who were fortunate to call him friend. These stirring accounts tenderly reveal the extraordinary man behind the illusion—a man whose legacy is not confined to his magical feats, but etched indelibly in the hearts of those who knew him.

The Lasting Impact of a Life Well-Lived

Alexander Herrmann's legacy extends far beyond the realm of magic. His life was not only about astonishing audiences with his spellbinding illusions, but also about leaving an indelible mark on the world through his actions and values. As we reflect on his enduring influence, it becomes apparent that Herrmann's impact transcends the boundaries of time and space. One of the most profound aspects of Herrmann's lasting impact is his unwavering commitment to kindness and compassion. Throughout his career, he exemplified the virtue of generosity, often using his talents to bring joy to those in need. Whether performing for underprivileged children or using his platform to raise awareness for charitable causes, Herrmann embodied the belief that magic should serve as a force for good in the world. Moreover, Herrmann's dedication to nurturing young talent has left an enduring impression on the magic community. His mentorship and encouragement inspired countless aspiring magicians to pursue their dreams, fostering a culture of camaraderie and support within the industry. Many magicians attribute their success to Herrmann's guidance, acknowledging him as a beacon of inspiration and guidance. Beyond his professional endeavors, Herrmann's personal integrity and ethics continue to serve as a compass for aspiring magicians and enthusiasts alike. His unwavering commitment to honesty and authenticity set a precedent for the art of magic, inspiring practitioners to uphold the highest moral standards in their performances. Herrmann's ethical approach transcended mere entertainment, elevating magic to a form of storytelling that celebrated truth and sincerity. In addition to his impact on magic, Herrmann's influence extended to the broader landscape of entertainment and beyond. His commitment to excellence and innovation set a standard for performers across various disciplines, demonstrating that true greatness arises from a genuine passion for one's craft. By pushing the boundaries of what was thought possible, Herrmann's legacy continues to inspire creative minds to embrace boldness and originality. Furthermore, Herrmann's enduring impact can be witnessed in the countless lives he touched, both directly and indirectly. The ripples of his kindness and wisdom have echoed through generations, shaping the artistic landscape and leaving an imprint on individuals who never had the privilege of witnessing his performances firsthand. It is a testament to his timeless appeal and universal relevance that Herrmann's influence remains palpable even in the digital age, where his legacy continues to captivate and inspire new audiences. As we contemplate the lasting impact of Alexander Herrmann's life well-lived, it is evident that his enduring legacy is woven into the fabric of history itself. His benevolence, mentorship, and artistic innovation have reverberated through time, reminding us that the power of magic extends far beyond mere illusion. Indeed, Alexander Herrmann's legacy serves as a testament to the transformative potential of a life dedicated to enchanting minds, uplifting spirits, and leaving an unerasable mark on the world.

Personal Life

A Glimpse into His Heart

Alexander Herrmann's compassionate nature and the values that guided his actions provided a captivating glimpse into the depths of his heart. Family ties and bonds were not just mere connections to Alexander but pillars of strength that shaped him as a person and as a magician. His upbringing in a loving and close-knit family instilled in him a deep sense of responsibility, compassion, and integrity. These values radiated through every aspect of his life, from his stage performances to his interactions with his loved ones. While pursuing his magical career, Alexander always made sure to keep his family at the center of his universe. The unwavering love and support he received from his family fostered a sense of security and grounding, allowing him to flourish in both his personal and professional realms. Family was not just a word to Alexander; it was a philosophy, a guiding force that infused warmth and humanity into everything he did. It was this very essence that endeared him to audiences across the globe. Reflecting on his journey, Alexander often spoke about how he found solace and inspiration in the smiles of his family, especially during trying times. Their unwavering belief in him fueled his determination to overcome obstacles and pursue his dreams with unwavering dedication. The bond he shared with his family transcended the boundaries of conventional relationships, evolving into an indispensable source of motivation and joy. This radiant connection served as a testament to the enduring power of love and the profound impact it had on Alexander's life and career. As we delve deeper into the realm of Alexander Herrmann's personal life, it becomes abundantly clear that his family ties and bonds were not just a peripheral part of his existence; they were the very core of his being.

Family Ties and Bonds

Alexander Herrmann's family played a pivotal role in shaping the man behind the magician. From his early years, family ties and bonds were a source of love, support, and inspiration for Alexander. The youngest of fourteen siblings, Alexander was born into a large and close-knit family in Paris. His childhood was marked by the warmth of familial connections, and his memories often revolved around the shared laughter, joy, and occasional squabbles with his brothers and sisters. Their bond was rooted in deep affection and an unwavering commitment to each other's well-being. Herrmann's magical journey was intertwined with the influence of his elder brother, Compars Herrmann, a renowned magician in his own right. Under Compars' guidance and mentorship, Alexander honed his skills and developed a profound appreciation for the art of magic. The bond between the two brothers extended beyond their professional collaboration; it was a testament to the strength of their familial relationship. As he embarked on his own path to stardom, Alexander remained closely connected to his family. Despite the demands of his burgeoning career, he made it a priority to stay connected with his siblings and extended family members. Whether through written correspondence or personal visits, he cherished every opportunity to share his successes, seek advice, and offer support to his loved ones. His family, in turn, provided a nurturing environment that allowed him to flourish as an artist and as a person. The unwavering support and encouragement from his family during both triumphant and challenging times bolstered Alexander's spirit and resolve. Their pride in his accomplishments became his source of strength, while their wisdom offered guidance through the complexities of life. Even as he dazzled audiences around the world, it was the familiar faces in the crowd – those of his beloved family members – that filled his heart with joy and gratitude. In tracing the tapestry of Alexander Herrmann's life, it becomes evident that family ties and bonds served as the cornerstone of his existence. His unwavering love and devotion to his family defined him not just as a celebrated magician, but also as a compassionate and empathetic individual whose essence was shaped by the love and unity that only a close-knit family could provide.

A Love Story: Alexander and Adelaide

Alexander Herrmann's life as a renowned magician was undeniably captivating, but the most enchanting and cherished aspect of his world was his profound love story with Adelaide. Their bond transcended time and space, weaving an extraordinary tale of devotion, unwavering support, and endearing companionship. Adelaide, a beacon of grace and elegance, captured Alexander's heart with her warmth and ethereal presence. It was a love that blossomed amidst the whirlwind of performances and travels, enduring the tests of distance and time. From the moment they met, their connection sparked a flame that illuminated the darkest corners of their lives, bringing light and love into each other's hearts. Their love was a testament to the enduring power of human connection, thriving against all odds. Each tender gesture, every stolen glance, and the unspoken understanding between them formed a narrative more enchanting than any illusion Alexander could conjure on stage. Adelaide was not just his partner in life; she was his muse, his confidante, and his unwavering source of inspiration. She stood beside him through triumphs and tribulations, offering solace in moments of doubt and celebrating every milestone with profound joy. Their love story became an essential part of Alexander's identity, shaping him as both a magician and a man. It was a union that exuded resilience, compassion, and a deep-seated understanding of each other's desires and aspirations. Together, they navigated through life's intricate tapestry, finding solace in each other's embrace and deriving strength from their shared dreams. Their love became a sanctuary, a refuge from the chaotic world beyond, where they could revel in the simple pleasures of companionship. As

Alexander dazzled audiences with his magical feats, Adelaide remained his pillar of unwavering support, offering guidance and embracing the complexities of his calling with grace. Their love story embodies the very essence of magic—an inexplicable force that binds two souls together, surpassing the constraints of the mortal realm. Beyond the glittering lights of the stage, their love thrived in quiet moments of tenderness, in heartfelt conversations, and in the tranquil rhythm of their intertwined lives. The legacy of Alexander Herrmann is incomplete without acknowledging the profound impact of his enduring love for Adelaide. It was a love story that transcended the boundaries of time, eternally woven into the fabric of his remarkable journey as a magician and as a man.

Friendships that Shaped Him

Alexander Herrmann was not only shaped by his love for magic and his dedication to his art, but also by the deep and lasting friendships he forged throughout his life. His relationships with fellow magicians, performers from other disciplines, and individuals from various walks of life provided a rich tapestry of support, inspiration, and camaraderie that deeply impacted his personal and professional journey. One of the most influential friendships in Herrmann's life was with the famed escape artist Harry Houdini. Their mutual admiration and shared passion for magic led to a profound bond that transcended professional respect. Houdini's fearlessness and innovative approach to escapology left an indelible mark on Herrmann, influencing the evolution of his own performances and pushing the boundaries of his magical craft. Beyond the realm of magic, Herrmann also found profound friendship in the company of renowned artists, writers, and intellectuals. These relationships enriched his perspective and creativity, fueling his performances with depth and nuance. The genuine connections he formed with these individuals extended far beyond the superficial trappings of fame, offering him a sense of kinship and belonging that sustained him during both triumphs and tribulations. It was within these relationships that Herrmann found unwavering support, wise counsel, and unwavering encouragement as he navigated the complexities of his career and personal life. These friendships were not only sources of joy and laughter, but also pillars of strength during moments of doubt and adversity. As he traveled the world, charming audiences with his illusions and enchanting feats, he carried with him the warmth and wisdom gleaned from these meaningful connections. The impact of these friendships is felt in the enduring resonance of Herrmann's performances, characterized by a depth of emotion and artistry that transcends mere spectacle.

Cherished Moments Away from the Spotlight

As much as Alexander Herrmann thrived in the enchanting world of magic and performance, he also cherished moments away from the spotlight. These were the times when he could simply be himself, free from the expectations and pressures of his public persona. Whether it was escaping to the countryside for a leisurely stroll or spending quiet evenings with his closest confidants, Herrmann treasured these respites from the bustling stage life. Amidst the wonder and allure of his magical feats, Herrmann sought solace in the ordinary joys of life – perhaps savoring a warm cup of tea as the sun dipped below the horizon or finding peace in the laughter shared among dear friends. One particular retreat that held a special place in Herrmann's heart was a quaint cabin nestled amidst towering pines and surrounded by nature's serene symphony. It was here that he could revel in the simple pleasures of existence, feeling the gentle embrace of solitude and basking in the beauty of the natural world. During these tranquil interludes, Herrmann often found inspiration for his illusions and performances, drawing from the harmony and mystery of the wilderness. The respite provided by such sanctuaries allowed him to recharge and reconnect with his innermost thoughts, strengthening the profound connection between his art and the essence of life itself. These cherished moments also offered Herrmann the opportunity to engage in pursuits beyond the realm of magic. Whether delving into profound conversations with kindred spirits, immersing himself in literature, or exploring new artistic mediums, he reveled in the multifaceted tapestry of human experience. In these intimate gatherings, away from the dazzle of the stage, Herrmann glimpsed the intricate beauty of human connection, nurturing friendships that transcended the boundaries of showmanship. Moreover, he found solace in the perennial presence of his beloved Adelaide, who illuminated his life with unwavering support and profound understanding. Together, they shared countless tender moments, finding joy in the simplest gestures and weaving a tapestry of love that extended far beyond the footlights. Their bond symbolized the enduring power of companionship, providing Herrmann with an anchor amidst the tempestuous seas of fame and fortune. In essence, these cherished moments away from the spotlight were irreplaceable fragments of Herrmann's life. They granted him a sanctuary from the bewitching allure of the stage, offering invaluable opportunities for reflection, creativity, and genuine connections. Emanating warmth and authenticity, these private interludes enriched Herrmann's spirit, infusing his performances with a depth and sincerity that captivated audiences worldwide.

Struggles and Triumphs of a Magician's Life

Alexander Herrmann's life was a tapestry woven with both struggles and triumphs, for the path of a magician is not always strewn with roses. Behind the captivating performances and the enigmatic smile lay a man who faced his share of challenges. As he navigated the world of magic, Herrmann encountered numerous hurdles that tested his determination and resilience. The relentless pursuit of mastering his craft often led to moments of self-doubt and uncertainty. The pressure to continuously innovate and astound his audience placed immense weight on his shoulders. It was a constant battle to strike the delicate balance between creating illusions that mesmerized the crowds and preserving the authenticity of his art. Amidst these struggles, Herrmann found solace in the unwavering support of his loved ones, who stood by him through every adversity. Their belief in his talent and unwavering encouragement became his anchor during turbulent times. However, every setback was met with a triumph that fueled his spirit and invigorated his passion. Each successful performance, every standing ovation, and the profound impact he left on his audience served as a testament to his perseverance. Herrmann's relentless dedication and unyielding determination bore fruits of unparalleled excellence. His ability to infuse wonder and awe into every act brought him accolades and recognition far and wide. The journey was rife with hardships, yet it was these very trials that sculpted him into the iconic figure he came to be. Through unwavering resolve and an unshakeable commitment to his art, Herrmann transcended every obstacle that came his way. His triumphs were not merely his own; they reflected the culmination of years of toil and sacrifice. Beyond the glittering stage and the resounding applause lay a story of resilience and tenacity. Each mesmerizing illusion and every gasp of amazement from his audience spoke volumes about the indomitable spirit of a magician who turned adversities into opportunities. The struggles could never overshadow the brilliance of his triumphs, for they illuminated his path and etched his name in the annals of magical history. Alexander Herrmann's life was a masterclass in perseverance and an illustration of the fact that every triumph is sweeter when it follows struggle.

Balancing Fame and Family

Balancing a life of fame and family was an intricate dance for Alexander Herrmann. As his star rose in the world of magic, so did the demands on his time and energy. Yet amidst the whirlwind of tours, performances, and the allure of the spotlight, Herrmann always sought to carve out moments for his beloved family. The ever-present challenge of ensuring that neither his dedication to his art nor his commitment to his loved ones wavered became a profound aspect of Herrmann's personal journey. Herrmann's dedication to his craft often took him far from home, captivating audiences across continents. His name and reputation as a renowned magician preceded him wherever he went, bringing both admiration and obligations. However, tethered to this illustrious persona was a man who longed for the comforting embrace of his family. Despite the distance, Herrmann constantly strived to maintain a delicate equilibrium between his thriving career and his responsibilities as a devoted husband and father. The magical world on stage was a stark contrast to the world at home, where the conjurer of illusions transformed into a caring husband and doting father. He cherished the fleeting moments of normalcy, relishing simple pleasures such as family dinners and holidays spent in each other's company. Even in the midst of his relentless schedule, Herrmann ensured that family remained at the heart of his existence. In the quiet corners of his mind, the laughter of his children and the warmth of his wife's presence provided solace, grounding him amidst the whirlwind of fame. Amidst the applause and adulation, Herrmann's private life was his sanctuary. It was in these intimate spaces that he found refuge from the demanding expectations of his public persona. He recognized the importance of nurturing familial bonds, understanding that they were the bedrock upon which his life rested. Whether it was stealing precious moments during breaks in tours or eagerly returning home after a successful performance, Herrmann consistently strived to seamlessly integrate his thriving career with the nurturing of his family. Even when the pressures of his profession threatened to consume him, Herrmann made it a point to prioritize his role as a dedicated family man. Every decision, every step he took, reflected a conscious effort to maintain harmony between two worlds that held equal significance in his life. His commitment to balancing fame and family epitomizes the enduring legacy of a man who understood that true fulfillment lies not just in his celebrated achievements but also in the love and joy that blossomed within the walls of his own home.

Passions Beyond Magic

While magic encompassed a significant portion of Alexander Herrmann's professional life, his interests and passions extended far beyond the realm of illusions and sleight of hand. One of the most profound aspects of Herrmann's character was his unwavering love for literature. He possessed a voracious appetite for books, with an extensive library that spanned various genres, from classic literature to contemporary works. Often seen immersing himself in the words of renowned authors, Herrmann found solace and inspiration within the pages of a well-crafted story. His passion for literature not only enriched his personal life but also seeped into his performances, lending an intellectual depth and storytelling prowess to his magical acts. Beyond literature, Herrmann harbored a deep appreciation for music. The melodious strains of symphonies and the delicate notes of chamber music held a special place in his heart. He derived immense joy from attending concerts and engaging in discussions about compositions and musical techniques with fellow enthusiasts. It is said that, at times, the magician would meld magic with melody, creating unforgettable performances where the surreal met the sonorous. This harmonious marriage of music and magic served as a testament to Herrmann's multifaceted nature and his ability to infuse diverse art forms into a captivating tapestry of entertainment. Moreover, Herrmann's keen interest in philanthropy distinguished him as a compassionate and empathetic individual. He devoted substantial time and resources to charitable causes, endeavoring to make a positive impact on the lives of those less fortunate. From organizing benefit shows in aid of orphanages to supporting educational initiatives, Herrmann wielded his influence to effect meaningful change in the world around him. His altruism, coupled with his charismatic stage presence, enabled him to rally support for numerous humanitarian endeavors, leaving an indelible mark on both the realms of magic and social welfare. In essence, Alexander Herrmann's passions transcended the confines of his profession, enriching his life with literary, musical, and philanthropic pursuits that mirrored the depth of his character. These passions not only added layers to his public persona but also provided invaluable sources of fulfillment and purpose in his private moments. They reflected the man behind the magician—a complex, compassionate soul whose legacy extends far beyond the enchanting world of magic.

Reflections and Inner Thoughts

In moments of quiet contemplation, Alexander Herrmann often delved into his inner thoughts, seeking to understand the deeper meaning behind his craft and his place in the world. His reflections were not just about magic, but also about life itself. He pondered the impact of his performances on his audiences, striving to touch their hearts and leave a lasting impression beyond mere amusement. Herrmann held a deep appreciation for the art of magic, understanding its power to evoke wonder and joy in people's lives. As he gazed into the starry night sky or strolled through nature's serene landscapes, a sense of awe enveloped him. He found inspiration in the beauty of the natural world, drawing parallels between the mysteries of nature and the wonder of his illusions. The intricate patterns of a flower petal or the graceful flight of a bird sparked his creativity, infusing his magic with a profound connection to the universe. Yet, amidst the adulation and applause, there were moments of solitude where Herrmann sought solace in his thoughts. He mulled over the delicate balance between his public persona and his private self, recognizing the vulnerability that lay beneath his charismatic stage presence. The weight of expectation that came with his elevated status as a renowned magician often left him grappling with his own humanity, yearning for deeper connections beyond the fleeting admiration of his fans. His inner turmoil and struggles shaped a more introspective side of Herrmann, one that was seldom revealed to the world. It was during these times that he confronted his fears and uncertainties, finding refuge in the quiet refuge of his own mind. Through introspection, he sought to reconcile the demands of fame with his fundamental desires for authenticity and emotional fulfillment. Deeply empathetic by nature, Herrmann's reflections extended to those around him. He contemplated the enduring impact of his art on future generations, aspiring to leave a legacy that transcended entertainment. His inner thoughts were imbued with a genuine concern for the well-being of others, driving him to use his talents not just for personal gain, but for the betterment of society as a whole. Ultimately, Herrmann's cherished reflections and inner thoughts offered a glimpse into the inner workings of a man who strived for meaningful connections, both in his performances and in his personal encounters. These contemplative moments laid bare the tender soul of a magician whose essence went far beyond the allure of his wondrous illusions.

The Essence of Herrmann

The essence of Alexander Herrmann, known to the world as Herrmann the Great, transcends mere illusions and magical feats. It lies in the depth of his character, the sincerity of his emotions, and the impact he left on those around him. Beyond the glittering stage and amidst the whispers of wonder, there existed a man whose essence was woven with threads of passion, empathy, and unwavering dedication. At the core of Herrmann's essence was an unyielding commitment to his art. His relentless pursuit of perfection in magic was propelled by a genuine love for captivating audiences and igniting their imaginations. Every illusion he crafted, every performance he delivered, bore the imprint of his fervent desire to bring joy and astonishment to all who encountered his magic. This unwavering dedication not only defined him as a magician but also endeared him to countless admirers worldwide. However, beyond the enigma of his craft, lay a compassionate soul that sought to touch lives beyond the confines of the stage. Herrmann's essence emanated from the kindness he exuded, the empathy he extended, and the genuine connections he fostered. Whether comforting a young fan disillusioned by life's harsh realities or offering solace to a fellow performer in times of struggle, Herrmann's empathy knew no bounds. His ability to empathize and uplift others echoed the very essence of humanity, transcending the boundaries of entertainment. The essence of Herrmann also flourished within the realms of creativity and innovation. His insatiable curiosity and thirst for originality propelled him to explore uncharted territories of magic, constantly evolving and redefining the art form. His legacy is not merely the sum of his performances but is equally attributed to the trailblazing spirit that continues to inspire magicians across generations. The essence of Herrmann resonates through the enduring impact of his contributions to the world of magic. Above all, the essence of Herrmann shines through the profound influence he had on those who were fortunate enough to intersect his life's path. His presence instilled courage, ignited dreams, and imparted wisdom to aspiring magicians and individuals from all walks of life. The indelible mark he left on hearts and minds encapsulates the true essence of an extraordinary man whose legacy extends far beyond the realm of magic. In understanding the essence of Herrmann, one must recognize the amalgamation of unshakeable passion, genuine empathy, unwavering innovation, and enduring influence. It is these qualities that compose the inner fabric of a magician whose essence continues to weave its enchanting spell upon the world, long after the curtain has fallen.

Building a Legacy

Reflecting on a Life of Magic

Alexander's journey in magic was as much about self-reflection as it was about performing. Throughout his illustrious career, he constantly sought to understand the essence of his passion and how it shaped his legacy. Reflecting on the intricacies of his craft became a profound exercise in introspection, allowing him to delve deep into the roots of his artistry. Each performance became a canvas for self-discovery, a platform for him to express his innermost thoughts and emotions. As Alexander honed his skills, he realized that magic wasn't merely about captivating an audience; it was about channeling his own experiences and vulnerabilities into every illusion. This introspective approach not only elevated his performances but also laid the groundwork for future magicians. By openly sharing his journey of self-discovery, he became an inspiration for aspiring magicians, encouraging them to embrace their genuine selves in their magical endeavors. Furthermore, Alexander's reflections helped him establish a profound connection with his audience. His performances were no longer just displays of skill; they became heartfelt narratives that resonated deeply with those who witnessed them. By baring his soul through his illusions, he created an emotional bond with his spectators, leaving them captivated and spellbound. These reflections ultimately defined Alexander's enduring legacy, emphasizing the importance of authenticity and self-awareness in the world of magic. His profound understanding of the transformative power of introspection enabled him to impact generations of magicians and instill in them the value of connecting with both themselves and their audiences on a deeper level. Through his reflective approach, Alexander Herrmann carved out a unique path in the realm of magic, one that continues to inspire and guide future magicians in planting the seeds for their own magical legacies.

Planting Seeds for Future Magicians

As Alexander Herrmann's illustrious career reached its pinnacle, he turned his attention to preserving and nurturing the future of magic. Realizing the importance of passing on his knowledge and expertise, Herrmann made it his mission to plant seeds for the next generation of magicians. With unwavering passion and dedication, he sought out promising young talents, offering guidance, mentorship, and opportunities to develop their skills. Through workshops, lectures, and personal interactions, Herrmann shared the secrets of his craft, instilling in budding magicians a deep appreciation for the art form. Herrmann also understood the significance of fostering creativity and innovation within the magical community. He encouraged aspiring magicians to think outside the box, experiment with new techniques, and push the boundaries of traditional magic. By championing originality and ingenuity, Herrmann envisioned a future where magic continuously evolved and captivated audiences in groundbreaking ways. In addition to nurturing individual talents, Herrmann established initiatives aimed at promoting magic education in schools and communities. Believing in the transformative power of magic as an educational tool, he tirelessly advocated for its inclusion in curriculums, emphasizing its ability to stimulate critical thinking, creativity, and confidence in young minds. Through partnerships with educational institutions and outreach programs, Herrmann laid the groundwork for a widespread appreciation of magic and its potential to inspire and empower future generations. Furthermore, Herrmann recognized that creating a supportive and inclusive environment was essential for cultivating diverse talent in the world of magic. He actively worked to eliminate barriers and prejudice within the industry, paving the way for individuals from all walks of life to pursue their magical aspirations freely. This dedication to inclusivity and equal opportunity not only enriched the magical community but also set a precedent for a more unified and harmonious future for the art of magic. The impact of Herrmann's efforts in planting seeds for future magicians reverberates through time, as countless magicians around the world continue to draw inspiration from his legacy. Through his profound commitment to nurturing the next generation, Herrmann ensured that the enchanting world of magic would endure, flourish, and inspire wonder for years to come.

Innovations that Redefined the Craft

In the annals of magical history, there are moments when an individual's creativity and vision transcend the conventional boundaries of the art and bring about revolutionary change. Alexander Herrmann was undeniably one such visionary whose innovations redefined the very fabric of the magic craft. His relentless pursuit of perfection and his passion for pushing the boundaries propelled him to create groundbreaking illusions that captivated audiences and left fellow magicians in awe. One of Herrmann's most remarkable innovations was his introduction of elaborate stage sets and props, transforming magic performances into grand spectacles. With meticulous attention to detail, he engineered illusions that seamlessly integrated with their surroundings, enhancing the overall impact of his acts. The utilization of innovative mechanical contrivances and cutting-edge technology elevated the art form to new heights, setting a standard that inspired generations to come. Furthermore, Herrmann's pioneering use of lighting and sound effects revolutionized the ambiance of his performances, immersing spectators in a sensory experience like never before. The integration of music, carefully choreographed movements, and dramatic lighting enhanced the storytelling aspect of his illusions, transporting audiences into a world of wonder and enchantment. Additionally, Herrmann's contributions extended to the realm of magical apparatus. He meticulously designed and constructed sophisticated devices that became the hallmark of his performances. From intricately crafted cabinets to mesmerizing optical illusions, each prop bore the imprint of his unparalleled creativity and ingenuity. By constantly refining and perfecting these apparatus, he set a new benchmark for craftsmanship within the magical community. Moreover, his inventive approach to the presentation of classic illusions breathed new life into age-old tricks, infusing them with a modern flair that captured the imagination of contemporary audiences. Through his innovative interpretations of traditional magic, Herrmann reshaped the perception of what was possible within the art form, inspiring a wave of creativity and reinvention among aspiring magicians worldwide. Ultimately, Alexander Herrmann's innovations not only reshaped the landscape of magic but also paved the way for future magicians to dream bigger, think bolder, and dare to defy the limits of what magic could achieve. His legacy as a pioneer continues to inspire and influence the evolution of magic, ensuring that his innovations remain eternally woven into the tapestry of magical history.

Mentorship and Inspiration to Others

Mentorship and inspiration are vital components of Alexander Herrmann's enduring legacy in the world of magic. Throughout his illustrious career, Herrmann recognized the importance of passing on knowledge and expertise to the next generation of magicians. His commitment to mentorship extended beyond simply teaching tricks; he sought to instill the values of dedication, creativity, and showmanship in his protégés. By sharing his insight and experiences with aspiring magicians, Herrmann aimed to inspire them to push boundaries and cultivate their own unique styles. Herrmann's mentorship was characterized by patience, encouragement, and a genuine desire to see others succeed. His empathetic approach fostered an environment where his apprentices felt supported and empowered to explore their potential. Beyond his direct influence,

Herrmann also championed the broader community of magicians, regularly offering advice and guidance to newcomers in the field. Recognizing the transformative power of shared knowledge, he actively contributed to the enrichment of magical arts, thereby shaping the future of the craft. Herrmann's belief in the importance of mentorship stemmed from his profound respect for the art of magic and the desire to ensure its continuity for generations to come. He understood that nurturing emerging talent was integral to preserving the beauty and wonder of magic as an art form. By embodying the qualities of a dedicated mentor, Herrmann not only left an indelible mark on the world of magic but also established a blueprint for how magicians could uplift and inspire one another. Through mentorship, Herrmann set a precedent for the cultivation of a supportive and interconnected community, fostering an environment conducive to growth and innovation within the magical realm. His commitment to lifting others up through guidance and support serves as a testament to the enduring impact of a generous spirit and a willingness to share one's gifts with the world.

Embracing the Responsibility of Influence

As a steward of the magical arts, Alexander Herrmann embraced his responsibility to influence both current and future generations of magicians. Understanding the profound impact his craft could have on aspiring illusionists, Herrmann dedicated himself to upholding the highest standards of professionalism, integrity, and artistry within the magical community. His commitment extended beyond mere performance, encompassing a genuine desire to cultivate a culture of respect, collaboration, and continuous improvement. In fulfilling this duty, Herrmann actively sought opportunities to mentor emerging talents, recognizing the invaluable role that guidance and encouragement play in shaping the trajectory of burgeoning magicians' careers. This nurturing approach was crucial not only in honing technical skills but also in developing the character and ethical compass of those entering the captivating yet demanding world of magic. Through his mentorship, Herrmann imparted not just tricks of the trade but also wisdom garnered from a lifetime dedicated to the pursuit of wonder and spectacle. Furthermore, embracing the responsibility of influence entailed championing inclusivity and diversity within the magic community. Herrmann fervently believed that magic should be accessible to all, breaking down barriers and prejudices that might hinder individuals from finding their voice and expression through the art form. By fostering an environment that welcomed magicians from various backgrounds and perspectives, Herrmann enriched the magical landscape with a vibrant tapestry of creativity and innovation, ensuring that the legacy of magic would continue to evolve and thrive for generations to come. Equally important was Herrmann's unwavering commitment to transparency and authenticity, understanding that the influence he wielded carried the weight of setting an example for aspiring magicians. By promoting ethical conduct and honesty in both performance and professional conduct, Herrmann set the standard for integrity within the magical arts, instilling in others the belief that magic's greatest power lies not in deception but in the genuine connection, inspiration, and awe it fosters. In summary, Herrmann's embrace of the responsibility of influence illuminated the path for countless magicians, offering guidance, inspiration, and assurance that the legacy of magic would endure through their dedication to shaping the future of the art form.

Preserving the Art Form for Generations

The preservation of the art of magic is a duty that transcends individual ambition. It involves safeguarding not only the secrets and techniques but also the spirit and essence of this timeless craft. Preserving the art form for generations requires a deep commitment to knowledge transfer, respect for tradition, and the continual evolution of magical expression. Magicians are entrusted with the responsibility of ensuring that the wonders and mysteries of magic endure beyond their own performances. This task involves embracing the role of custodian, mentor, and guardian of an illustrious legacy. It demands a mindset that extends beyond personal gain and places emphasis on the broader cultural impact of magic. Preserving the art form is a labor of love that necessitates an unwavering dedication to the enrichment and enlightenment of future generations. Through passing down the wisdom garnered from years of experience, magicians foster a sense of continuity and connection that transcends time. It's about imparting not just the technical skills, but also the storytelling prowess, showmanship, and profound understanding of human psychology that form the foundation of exceptional magic. With each apprentice they nurture, magicians plant seeds that will blossom into a new generation of spellbinders, each contributing their unique flourishes to the wondrous tapestry of magic. Furthermore, the preservation of magic demands a heightened awareness of the societal and cultural context in which it thrives. By aligning with the values and sensibilities of each era, while upholding the enduring principles of enchantment, magicians ensure that the art remains relevant and resonant. This balance between honoring tradition and embracing progress fosters an ongoing dialogue between past, present, and future within the magical community, enriching the art form through diverse perspectives and innovations. Preserving the art form for generations is not merely a theoretical concept; it is a living commitment. It involves the constant toil of passionate individuals who understand that the true magic lies not only in the execution of illusions but in the perpetuation of wonder and awe throughout the ages.

The Impact of Family Support

Family support plays a significant role in the life and legacy of Alexander Herrmann. From his early days as a budding magician to the height of his career, Herrmann's family stood as pillars of unwavering encouragement and strength. At every pivotal moment, they were there to provide guidance, reassurance, and invaluable assistance. Their belief in his talent, even during moments of uncertainty, fueled Herrmann's determination and passion for magic. It was within the walls of his home that he found solace, acceptance, and the freedom to pursue his dreams. The unconditional love and support from his family laid the foundation for his success. As Herrmann's fame grew, his family remained his constant source of inspiration and grounding. Their unwavering loyalty and commitment allowed him to navigate the challenges and triumphs of his illustrious career. Beyond mere encouragement, his family became his confidants and collaborators, contributing their insights and enthusiasm to his acts. Together, they celebrated the milestones, weathered the storms, and embraced the adventures that came with his magical journey. The impact of family support extended far beyond personal achievements; it shaped Herrmann's character and deeply influenced his interactions with others. His dedication to his craft and the values he upheld were instilled by the values of unity and resilience that his family embodied. They exemplified the power of solidarity and solidarity in pursuit of one's passions, leaving an indelible mark on Herrmann's legacy. From the applause of the audience to the quiet moments of reflection, Herrmann knew that his family's unwavering support had been the bedrock of his magical odyssey. Their love and encouragement continue to reverberate through the annals of history, reminding aspiring magicians of the profound impact and significance of familial bonds in shaping a lasting legacy.

Philanthropy and Giving Back

The legacy of Alexander Herrmann extends far beyond his remarkable achievements in the world of magic. A philanthropist at heart, Herrmann dedicated himself to giving back to the community and supporting causes close to his heart. Understanding the importance of using his success for the betterment of others, he established charitable programs aimed at nurturing young talents in the art of magic, providing resources and mentorship to aspiring magicians from underprivileged backgrounds. Herrmann firmly believed in the transformative power of education and creativity. Through his philanthropic initiatives, he sought to make a meaningful impact on the lives of aspiring magicians, offering scholarships, workshops, and educational opportunities to those eager to pursue their passion for the mystical arts. His unwavering commitment to nurturing the next generation of magicians not only ensured the preservation of the craft but also provided hope and inspiration to countless individuals striving to overcome adversity and achieve their dreams. In addition to supporting budding magicians, Herrmann was deeply involved in various charitable endeavors that aimed to enrich the lives of children and families. He worked tirelessly to bring the wonder of magic to hospitals, orphanages, and communities in need, using his talent to entertain and uplift those facing difficult circumstances. His performances brought joy and respite to countless individuals, proving that magic has the extraordinary ability to transcend barriers and instill hope in the hearts of all who witness it. Furthermore, Herrmann recognized the importance of environmental conservation and sustainability. He actively supported environmental initiatives, participating in tree-planting campaigns, wildlife conservation projects, and efforts to raise awareness about ecological challenges. His dedication to preserving the natural world mirrored his reverence for the art of magic, emphasizing the profound responsibility we hold in safeguarding the wonders of our planet for future generations. The impact of Herrmann's philanthropy continues to resonate today, with his charitable legacy serving as a testament to the enduring significance of kindness and generosity. Through his benevolent actions, he demonstrated that true magic lies not only in the illusions performed on stage but also in the ability to touch lives, inspire positive change, and leave behind a lasting legacy of compassion and goodwill.

Facing Challenges with Grace

In the journey of any great magician, there are bound to be challenges that test the very essence of one's being. For Alexander Herrmann, these challenges were not mere stumbling blocks but opportunities for growth and resilience. The path to success is often riddled with unexpected obstacles, and it is how one confronts and overcomes these trials that truly define a legacy. Through both personal and professional adversities, Herrmann exemplified unwavering grace and fortitude, inspiring admiration and respect from contemporaries and future generations alike. Despite the numerous tribulations faced, Herrmann remained steadfast in his pursuit of greatness, demonstrating an unyielding determination to triumph over every setback. Whether it was navigating the intricacies of an ever-evolving industry or transcending personal hardships, he approached each hardship with an admirable composure and resolve. His ability to face these challenges with grace serves as a testament to his remarkable character and unwavering dedication to his craft. It is within the crucible of adversity that true leaders emerge, and Herrmann's tenacity in such circumstances only solidifies his enduring influence on the world of magic. Beyond performing awe-inspiring illusions on stage, Herrmann's ability to maintain poise in the face of adversity left an indelible mark on those who witnessed his resilience. Moreover, his example continues to inspire aspiring magicians to navigate their own obstacles with similar dignity and perseverance. Facing challenges with grace is not merely a reflection of strength in times of turmoil; it is an embodiment of humility, empathy, and an unwavering commitment to one's passions. Herrmann's dedication to maintaining his artistry amidst adversity is a testament to the values he held dear and the reverence he held for the art of magic. By embracing challenges with grace, Herrmann elevated his art beyond mere entertainment; he transformed it into a platform for resilience and empowerment. Ultimately, his legacy lies not only in his masterful performances but in his unwavering ability to confront life's trials with grace and dignity, leaving an indelible mark on the world of magic and beyond.

A Legacy Etched in Time

Alexander Herrmann's enduring impact on the magical arts is a testament to the unwavering passion and commitment he possessed throughout his illustrious career. As time passed, his legacy continued to shape and influence the world of magic, leaving an indelible mark that transcended generations. The culmination of his achievements, from pioneering innovative techniques to mentoring aspiring magicians, solidified his position as a timeless icon in the realm of illusion. Beyond the mere mastery of his craft, Herrmann's philanthropic endeavors reflect a deep sense of responsibility towards nurturing future talents and preserving the rich tapestry of magic for posterity. His unwavering spirit in the face of adversity and the graceful manner in which he met challenges serve as an enduring example for those who strive to follow in his footsteps. Each illusionist inspired by Herrmann becomes a living vessel of his legacy, ensuring that his influence persists beyond the constraints of mortality. Furthermore, the familial support that anchored Herrmann during his journey plays a pivotal role, as the synergy between his personal and professional life created a foundation upon which his legacy could thrive. The values and principles he upheld continue to resonate, serving as guiding beacons for those enchanted by the allure of magic. It is within these values that the essence of Herrmann's enduring legacy can be found - in the generosity, resilience, and innovation that encapsulate his contribution to the world of magic. This legacy, etched in time, stands as a timeless reminder of the transformative power of dedication and the profound impact one individual can have on an entire art form.

The Final Act

A Glimpse Behind the Curtain

As the date of Alexander Herrmann's final performance approached, there was an air of poignant anticipation surrounding the great magician. Those close to him spoke of the meticulous attention to detail that defined his preparations for this momentous occasion. Walking backstage at the grand theater where he would soon mesmerize his audience one last time, one could sense the charged atmosphere of focused energy and profound significance. The familiar scent of polished wood and the murmur of hushed conversations filled the air as Herrmann oversaw every aspect of the stage set-up with an unwavering commitment to perfection. Amidst the controlled chaos of last-minute adjustments, his calm demeanor gave no hint of the torrential emotions swirling within. Observing Herrmann rehearsing with steadfast determination, one could glimpse the essence of his artistry – a seamless blend of technical mastery and emotive storytelling. Each movement, each gesture seemed imbued with deep meaning, reflecting a lifetime of dedication to the craft. Behind the scenes, the seemingly effortless illusions were honed to an exquisite precision, ensuring that every flourish and sleight would enrapture the audience one final time. More than just a masterful magician, Herrmann was a consummate performer, infusing each act with an indefinable magic that transcended the boundaries of reality. Among the flurry of activity, moments of quiet introspection revealed a man grappling with the weight of both his legacy and mortality. In those intimate instants, glimpses of vulnerability surfaced, offering a rare insight into the profound emotional journey that shaped his final performance. His eyes held the wisdom of decades spent in pursuit of enchantment, while his movements reflected a graceful acceptance of life's fleeting nature. It was as though every practiced flourish and enigmatic smile carried the weight of farewell, leaving an indelible mark upon the very fabric of his being. In the hush of the dimly lit backstage area, one could feel the reverence with which Herrmann prepared for his swansong. Every detail, from the placement of props to the intonation of his whispered incantations, was infused with purpose and meaning. Here, behind the curtain, a maestro molded illusion into reality, weaving ephemeral wonders into the tapestry of existence. And as the hour drew near, the anticipation grew, carrying with it the unspoken knowledge that this final performance would etch itself into the annals of history, transcending mere magic to become a timeless testament to the human spirit.

The Last Performance

As the final curtain drew near for Alexander Herrmann, the anticipation and emotions surrounding his last performance were palpable. The venue buzzed with a unique blend of excitement and nostalgia, as fans and colleagues from across the globe gathered to witness the magician's farewell act. The atmosphere was electric, charged with a sense of history in the making and a profound respect for the man who had mesmerized audiences for decades. Herrmann's last show wasn't just another spectacle; it was a poignant display of mastery and artistry that transcended the boundaries of conventional entertainment. Each illusion, every sleight of hand, and meticulously choreographed movement carried the weight of a lifetime dedicated to perfecting an ancient craft. As he took center stage for the final time, the magician's presence commanded attention, his trademark charisma now tinged with a bittersweet undercurrent. Throughout the performance, whispers of awe and admiration reverberated through the audience, punctuated by gasps of wonder at Herrmann's unparalleled skill. Every trick seemed imbued with profound significance, serving as a testament to a legacy marked by innovation and unwavering dedication. Spectators found themselves caught in a whirlwind of emotions, oscillating between spellbound fascination and a growing awareness of the impending loss. The culmination of the evening arrived with a grand finale that surpassed all expectations. In a mesmerizing display of showmanship, Herrmann executed his most iconic illusions with an unmatched finesse, leaving the crowd suspended in a state of collective disbelief and reverence. His final bow echoed the sentiments of gratitude and admiration that permeated the auditorium, a poignant acknowledgment of the profound impact his artistry had made on countless lives. As the lights dimmed and the applause resounded, an indelible sense of closure and reverence filled the space. It was more than just the end of a performance; it marked the conclusion of an era—an era defined by the enigmatic allure of Alexander Herrmann. The echoes of his final act lingered in the hearts and minds of those present, forever etched into the annals of magical history, ensuring that his legacy would endure beyond the stage and into eternity.

An Unexpected Exit

The world of magic was left reeling when news of Alexander Herrmann's sudden passing spread like wildfire. Fans, fellow magicians, and admirers were plunged into disbelief as the realization set in that the illustrious performer had taken his final bow. The shock and sadness rippled through every corner of the entertainment industry, where Herrmann had been a revered figure. His untimely departure created an irreplaceable void, leaving many struggling to comprehend the unexpected exit of a man who had captured the imaginations of millions. As the details of his passing emerged, the public clung onto memories of his captivating performances, unable to fathom that such a force in the magical realm could suddenly be silenced. The outpouring of grief and heartfelt tributes from around the globe bore testimony to the profound impact Herrmann had made in his lifetime. It was a stark reminder of how swiftly life can change and serve as a poignant reflection on the impermanence of even the most extraordinary legacies. The magic community mourned the loss of a luminary, while the wider world grappled with bidding adieu to a beloved entertainer whose unique brand of enchantment had transcended cultural boundaries.

The News Spreads

The news of Herrmann's passing spread like wildfire, igniting a wave of disbelief and sorrow across the city. People emerged from their homes with an air of solemnity, gathering in quiet clusters on street corners and at cafes to mourn the loss of a beloved figure. It was as if the entire city had collectively bowed its head in shared grief. The once bustling streets now bore a quietude that resonated with the weight of the somber tidings. Every conversation seemed to gravitate towards the profound impact Herrmann had made during his lifetime. His magical performances had captivated hearts and minds, transcending barriers of age, class, and culture. Citizens recalled cherished memories of witnessing his acts of wonder and marvel, and the realization that such enchantment would no longer grace their lives cast a pall over the community. Among the newsbearers, the city's children stood out, their young faces etched with a blend of innocence and melancholy, for they had grown up under the spell of Herrmann's artistry. Parents found themselves navigating delicate discussions with their little ones, seeking to console them amidst their own heartfelt lamentations. The local schools, typically abuzz with youthful exuberance, now echoed with subdued whispers and reflective gazes, bearing testimony to the depth of impact Herrmann had left on the next generation. Throughout the day, tributes began to materialize spontaneously. Floral bouquets, notes of gratitude, and tokens of remembrance adorned the bustling square at Herrmann's theater, transforming it into a poignant centerpiece of collective homage. A sense of unity permeated the city as acquaintances and strangers alike found solidarity in their shared sorrow. The newspapers swiftly disseminated the grim news, devoting entire sections to commemorating Herrmann's life and legacy. Elegies penned by prominent citizens adorned the fronts of dailies, each offering personal recollections of how Herrmann's magic had touched their lives. Readers combed through the tributes, finding solace and catharsis in the words of fellow mourners. As evening descended, the city's skyline twinkled with a blend of sunlight-drenched windows and the first embers of streetlights. An ethereal quality tinged the atmosphere, as if the world itself paid silent tribute to the departing maestro of enchantment. Herrmann's absence was palpable, yet his spirit lingered in the hearts of all those who had been moved by his wondrous art. The indelible mark of his legacy continued to resonate across the city, a testament to the enduring power of magic, love, and remembrance.

A City in Mourning

The news of Herrmann's sudden passing sent shockwaves through the city, and an air of mourning descended upon its inhabitants. People from all walks of life, whether they were ardent fans or mere admirers of the great magician, felt a profound sense of loss. The once lively streets now seemed quieter, the excitement replaced by a somber, reflective atmosphere. As the word spread, businesses closed their doors early out of respect for Herrmann, and even the bustling markets seemed to lose their usual vigor. It was as though the city itself had paused to acknowledge the departure of a beloved figure. Gatherings spontaneously formed at street corners and cafes, with groups of individuals engaging in heartfelt conversations about the impact Herrmann had on their lives. His performances had been a source of joy and wonder for so many, and now, his absence was keenly felt. Strangers became connected through shared memories and anecdotes, recounting the moments when they had witnessed Herrmann's enchanting acts. The outpouring of sorrow was palpable, bringing a sense of unity and solidarity to the community. Tributes began to emerge throughout the city, with impromptu displays of flowers, cards, and mementos adorning the entrances of theaters where Herrmann had once graced the stage. These poignant gestures served as a testament to the profound impact that Herrmann had made on the lives of those who had been touched by his artistry. Even the local newspaper ran special editions dedicated to honoring Herrmann's legacy, filled with touching stories and commemorative messages from readers who wished to express their deep gratitude for the magic he had woven into their lives. Amidst the collective grief, there was also a stirring determination to keep Herrmann's spirit alive. Plans began to surface for a memorial event, where people could come together to pay their respects and celebrate the indelible mark Herrmann had left on their city. The outpouring of support and affection for Herrmann's memory was a testament to the enduring impact of his art. The city may have been in mourning, but it was also embracing the opportunity to honor and preserve the magic that had touched so many lives.

Heartfelt Tributes

The passing of Alexander Herrmann marked the end of an era, leaving a palpable void in the hearts of countless individuals. As news of his departure spread like wildfire, a profound sense of loss shrouded cities and towns that had once been graced by the magician's mesmerizing performances. Amidst this collective grief, an outpouring of poignant tributes began to emerge, painting a vivid tapestry of Herrmann's impact on the lives he had touched. From esteemed colleagues to devoted fans, testimonials poured in from every corner of the globe, each one bearing witness to the indelible mark left by the legendary illusionist. Fellow magicians recounted personal anecdotes of Herrmann's mentorship and camaraderie, highlighting the unwavering support and generosity that had endeared him to so many within the magical fraternity. Their shared reverence for his artistry manifested in heartfelt eulogies that celebrated not only his unparalleled skill but also his gracious demeanor and boundless passion for the craft. Beyond the confines of the magic community, ordinary citizens sought solace in sharing their cherished memories of witnessing Herrmann's extraordinary feats. Their poignant recollections painted a portrait of a man whose performances had transcended mere entertainment, embedding themselves as enduring sources of wonderment and inspiration. To these individuals, Herrmann had symbolized a conduit to the enchanting realm of possibility, weaving awe-inspiring narratives that imbued their lives with a touch of magic. In response to this overwhelming outpouring of adoration, tributes and memorials sprung up in countless locales synonymous with Herrmann's illustrious career. Theatres where he had once enthralled audiences became hallowed grounds, adorned with flowers, handwritten notes, and mementos that bore testament to the profound impact he had made. Devotees young and old congregated to pay their respects, forming a collective tapestry of love and gratitude that served as an emblem of the magician's enduring legacy. As the tributes continued to pour in, it became evident that Alexander Herrmann's influence extended far beyond the realms of entertainment. His artistry had permeated the cultural fabric of society, leaving an indelible impression on generations past and present. Whether through his astonishing illusions or his unwavering commitment to his craft, Herrmann had left an ineffaceable mark that would echo throughout history, inspiring future generations to embrace the transformative power of magic.

Family and Farewell

The passing of Alexander Herrmann, known to many as Herrmann the Great, took a toll on more than just his adoring fans and the magic community at large. Behind the renowned illusionist stood a close-knit family who had been a part of his journey from the very beginning. As news of his demise spread across the world, his loved ones found themselves in the midst of an outpouring of condolences and kind words from individuals whose lives had been touched by Herrmann's incomparable artistry. But amidst the public acclaim, it was within the intimate circle of his family that the true depth of Herrmann's impact became unequivocally evident. His immediate family, including his devoted wife, children, and siblings, found themselves not only grappling with profound grief but also shouldering the responsibility of preserving and advancing his legacy. The weight of this monumental task was tempered by the overwhelming support and solidarity they received from those who had witnessed Herrmann's greatness both on and off the stage. In the days following his passing, the Herrmann household became a place of solace and reminiscence, where cherished memories were swapped, tears flowed freely, and plans for how best to honor and perpetuate his artistic contributions were earnestly discussed. While bidding farewell to a beloved patriarch and luminary of magic, the Herrmann family also had to contend with the hard realities of saying goodbye to a loved one. Funeral arrangements and tributes occupied their thoughts, serving as poignant reminders of the colossal void left behind by Herrmann's absence. It was during this time that his family unearthed an assortment of personal effects, each laden with sentimental value and carrying profound emotional resonance. These tangible mementos—be it his trusty deck of cards, a well-worn top hat, or photographs capturing moments of joy and triumph—served to reignite the warmth of his presence and reinforce his enduring influence within their hearts. Amidst the emotional turbulence, the Herrmann family found themselves bolstering one another, drawing strength and compassion from their shared love for him. Their unity and unwavering determination to honor his memory offered a poignant testament to the profound bond that held them together. As final farewells were exchanged and the curtain fell on Herrmann's earthly chapter, his family emerged from the crucible of grief with a renewed resolve to champion his timeless legacy. For them, honoring Herrmann's life's work was not merely an obligation; it was a solemn privilege and an expression of profound love. Through the tumultuous aftermath of his passing, the Herrmann family remained resolute in preserving the enchanting legacy of their beloved patriarch and ensuring that the luster of his artistry would endure for generations to come.

A Legacy Etched in Time

Alexander Herrmann's influence on the world of magic is so profound that his legacy is truly etched in time. His contributions to the art form have left an indelible mark, shaping the way we perceive and appreciate magic today. Through his unparalleled skill, unwavering dedication, and relentless passion, Herrmann not only captivated audiences around the globe but also inspired countless aspiring magicians. His commitment to perfection and innovation set a standard that continues to drive and motivate magicians of all generations. The impact of his performances, teachings, and creative flair continues to reverberate through the annals of magical history, reminding us of his enduring influence. Beyond the confines of the stage, Herrmann's philanthropic endeavors and generous spirit endeared him to communities far and wide. His charitable contributions and acts of kindness enriched the lives of many, embodying the true essence of an iconic figure whose influence transcends entertainment. Whether it was sharing the wonder of magic with underprivileged children or supporting charitable causes, Herrmann's compassion mirrored the magic he brought to the world. His legacy extends far beyond the realm of illusions and sleight of hand, resonating deeply with those who were touched by his performances and goodwill. Today, as we reflect on the lasting impact of Alexander Herrmann, we are reminded of the artistry, the generosity, and the boundless spirit that defined his life. His legacy continues to inspire new generations of magicians, ensuring that his name will forever remain synonymous with the captivating allure of magic.

Reflections from Contemporaries

As news of Alexander Herrmann's passing reverberated through the global magic community, an outpouring of poignant reflections and tributes from his contemporaries flooded in, painting a vivid portrait of the indelible mark Herrmann had left on the world of magic. The sentiments expressed by fellow magicians spoke not only to the unparalleled artistry and showmanship that characterized Herrmann's performances but also to the profound impact he had on shaping the trajectory of modern magic. Countless magicians, from vaudeville acts to esteemed illusionists, shared stories of how Herrmann's revolutionary techniques and captivating stage presence had inspired them in their own artistic pursuits. Renowned magician Robert-Houdin described Herrmann as a "pioneer whose innovative approach to magic transcended traditional boundaries, forever altering the landscape of our craft." Similarly, contemporary illusionist Harry Kellar fondly reminisced about Herrmann's mentorship and how his guidance had paved the way for Kellar's own illustrious career. These heartfelt accounts underscored the immense respect and admiration that Herrmann commanded within the fraternity of magicians, solidifying his legacy as a luminary whose influence extended far beyond his era. Furthermore, several contemporaries delved into the profound impact of Herrmann's enduring performances, which had captivated audiences across continents. Their recollections painted a vivid tapestry of awe-inspiring illusions and masterful sleight of hand that had audiences spellbound, often at a loss to discern reality from enchantment. Eulogies and testimonials underscored the timeless allure of Herrmann's art, highlighting its profound resonance across generations and cultures. It is evident that Herrmann's enduring contributions to the world of magic shall continue to serve as a wellspring of inspiration and innovation for present and future practitioners alike, perpetuating his legacy as an iconic figure in the annals of magical history.

The Enduring Magic of Herrmann

Alexander Herrmann's impact on the world of magic continues to reverberate through the ages. His artistry, innovation, and dedication to his craft have left an indelible mark on the history of magic, captivating audiences and inspiring future generations of magicians. As we reflect on Herrmann's legacy, it becomes evident that his enduring magic goes beyond his spellbinding performances. One of the most remarkable aspects of Herrmann's enduring magic is the timeless appeal of his illusions. Even in today's modern era, where technology and special effects dominate entertainment, the elegance and ingenuity of Herrmann's illusions continue to captivate and mystify audiences. The seamless blend of showmanship, storytelling, and technical skill in Herrmann's performances transcends time, making his magic as mesmerizing today as it was in the past. Moreover, Herrmann's influence extends far beyond the confines of the stage. His undying passion for sharing the art of magic has inspired countless individuals to pursue their own magical dreams. From aspiring magicians to seasoned professionals, Herrmann's teachings and principles have served as a guiding light, shaping the very fabric of the magic community. His emphasis on creativity, dedication, and showmanship has become a cornerstone of magical performance, ensuring that his legacy lives on in the hearts and minds of those who are touched by his magic. Herrmann's enduring magic also lies in the profound emotions evoked by his performances. Beyond the spectacle of magic, Herrmann possessed a rare ability to connect with his audience on a deep, emotional level. His performances were not merely displays of skill and trickery, but immersive experiences that stirred wonder, awe, and joy in the hearts of all who witnessed them. This emotional resonance has etched Herrmann's name in the annals of magical history, ensuring that his impact endures through the power of human connection. Finally, the enduring magic of Herrmann is embodied in the collective memories and testimonials of those who had the privilege of witnessing his artistry firsthand. Countless tales of astonishment, laughter, and pure amazement serve as testaments to the lasting impression Herrmann made on all who crossed paths with him. These cherished moments serve as poignant reminders of the enchanting legacy he has left behind, weaving a tapestry of wonder and delight that transcends time and space. In honoring the enduring magic of Alexander Herrmann, we pay homage to a true maestro of his craft, whose influence continues to resonate across generations. Through his timeless illusions, profound teachings, emotional impact, and cherished memories, Herrmann's magic remains as vibrant and awe-inspiring today as it was during his illustrious lifetime. It is a testament to his unparalleled artistry and unwavering spirit, ensuring that the legacy of the great Herrmann will endure for eternity.

Herrmann's Legacy After His Death

The Impact of His Performances

Herrmann's shows captivated audiences worldwide, leaving a lasting impression on the art of magic. His performances were not just displays of skill and showmanship; they were transformative experiences that left an indelible mark on all who witnessed them. Through his groundbreaking use of elaborate stagecraft, dazzling illusions, and charismatic showmanship, Herrmann elevated the perception of magic from mere trickery to a sophisticated form of entertainment and artistry. His innovative approach to combining storytelling with magical effects set a new standard for modern magic shows. As a result, Herrmann's legacy lives on in every magician who has been inspired by his trailblazing performances. At the heart of Herrmann's impact was his ability to transport audiences to a realm where the impossible became possible. His mastery of illusion and innovation in theatrical presentation set him apart as a true pioneer of the magical arts. Whether he was performing grand illusions on a lavish stage or engaging in more intimate close-up magic, Herrmann possessed the rare gift of captivating audiences of all ages and backgrounds. His influence stretched far beyond the confines of the theater, permeating popular culture and shaping the public's perception of magic. Moreover, Herrmann's legacy endures in the techniques and styles adopted by contemporary magicians. The enduring appeal of his performances lies in their ability to evoke wonder and imagination, transcending language and cultural barriers. By weaving elements of mystery, suspense, and humor into his acts, Herrmann ensured that his shows resonated with diverse audiences around the world. His performances epitomized the transformative power of magic, inspiring countless individuals to pursue careers in illusion and enchantment. In summary, the impact of Herrmann's performances reverberates through the annals of magical history, forever influencing the trajectory of the art form. His mesmerizing shows continue to shape the evolution of magic, serving as a testament to his enduring legacy and undying passion for enchanting audiences.

Pioneering Modern Magic Shows

Alexander Herrmann's impact on the world of magic extended far beyond his own performances. One of his most significant contributions was in pioneering modern magic shows, setting a new standard for theatricality and spectacle. Herrmann understood the importance of creating a compelling narrative and captivating visuals to enhance the experience for the audience. His shows were meticulously crafted productions that seamlessly integrated storytelling, music, and stunning illusions, elevating the art form to a new level of grandeur and sophistication. Herrmann's innovative approach to staging magic laid the groundwork for the extravagant productions that would become synonymous with modern-day magicians such as David Copperfield and Siegfried & Roy. By introducing elaborate set designs, special effects, and choreographed performances, Herrmann transformed the perception of magic from simple tricks into a full-scale theatrical extravaganza. His influence can be seen in the dazzling spectacles that continue to captivate audiences around the world today. Moreover, Herrmann's emphasis on showmanship and entertainment value revolutionized the way magicians engaged with their audiences. He recognized the power of building an emotional connection with spectators and leaving them in awe. This focus on the overall experience, rather than just the mechanics of the tricks, reshaped the entire landscape of magic performance. Magicians following in Herrmann's footsteps learned to prioritize storytelling and audience engagement, forever changing the dynamics of magic shows. Furthermore, Herrmann's legacy in pioneering modern magic shows is evident in the enduring popularity and relevance of magic as a form of entertainment. His ability to create immersive and unforgettable experiences paved the way for the continued evolution and expansion of magic in popular culture. From television specials to large-scale stage productions, his influence continues to inspire present-day magicians to push the boundaries of creativity and theatricality, ensuring that the legacy of Alexander Herrmann lives on in every mesmerizing magic show.

Inspiration for Future Magicians

Alexander Herrmann's legacy is not just a collection of performances and tricks. It transcends time, inspiring generations of magicians to come. His pioneering spirit in pushing the boundaries of magic shows has left an indelible mark on the art of illusion. The very essence of his performances continues to stir the imagination and creativity of aspiring magicians around the world. Herrmann's ability to captivate audiences with his seamless blend of storytelling and spellbinding illusions serves as a masterclass for budding magicians. He has set a standard that encourages performers to delve deeper into the intricacies of their craft, challenging them to innovate and evolve the art form. His influence can be seen in the way modern magicians approach their acts, striving for excellence while infusing their performances with a touch of Herrmann's magic. Beyond the technical aspects, Herrmann's dedication to entertaining and enchanting his audience serves as a poignant reminder for future magicians. His commitment to creating experiences that transcend mere tricks or illusions reminds them that magic is not just about clever techniques, but about forging a profound connection with the spectators. In today's world, where technology often threatens to overshadow the wonder of live performances, Herrmann's legacy inspires magicians to keep the authentic charm of magic alive. Moreover, Herrmann's influence extends beyond the stage, permeating the very philosophy of magic itself. His emphasis on showmanship, theatricality, and the art of illusion as a vehicle for storytelling continues to shape the way magicians conceive and present their acts. By demonstrating that magic is not confined to bewilderment but can be a powerful medium for conveying emotions and narratives, he compels future magicians to consider the broader impact of their craft. Ultimately, Herrmann's enduring influence not only shapes the technical prowess of future magicians but also fosters a deep reverence for the art of illusion itself. His legacy kindles a passion within aspiring magicians, urging them to preserve the enchantment and mystery of magic while embracing innovation and modernity. As they embark on their own magical journeys, they carry with them the torch of inspiration ignited by Alexander Herrmann, ensuring that his timeless legacy continues to inspire awe and wonder for generations to come.

Preserving the Art of Illusion

Preserving the Art of Illusion is a task that transcends time, and Alexander Herrmann's influence plays a significant role in this noble endeavor. The timeless allure of magic has always relied on the preservation and passing down of tricks, techniques, and knowledge from one generation to the next. Herrmann's unique stage presence and dramatic performances have left an indelible mark on the art of illusion, inspiring magicians around the world to uphold the traditions of their craft and continue to captivate audiences with wonder and mystery. From grand theaters to intimate venues, the legacy of preserving and advancing the art of illusion has thrived due in no small part to the enduring impact of Alexander Herrmann. The custodians of magic understand the importance of keeping classic illusions alive, while also embracing innovation to push the boundaries of what is possible. Through mentorship, apprenticeship, and educational initiatives, the intricate secrets of the trade are carefully handed down from seasoned professionals to aspiring magicians. As they learn the intricacies of mastering sleight of hand, misdirection, and audience engagement, these successors become integral in upholding the legacy of great magicians like Herrmann.

By fostering an environment of respect for the history and tradition of magic, they ensure that future generations will marvel at the same wonders that have enthralled audiences for centuries. Furthermore, the preservation of the art of illusion extends beyond the technical aspects of magic. It encompasses the cultivation of a sense of wonder and amazement, sparking creativity and imagination in both performers and spectators. Through dedicated efforts to preserve the allure of magic, magicians and enthusiasts alike strive to capture and inspire the spirit of intrigue and fascination that lies at the core of this enchanting art form. With each new performance, each shared revelation of a secret, and each instance of passing on the torch, the magical legacy of Alexander Herrmann and his contemporaries remains vibrantly preserved for future generations to cherish. In conclusion, the ongoing commitment to preserving the art of illusion stands as a testament to Alexander Herrmann's lasting impact on the world of magic. The dedication of magicians worldwide to honor the traditions, innovate responsibly, and nurture the next wave of talent ensures that the enigmatic and captivating nature of magic endures, continuing to captivate and inspire audiences for years to come.

Family and Successors in Magic

Alexander Herrmann's legacy extended beyond his own performances, leaving a lasting impression on the world of magic. His influence continued through his family members and successors who carried on his artistry and contributed to the evolution of magic as a performing art. Following Alexander Herrmann's passing, his wife Adelaide Herrmann bravely took the reins of his magic show, becoming one of the first female magicians to achieve international recognition. Adelaide honored her late husband's legacy by mastering his illusions and captivating audiences with her own unique style. She became a trailblazer for women in magic, paving the way for future generations of female magicians. The Herrmann dynasty further flourished through the contributions of Leon Herrmann, Alexander's nephew, who continued the family's magical tradition. Taking up the mantle of Herrmann the Great, he ensured that the family's prestigious name remained at the forefront of the magic industry. With intricate performances and innovative illusions, Leon upheld the legacy of his uncle, captivating audiences around the world. Arthur Herrmann, Alexander's brother, also played a pivotal role in preserving the family's magical heritage. He passed down invaluable knowledge and techniques, serving as a mentor to aspiring magicians and ensuring that the Herrmann legacy remained a cherished part of the magical community. Beyond the family circle, Alexander Herrmann's influence reached numerous protégés and apprentices who were inspired by his skill and showmanship. Many of these individuals went on to become renowned magicians in their own right, spreading the art of magic to new horizons while honoring Herrmann's legacy. It is through the dedication and passion of these individuals that the spirit of Alexander Herrmann lives on, continuing to inspire and enchant audiences with the timeless wonder of magic. Their commitment to the art form ensures that the Herrmann legacy remains an enduring force, shaping the trajectory of magic for generations to come.

Cultural Significance

The cultural significance of Alexander Herrmann's legacy in magic cannot be overstated. Throughout his illustrious career, Herrmann captivated audiences and left an indelible mark on the art of illusion. His performances transcended mere entertainment, becoming part of the cultural fabric of the societies in which he performed. Herrmann's ability to weave storytelling, mystery, and amazement into his acts not only entertained but also inspired and influenced generations of spectators, shaping their perceptions of magic and the impossible. As a result, Herrmann became a prominent figure in popular culture, and his influence extended far beyond the confines of the stage. Through his pioneering performances, Herrmann introduced new dimensions to live entertainment, setting the stage for the modern magic shows that continue to enthrall audiences today. His innovative techniques and showmanship paved the way for future magicians, shaping the very essence of magic as a performing art. Beyond the realm of live performances, Herrmann's impact on popular culture is evident in various forms of media, including literature, film, and visual arts. His mystique and charisma have been perpetuated in countless artistic interpretations, fueling fascination with the art of magic and further embedding its presence in cultural narratives. In addition to his artistic contributions, Herrmann's cultural significance is underscored by his role as a symbol of perseverance and determination. His ability to overcome adversity and achieve unparalleled success served as an inspirational narrative for aspiring artists and individuals facing their own challenges. Furthermore, the enduring allure of Herrmann's legacy continues to inspire new generations of magicians to push the boundaries of the art form, ensuring that his cultural impact remains relevant and enduring. Herrmann's enduring cultural significance extends to historical recognition, memorialization, and the continued integration of his influence into popular culture. Through these facets, his legacy continues to resonate profoundly, solidifying his place as an icon in the cultural tapestry of magic.

Historical Recognition

Alexander Herrmann holds a special place in the annals of magic history, not only for his mesmerizing performances but also for the indelible mark he left on the art form. His contributions to the world of illusion and entertainment have earned him profound historical recognition that continues to resonate to this day. Herrmann's enduring impact on the cultural landscape is evident through the widespread influence he exerted during his time and beyond. His innovative techniques and groundbreaking stagecraft challenged conventions and set new standards for magicians around the world. By pushing the boundaries of traditional magic, Herrmann cemented his legacy as a trailblazer, inspiring future generations of performers. Moreover, Herrmann's historical recognition is underscored by the significant role he played in popularizing magic as a mainstream form of entertainment. His ability to captivate audiences across diverse settings and demographics propelled magic into the spotlight, garnering newfound respect and appreciation for the craft. This heightened visibility not only elevated Herrmann's own status but also laid the groundwork for the thriving magic industry we witness today. Beyond his artistic achievements, historical recognition for Herrmann also stems from his pivotal role in bridging different cultures through the universal language of magic. As an international sensation, Herrmann transcended geographical and linguistic barriers, captivating hearts and minds across continents. His tours across Europe and beyond not only showcased the artistry of magic but also fostered cultural exchange and understanding, leaving an indelible mark on global entertainment history. Furthermore, Herrmann's historical recognition is upheld by the numerous accolades and honors bestowed upon him during and after his lifetime. From prestigious awards to accolades from monarchs and dignitaries, Herrmann's contributions to the world of magic were celebrated on a grand scale, solidifying his status as an iconic figure in the narrative of magic's evolution. In conclusion, the historical recognition of Alexander Herrmann is a testament to his profound impact on the world of magic. His enduring influence, unparalleled showmanship, and contributions to the cultural fabric of society have secured his place in history as a luminary whose legacy continues to inspire and captivate audiences worldwide.

Memorials and Tributes

The legacy of Alexander Herrmann has been immortalized through countless memorials and tributes. Magicians and fans, both past and present, have paid homage to the master magician in various forms. His influence on the world of magic is undeniable, and as a result, numerous tributes have been established to celebrate his contributions. From statues and plaques dedicated to his memory in his hometown to annual magic festivals held in his honor, Herrmann's presence continues to be felt long after his passing. Dedicated followers of his work have worked tirelessly to preserve his memory, ensuring that his impact on the art of illusion remains enduring. Furthermore, magicians worldwide continue to pay tribute to Herrmann by incorporating elements of his signature acts into their own performances. This serves as not only a homage to the great magician but also as a way to keep his timeless magic alive for new generations. The magic community has come together to establish scholarships, awards, and grants in Herrmann's name, fostering the growth of future talents and carrying forward his spirit of innovation. In addition to these efforts, numerous documentaries, films, and books have been produced to narrate and commemorate the illustrious career of Alexander Herrmann. These works not only serve to educate the public about his magical innovations but also ensure that his extraordinary legacy remains an integral part of the history of magic. Moreover, magic enthusiasts continue to organize special events and exhibitions dedicated to showcasing Herrmann's life and achievements, allowing audiences to delve deeper into the captivating world of one of the greatest magicians of all time. Through these multifaceted memorials and tributes, Alexander Herrmann's profound impact on the art of magic continues to be celebrated, explored, and cherished by enthusiasts and professionals alike.

Magic Organizations Influenced by Herrmann

Alexander Herrmann's legacy extends far beyond his mesmerizing performances and groundbreaking illusions. His impact on the world of magic is also evident through the profound influence he had on magic organizations around the globe. To this day, many magic societies and clubs draw inspiration from Herrmann's innovative techniques, showmanship, and dedication to advancing the art of illusion. One of the most significant ways in which Herrmann's influence can be seen is in the establishment and growth of magic societies that aim to preserve and promote the rich traditions of magic. These organizations often look to Herrmann as a guiding light, embracing his values of excellence, creativity, and the relentless pursuit of magical innovation. Herrmann's emphasis on the importance of community and collaboration within the magic fraternity has inspired the formation of numerous magical societies fostering a sense of camaraderie among magicians, providing platforms for knowledge sharing, mentorship, and honing the craft of magic. The ethos of inclusivity and support championed by Herrmann continues to thrive within these organizations, shaping the experiences of budding and seasoned magicians alike. Furthermore, Herrmann's dedication to elevating the perception of magic as a sophisticated art form has led to the integration of educational initiatives within many magic societies. By promoting the scholarly study of magic history, theory, and performance techniques, these organizations uphold Herrmann's commitment to ensuring that the essence of magic endures as a respected cultural tradition. Through workshops, lectures, and publications, contemporary magic societies emulate Herrmann's belief in nurturing the talents of aspiring magicians and preserving the timeless allure of magic for future generations. In addition to upholding the traditional values and practices championed by Herrmann, modern magic organizations have also embraced technological advancements and digital platforms to expand their reach and engage with wider audiences, drawing inspiration from Herrmann's penchant for leveraging the latest innovations in entertainment and spectacle to captivate audiences across the globe. They honor Herrmann's spirit by embracing new media while staying true to the essence of magic as an art form that transcends time and space. By acknowledging and celebrating Alexander Herrmann's enduring influence, these magic organizations pay homage to a legendary figure whose pioneering vision continues to shape the landscape of magic, ensuring that his remarkable legacy remains an enduring source of inspiration for generations of magicians to come.

The Continuing Influence on Popular Culture

Alexander Herrmann's influence on popular culture extends far beyond the realms of magic and illusion. His groundbreaking performances and pioneering techniques have left an indelible mark, shaping the way magic is portrayed and perceived in mainstream media. Herrmann's legacy continues to resonate in various aspects of popular culture, influencing literature, theater, cinema, and even contemporary music. Literature has been profoundly impacted by Herrmann's magical feats, with numerous works of fiction and non-fiction drawing inspiration from his life and career. His enigmatic persona and captivating stage presence have served as a muse for many renowned authors, who have integrated elements of magic and illusion into their storytelling. The allure of Herrmann's performances continues to captivate audiences across different mediums, demonstrating the enduring appeal of his artistry. Similarly, the influence of Alexander Herrmann's performances is evident in the realm of theater, inspiring myriad productions that seek to reenact the sense of wonder and mystery that permeated his shows. Countless plays and musicals have been crafted to celebrate the art of illusion and pay homage to Herrmann's lasting impact on the world of entertainment. The echo of his performances reverberates through these theatrical spectacles, ensuring that his contributions are immortalized on the stage. Cinema, too, has felt the profound influence of Alexander Herrmann, with his legacy manifesting in iconic films that explore the enchanting realm of magic. From classic movies depicting the golden age of magic to contemporary blockbusters featuring enthralling illusions, the enduring fascination with Herrmann's legacy is palpable in cinematic representations of the art form. His ability to mesmerize audiences transcends time, making him an omnipresent figure in the visual storytelling landscape. Furthermore, the impact of Alexander Herrmann on popular culture extends to the realm of contemporary music, where his mystique and showmanship have inspired compositions that evoke the spirit of magic and wonder. Musicians and lyricists have drawn from the essence of Herrmann's performances, infusing their creations with mystical themes and enchanting melodies that reflect the allure of illusion. His influence can be discerned in the lyrical narratives and evocative harmonies that evoke a sense of enchantment, underscoring the enduring relevance of his artistic legacy. In conclusion, Alexander Herrmann's enduring influence on popular culture is a testament to the timeless appeal of his magical prowess. From literature to theater, cinema, and music, his transformative impact continues to shape and enrich the creative tapestry of popular culture, ensuring that his legacy remains woven into the fabric of entertainment for generations to come.

Remembering Herrmann

A Lasting Impression

Alexander Herrmann's legacy has left a profound and indelible impression on the world of magic, a lasting mark that continues to inspire and captivate performers and audiences alike. His mastery of the art of illusion and his innovative techniques have set a standard that magicians aspire to achieve even in the contemporary era. Herrmann's influence is profound, transcending time and leaving an enduring impact that resonates with those who admire and study his work. From his awe-inspiring stage presence to his revolutionary illusions, Herrmann's evocative performances continue to be emulated and revered. His enduring contribution to the magical arts stands as a testament to his unparalleled talent and commitment to his craft, ensuring that his name will forever be woven into the fabric of magic history. Those who have had the privilege of witnessing his performances or studying his techniques are often deeply moved by the elegance and mystery he brought to the stage. The whispers of Herrmann's enchanting performances continue to echo through generations, bearing witness to the timeless wonder he created. Through his artistic expression, he cultivated a profound connection with his audience, sparking a sense of marvel and fascination that lingers long after the curtain falls. This enduring impact reflects the depth of Herrmann's artistry and the emotion he infused into each moment of his performances. Even today, contemporary magicians and enthusiasts pay homage to Herrmann's unmatched skill and charismatic stage presence, recognizing him as a beacon of inspiration. The power of his artistry traverses time, stirring emotions and leaving a profound imprint on all who encounter his legacy.

Tributes from Contemporaries

The legacy of Alexander Herrmann extends far beyond his timeless performances and breathtaking illusions. Throughout his illustrious career, Herrmann garnered the deep admiration and respect of his fellow magicians, earning numerous heartfelt tributes that spoke to the impact he had on the art of magic. As contemporaries reflect on Herrmann's influence, it becomes clear that his contributions transcended mere entertainment, leaving an indelible mark on the magical community. Magicians of the time often marveled at Herrmann's mastery of sleight of hand and his ability to captivate audiences with his enigmatic stage presence. Countless letters and personal accounts attest to the profound inspiration that Herrmann provided for emerging talents, shaping the landscape of magic for generations to come. Furthermore, many esteemed magicians have lauded Herrmann's dedication to the craft and his unwavering commitment to maintaining the highest standards of showmanship. His innovative approach to magic, coupled with his relentless pursuit of perfection, set a benchmark that continues to inspire aspiring magicians today. The outpouring of admiration from contemporaries not only attests to Herrmann's extraordinary skill but also underscores the profound impact he had on the evolution of magic as an art form. From prestigious magic societies to intimate gatherings of peers, tributes celebrating Herrmann's unparalleled contributions resonate throughout the annals of magical history, serving as a testament to his enduring influence. These heartfelt expressions of reverence from esteemed colleagues reveal the depth of Herrmann's impact on the magical community and solidify his status as an icon in the realm of illusion and wonder. Even as time marches forward, these tributes ensure that Alexander Herrmann's remarkable legacy will forever be etched in the fabric of magic, inspiring awe and wonder for years to come.

Stories Told by Family and Friends

In the wake of Alexander Herrmann's passing, family members and friends gathered to share personal anecdotes that revealed the man behind the magician. Stories of his generosity and kindness were abundant, reflecting a side of Herrmann not often seen on stage. His niece recounted how he always made time for her, regaling her with tales of adventure from his travels. A childhood friend spoke of Herrmann's unwavering loyalty and compassion, emphasizing how he never forgot those who had helped him along the way. These intimate accounts painted a portrait of a man who transcended his public persona, showcasing a warmth and humility that endeared him to those closest to him. The stories also shed light on Herrmann's insatiable curiosity and relentless pursuit of perfection. His brother, compelled by emotion, revealed how Alexander would spend countless hours refining his illusions, driven by an unwavering commitment to his craft. Friends shared humorous anecdotes about Herrmann's determination and resilience, recounting incidents where he overcame seemingly insurmountable challenges with grace and humor. These personal recollections not only humanized the legendary magician but also emphasized the profound impact he had on those around him. Whether through simple gestures of kindness or tireless dedication to his art, Herrmann's influence extended far beyond the confines of the stage. Each story served as a testament to his enduring spirit and the lasting impression he left on all who knew him. It became evident that Herrmann's magic was not confined to the realm of trickery and illusion; it existed within the hearts and memories of those fortunate enough to have crossed paths with him. The anecdotes shared by family and friends crystallized Herrmann's legacy, ensuring that he would be remembered not only as a master magician but as a beloved and cherished individual whose spirit continues to inspire generations.

Preserving His Masterpieces

Preserving the masterpieces of Alexander Herrmann is not merely a task; it is a sacred duty. Each illusion, each sleight of hand, and each performance represented a culmination of dedication, artistry, and a touch of sheer magic that has mesmerized audiences for generations. The preservation of Herrmann's masterpieces is a tribute to his enduring legacy and an affirmation of his irreplaceable contribution to the world of magic. Every effort is being made to safeguard and maintain the original props, costumes, and scripts used by Herrmann during his illustrious career. Through meticulous conservation efforts, these artifacts are not just historical relics but living reminders of Herrmann's extraordinary talent and charisma. Each item holds within it the power to transport us back to a time when the impossible seemed achievable, and wonder was just an illusion away. In addition to physical preservation, there is a concerted endeavor to digitize and archive recordings of Herrmann's performances. By capturing his acts on film or audio, future generations can experience the same awe and inspiration that enraptured audiences of the past. These archives also serve as invaluable resources for scholars, historians, and aspiring magicians seeking to unravel the secrets behind Herrmann's enchanting performances. Moreover, replicas of Herrmann's iconic illusions are painstakingly recreated to ensure that modern audiences can witness the marvels that once captivated the world. These reproductions are crafted with an unwavering commitment to authenticity, aiming to recreate not only the mechanics of the illusions but also the essence of Herrmann's spellbinding presence. Furthermore, dedicated museums and private collectors proudly showcase select pieces from Herrmann's illustrious career. The allure of seeing an original Herrmann artifact in person, be it a prop, costume, or poster, is an experience that evokes a profound connection with the maestro himself. Such displays provide a tangible link between the past and the present, keeping Herrmann's spirit alive for enthusiasts and newcomers alike. The endeavors to preserve Alexander Herrmann's masterpieces are not solely about cherishing the past; they are about ensuring that his timeless artistry continues to inspire and enchant future generations. By safeguarding his legacy, we guarantee that the magic of Alexander Herrmann will endure for eternity.

The Influence on Modern Magic

Alexander Herrmann's impact on modern magic is immeasurable. His innovative techniques and brilliant illusions continue to inspire and influence magicians around the world. Through his dedication to the art form and his unwavering commitment to excellence, Herrmann left an indelible mark on the world of magic. The principles he espoused and the performances he delivered have set a standard that continues to be emulated today. One of Herrmann's greatest contributions to modern magic was his emphasis on showmanship and spectacle. He understood the importance of not just executing tricks flawlessly, but also captivating and engaging audiences throughout his performances. This focus on the theatricality of magic has become a hallmark of contemporary magicians, who strive to create unforgettable experiences for their spectators. Furthermore, Herrmann's willingness to push the boundaries of what was considered possible in magic paved the way for the evolution of the art. His daring spirit and willingness to take risks inspired future generations to explore new possibilities and develop their own unique styles. Additionally, Herrmann's use of storytelling within his magic performances revolutionized the way magicians connected with their audiences. By weaving narratives into his illusions, he created an emotional resonance that elevated his shows beyond mere trickery. This approach has influenced modern magicians to infuse their acts with storytelling elements, creating more immersive and memorable performances. Another aspect of Herrmann's legacy in modern magic is his impact on the technical aspects of the craft. His inventions and groundbreaking techniques have had a profound effect on the methods used by contemporary magicians. From his mastery of sleight of hand to his pioneering work in escapology, Herrmann's innovations continue to shape the way magic is performed today. As magicians continue to build on his foundation, they pay homage to his contributions while continually advancing the art form. In conclusion, Alexander Herrmann's influence on modern magic encompasses every facet of the craft. His artistic vision, technical prowess, and dedication to creating enchanting experiences live on through the magicians who continue to be inspired by his legacy.

Cultural Impact and Recognition

The cultural impact and recognition of Alexander Herrmann, also known as Herrmann the Great, cannot be overstated. His influence on the world of magic reverberates through time, leaving an indelible mark on both performers and enthusiasts alike. Herrmann's performances transcended mere entertainment, often delving into the realms of art and wonderment. His ability to captivate audiences with his spellbinding illusions and charismatic stage presence garnered him not only praise but also a place in the hearts of many. As a result, he became a cultural icon whose legacy continues to resonate today. Herrmann's recognition extended far beyond the confines of the stage. Through live performances, publications, and public appearances, he left an enduring impression on the collective consciousness. His contributions to the art of magic elevated its status, transforming it from mere trickery to a respected form of theatrical expression. This evolution not only impacted the entertainment industry but also influenced broader cultural attitudes towards magic and illusion. Moreover, Herrmann's impact was not limited to a particular demographic or geographic location. His tours spanned continents, captivating audiences across Europe and the United States. The universal appeal of his work introduced diverse communities to the art of magic, fostering an appreciation for the craft on a global scale. Throughout his career, Herrmann broke down cultural barriers, effectively uniting people through the shared experience of awe and amazement. In recognition of his profound influence, numerous artistic and cultural institutions have honored Herrmann's legacy. Museums showcase artifacts from his performances, preserving his masterpieces for future generations to behold. Academics study his techniques, analyzing the intricacies of his illusions to gain insight into the artistry behind his performances. Additionally, contemporary magicians and entertainers continue to draw inspiration from his repertoire, keeping his spirit alive in their own acts and paying homage to the enduring impact of his work. Furthermore, the cultural impact of Herrmann's legacy extends beyond the realm of magic itself. His influence has permeated literature, cinema, and popular culture. Countless books, films, and theatrical productions have drawn from his life and career, ensuring that his story remains embedded in the tapestry of artistic expression. Whether portrayed as a larger-than-life figure or as a source of inspiration for fictional characters, Herrmann's enduring presence underscores his significance within the broader cultural landscape. In conclusion, the cultural impact and recognition of Alexander Herrmann encompass a multifaceted legacy that resonates across centuries. By transcending geographical, generational, and artistic boundaries, Herrmann has solidified his position as a foundational figure in the history of magic and entertainment. His enduring influence serves as a testament to the power of performance to transcend time and leave an indelible mark on the fabric of human culture.

Legacy in Literature and Media

Alexander Herrmann's legacy is not confined to the stage but extends into literature and various forms of media, ensuring that his influence and impact on the world of magic continue to thrive. Numerous books, articles, and academic papers have been dedicated to the study of Herrmann's life and work, delving deep into his innovative techniques and legendary performances. These literary works serve as a testament to the enduring fascination with the man known as 'Herrmann the Great.' Moreover, Herrmann's illustrious career has been immortalized through documentaries and films, serving as both educational tools and captivating entertainment for audiences eager to witness the enigmatic allure of magic. The visual medium has allowed contemporary viewers to gain insight into the artistry and showmanship of this revered magician, solidifying his place in the annals of magical history. Furthermore, the digital age has seen an unprecedented surge in online content paying homage to Herrmann, with dedicated websites, social media pages, and digital archives preserving his mesmerizing feats for future generations to behold. These platforms not only keep his memory alive but also foster communities of enthusiasts who continue to celebrate his contributions to the world of illusion. Whether in print or on screen, Alexander Herrmann's presence resonates through time, continuing to captivate and inspire individuals across the globe, perpetuating his unparalleled legacy in literature and media.

Fan Clubs and Dedications

Fan clubs and dedications dedicated to honoring the legacy of Alexander Herrmann have sprouted across the globe, serving as testaments to the profound impact and enduring love for his magical prowess. Each fan club serves as a melting pot of devoted enthusiasts who share a common adoration for Herrmann's contributions to the world of magic. These communities often organize events, conventions, and gatherings where members can revel in their shared passion and celebrate the timeless allure of Herrmann's artistry. From hosting workshops that delve into the secrets behind Herrmann's most iconic illusions to staging charity fundraisers in his honor, these fervent admirers ensure that his name remains immortalized in the annals of magic history. Alongside these fan clubs, countless dedications have been established to pay homage to the indelible mark left by Herrmann. Impressive monuments, statues, and plaques have been erected in various locations, each symbolizing the enduring gratitude and reverence towards Herrmann's unparalleled magical dexterity. Furthermore, annual ceremonies and commemorative events are meticulously arranged to commemorate key milestones and illuminate the life and work of this maestro of magic. Admirers from all walks of life, young and old, continue to flock to these dedications, igniting an unyielding flame of admiration for Herrmann that transcends time and borders. The fervor for creating fan clubs and dedications stems from the desire to safeguard Herrmann's legacy for future generations. These initiatives seek to preserve his memory not just as a master illusionist, but as a pioneer whose innovative spirit forever changed the landscape of magic. The unwavering dedication displayed by fans and organizers alike underscores the enduring fascination with Herrmann's enchanting performances and extraordinary persona. Their concerted efforts ensure that his influence will continuously ripple through the currents of magic, casting an everlasting spell on the hearts and minds of all those enchanted by his mystifying art.

The Place in Magic History

Alexander Herrmann's place in magic history is both distinguished and enduring. His innovative techniques and captivating performances left an indelible mark on the art of magic, earning him a hallowed position among the great conjurers of all time. Through his unparalleled showmanship and groundbreaking illusions, Herrmann not only entertained audiences but also revolutionized the way magic was perceived and appreciated. His contributions to the world of magic have secured him a revered status that continues to inspire and influence generations of magicians. Herrmann's impact on magic history transcends mere admiration; it represents a pivotal moment in the development of the art form. His ability to blend tradition with innovation, master classic routines, and introduce new and daring acts set a standard that many aspiring magicians still strive to emulate. Moreover, Herrmann's commitment to excellence and his unwavering dedication to magic as an art form helped elevate the perception of magic from mere trickery to a respected and cherished form of entertainment. As a trailblazer in his field, Herrmann's influence extended far beyond his own performances. He shaped the evolution of magic by inspiring others to push the boundaries of what was thought possible, encouraging emerging magicians to explore their creativity, and motivating them to develop their own signature styles. His impact on the next generation of magicians cannot be overstated, and his legacy lives on in the work of those who continue to be inspired by his artistry and vision. Furthermore, Herrmann's contributions to magic history have been meticulously documented and celebrated, ensuring that his name and achievements will never fade into obscurity. Historians of magic recognize and honor the significance of his career, preserving his legacy for future enthusiasts and students of the craft. The influence of Herrmann's feats and innovations can be seen in the techniques and performances of contemporary magicians, reaffirming his enduring relevance and importance in the annals of magical history. In essence, Alexander Herrmann's place in magic history is affirmed not only by the applause of countless audiences during his lifetime but also by the lasting impact he has had on the world of magic. Each chapter of magic history acknowledges his influence, and each new magician who takes the stage carries with them a spark ignited by Herrmann's remarkable legacy.

Enduring Inspiration for Future Generations

The legacy of Alexander Herrmann continues to inspire and shape the future of magic. His timeless artistry transcends generations, leaving an indelible mark on the world of illusion and performance. As we reflect on his enduring influence, it becomes evident that his impact extends far beyond his own era, resonating with contemporary magicians and enchanting audiences worldwide. One key aspect of Herrmann's enduring inspiration lies in the innovative techniques and dazzling illusions he pioneered. His creative brilliance and unwavering dedication to his craft serve as a source of motivation for aspiring magicians, urging them to push the boundaries of what is possible. The very essence of Herrmann's magic lives on, sparking a sense of wonder and ambition in those who dare to follow in his footsteps. Moreover, the values and principles embodied by Herrmann continue to guide and inspire future generations of magicians. His unwavering commitment to excellence, showmanship, and the relentless pursuit of perfection sets a standard that serves as a beacon of inspiration for artists across the globe. From stage presence to the intricacies of trickery, Herrmann's enduring legacy imparts invaluable lessons that transcend time and circumstance. In addition to technical prowess, Herrmann's impact on the ethos of magic extends to the realm of creativity and storytelling. His ability to weave captivating narratives through his performances has left an indelible impression on the world of magic. Aspiring magicians are encouraged to delve into the depths of their imagination and embrace the power of storytelling, understanding that behind every remarkable illusion lies an emotive and compelling tale. The profound influence of Herrmann resonates within the fabric of modern magic, as contemporary magicians pay homage to his iconic style while infusing their own innovations. The adoration and reverence for Herrmann's work are evident in the countless tributes and adaptations that continue to grace stages around the world. Through these endeavors, his enduring inspiration fuels the evolution of magic, ensuring that his spirit remains ever-present in the art form he so passionately dedicated his life to. As we contemplate Herrmann's enduring inspiration for future generations, it becomes clear that his magic endures not only in the memories of his admirers but also in the very essence of the art itself. It is a testament to his unparalleled artistry and profound impact that his legacy will continue to captivate, motivate, and guide magicians for countless generations to come.

Did you love *In The Hands Of A Master Herrmann The Great's World Of Magic*? Then you should read *Jean Eugène Robert-Houdin The Father Of Modern Magic*[1] by Robert Jakobsen!

[2]

Step into the life of a legend—where precision meets enchantment and one man forever reshapes the art of magic.

Jean-Eugène Robert-Houdin wasn't just a magician; he was a visionary whose work transcended mere tricks and illusions, merging mechanical genius with a passion for the mystique of the unknown. From humble beginnings in a small French town, where he first tinkered with timepieces in his father's clock shop, Robert-Houdin's journey unfolds like an intricate illusion, layer upon layer of discovery, dedication, and revolutionary invention.

---

1. https://books2read.com/u/3nkEGB

2. https://books2read.com/u/3nkEGB

In an age where science and superstition clashed, Robert-Houdin rose to prominence, not just by dazzling audiences but by transforming magic into an art form that earned respect and admiration from royalty and laypersons alike. His ingenuity and mastery of mechanical marvels enthralled crowds at the Palais Royale, each performance more breathtaking than the last. As you delve into his story, you'll be transported to a Parisian stage lit by gaslight, where whispers of disbelief mingle with gasps of awe, and reality becomes as fluid as a well-timed sleight of hand.

Follow Robert-Houdin's journey, from his fateful transition from clockmaker to magician to his influence on the world stage, inspiring magicians for generations to come. What secrets did he conceal within his illusions? And what did he ultimately reveal about the human desire for wonder?

Will you join the audience, suspend your disbelief, and uncover the magic that changed history?

Milton Keynes UK
Ingram Content Group UK Ltd.
UKHW021915151124
451262UK00014B/1408

9 798227 688255